CURRENCY WARS

CURRENCY
WARS
THE MAKING
OF THE NEXT
GLOBAL
CRISIS

JAMES RICKARDS

PORTFOLIO / PENGUIN

PORTFOLIO / PENGUIN
Published by the Penguin Group
Penguin Group (USA) Inc., 375 Hudson Street,
New York, New York 10014, U.S.A.
Penguin Group (Canada), 90 Eglinton Avenue East, Suite 700,
Toronto, Ontario, Canada M4P 2Y3
(a division of Pearson Penguin Canada Inc.)
Penguin Books Ltd, 80 Strand, London WC2R 0RL, England
Penguin Ireland, 25 St Stephen's Green, Dublin 2, Ireland
(a division of Penguin Books Ltd)
Penguin Books Australia Ltd, 250 Camberwell Road, Camberwell,
Victoria 3124, Australia
(a division of Pearson Australia Group Pty Ltd)
Penguin Books India Pvt Ltd, 11 Community Centre, Panchsheel Park,
New Delhi – 110 017, India
Penguin Group (NZ), 67 Apollo Drive, Rosedale, Auckland 0632,
New Zealand (a division of Pearson New Zealand Ltd)
Penguin Books (South Africa) (Pty) Ltd, 24 Sturdee Avenue,
Rosebank, Johannesburg 2196, South Africa

Penguin Books Ltd, Registered Offices:
80 Strand, London WC2R 0RL, England

First published in 2011 by Portfolio / Penguin,
a member of Penguin Group (USA) Inc.

1   3   5   7   9   10   8   6   4   2

Library of Congress Cataloging-in-Publication Data

Rickards, James.
Currency wars : the making of the next global crisis / James Rickards.
p. cm.
Includes bibliographical references and index.
ISBN 978-1-59184-449-5
1. Currency crises. 2. Foreign exchange. 3. Financial crises. I. Title.

HG3851.3.R53 2011
332.4—dc23
2011026906

Printed in the United States of America
Set in Sabon LT Std
Designed by Elyse Strongin

For Ann, Scott, Ali, Will and Sally—with love and gratitude,
and to the memory of my father, Richard H. Rickards,
with the Old Breed in Peleliu, Okinawa and China

"And when the money failed in the land of Egypt, and in the land of Canaan, all the Egyptians came unto Joseph, and said, Give us bread: for why should we die in thy presence? For the money faileth."

Genesis 47:15, King James Version

CONTENTS

PREFACE

On August 15, 1971, a quiet Sunday evening, President Richard Nixon took to the airwaves, preempting the most popular television show in America, to announce his New Economic Policy. The government was imposing national price controls and a steep surtax on foreign imports and banning the conversion of dollars into gold. The country was in the midst of a crisis, the result of an ongoing currency war that had destroyed faith in the U.S. dollar, and the president had determined that extreme measures were necessary.

Today we are engaged in a new currency war, and another crisis of confidence in the dollar is on its way. This time the consequences will be far worse than those confronting Nixon. The growth in globalization, derivatives and leverage over the past forty years have made financial panic and contagion all but impossible to contain.

The new crisis will likely begin in the currency markets and spread quickly to stocks, bonds and commodities. When the dollar collapses, the dollar-denominated markets will collapse too. Panic will quickly spread throughout the world.

As a result, another U.S. president, possibly President Obama, will take to the airwaves and cyberspace to announce a radical plan of intervention to save the dollar from complete collapse, invoking legal authority already in place today. This new plan may even involve a return to the gold standard. If gold is used, it will be at a dramatically higher price in order to support the bloated money supply with the fixed quantity of gold available. Americans who had invested in gold earlier will be confronted with a 90 percent "windfall profits" tax on their newfound wealth, imposed in the name of fairness. European and Japanese gold presently stored in New York will be confiscated and converted to use in the service of the New Dollar Policy. No doubt the Europeans and Japanese will be given receipts for their former gold, convertible into New Dollars at a new, higher price.

Alternatively, the president may eschew a return to gold and use an array of capital controls and global IMF money creation to reliquify and stabilize the situation. This IMF global bailout will not be in old, nonconvertible dollars but in a newly printed global currency called the SDR. Life will go on but the international monetary system will never be the same.

This isn't far-fetched speculation. It has all happened before. Time and again, paper currencies have collapsed, assets have been frozen, gold has been confiscated and capital controls have been imposed. The United States has not been immune to these acts; in fact, America has been a leading advocate of dollar debasement from the 1770s to the 1970s, through the Revolution, the Civil War, the Great Depression and Carter-era hyperinflation. The fact that a currency collapse has not happened in a generation just implies that the next crash is overdue. This is not a matter of guesswork—the preconditions are already in place.

Today, the U.S. Federal Reserve, under the guidance of Chairman Ben Bernanke, is engaged in the greatest gamble in the history of finance. Beginning in 2007, the Fed fought off economic collapse by cutting short-term interest rates and lending freely. Eventually rates reached zero, and the Fed appeared to be out of bullets.

Then, in 2008, the Fed found a new bullet: quantitative easing. While the Fed describes the program as an easing of financial conditions through the lowering of long-term interest rates, this is essentially a program of printing money to spur growth.

The Fed is attempting to inflate asset prices, commodity prices and consumer prices to offset the natural deflation that follows a crash. It is basically engaged in a game of tug-of-war against the deflation that normally accompanies a depression. As in a typical tug-of-war, not much happens at first. The teams are evenly matched and there is no motion for a while, just lots of tension on the rope. Eventually one side will collapse, and the other side will drag the losers over the line to claim victory. This is the essence of the Fed's gamble. It must cause inflation before deflation prevails; it must win the tug-of-war.

In a tug-of-war, the rope is the channel through which stress is conveyed from one side to the other. This book is about that rope. In the contest between inflation and deflation, the rope is the dollar. The dollar bears all the stress of the opposing forces and sends that stress around the world. The value of the dollar is the way to tell who is winning the tug-of-war. This particular tug-of-war is actually a full-on currency war, and it is not really a game but an attack on the value of every stock, bond and commodity in the world.

In the best of all possible worlds for the Fed, asset values are propped up, banks get healthier, government debt melts away and no one seems to notice. Yet, by printing money on an unprecedented scale, Bernanke has become a twenty-first-century Pangloss, hoping for the best and quite unprepared for the worst.

There is a very real danger that the Fed's money printing could suddenly morph into hyperinflation. Even if inflation does not affect consumer prices, it can show up in asset prices leading to bubbles in stocks, commodities, land and other hard assets—bubbles that are prone to burst like tech stocks in 2000 or housing in 2007. The Fed claims to have the tools needed to avert these outcomes, but those tools have never been tried in these circumstances or on such a large scale. The Fed's remedies—higher rates and tight money—are likely to lead straight to the kind of depression the Fed set out to avoid in the first place. The U.S. economy is resting on a knife's edge between depression and hyperinflation. Millions of investors, business owners and workers wonder how much longer the Fed can balance the knife.

Worse yet, none of this happens in a vacuum. If the Fed's policy manipulations were limited to the U.S. economy, that would be one thing, but they are not. The effects of printing dollars are global; by engaging in quantitative easing, the Fed has effectively declared currency war on the world. Many of the feared effects of Fed policy in the United States are already appearing overseas. Printing dollars at home means higher inflation in China, higher food prices in Egypt and stock bubbles in Brazil. Printing money means that U.S. debt is devalued so foreign creditors get paid back in cheaper dollars. The devaluation means higher unemployment in developing economies as their exports become more expensive for Americans. The resulting inflation also means higher prices for inputs needed in developing economies like copper, corn, oil and wheat. Foreign countries have begun to fight back against U.S.-caused inflation through subsidies, tariffs and capital controls; the currency war is expanding fast.

While Fed money printing on a trillion-dollar scale may be new, currency wars are not. Currency wars have been fought before—twice in the twentieth century alone—and they always end badly. At best, currency wars offer the sorry spectacle of countries stealing growth from trading partners. At worst, they degenerate into sequential bouts of inflation, recession, retaliation and actual violence as the scramble for resources leads to invasion and war. The historical precedents are sobering enough, but the dangers today are even greater, exponentially increased by the scale and complexity of financial linkages throughout the world.

Baffling to many observers is the rank failure of economists to foresee or prevent the economic catastrophes of recent years. Not only have their theories failed to prevent calamity, they are making the currency wars worse. The economists' latest solutions—such as the global currency called the SDR—present hidden new dangers while resolving none of the current dilemmas.

Among the new dangers are threats not just to America's economic well-being but to our national security as well. As national security experts examine currency issues traditionally left to the Treasury, new threats continually come into focus, from clandestine gold purchases by China to the hidden agendas of sovereign wealth funds. Greater than any single threat is the ultimate danger of the collapse of the dollar itself. Senior military and intelligence officials have now come to the realization that America's unique military predominance can be maintained only with an equally unique and predominant role for the dollar. If the dollar falls, America's national security falls with it.

While the outcome of the current currency war is not yet certain, some version of the worst-case scenario is almost inevitable if U.S. and world economic leaders fail to learn from the mistakes of their predecessors. This book examines our current currency war through the lens of economic policy, national security and historical precedent. It untangles the web of failed paradigms, wishful thinking and arrogance driving current public policy and points the way toward a more informed and effective course of action. In the end, the reader will understand why the new currency war is the most meaningful struggle in the world today—the one struggle that determines the outcome of all others.

PART ONE

WAR GAMES

CHAPTER 1

Prewar

"The current international currency system is the product
of the past."

Hu Jintao,
General Secretary of the Communist Party of China,
January 16, 2011

The Applied Physics Laboratory, located on four hundred acres of former farmland about halfway between Baltimore and Washington, D.C., is one of the crown jewels of America's system of top secret, high-tech applied physics and weapons research facilities. It operates in close coordination with the Department of Defense, and its specialties include advanced weaponry and deep space exploration. Lab officials are proud to tell visitors that the earth's moon and every planet in the solar system has a device developed at APL either on its surface or passing nearby.

The Applied Physics Lab was set up in haste in 1942, shortly after the Pearl Harbor attack, to bring applied science to the problem of improving weaponry. Much of what the U.S. military was using in the early days of World War II was either obsolete or ineffective. The lab was originally housed in a former used-car dealership, requisitioned by the War Department, on Georgia Avenue in Silver Spring, Maryland. It operated in secrecy from the start, although in the early days the secrecy was enforced with just a few armed guards rather than the elaborate sensors and multiple security perimeters used today. APL's first mission was to develop the variable time, or VT, proximity fuse, an antiaircraft fuse used to defend naval vessels from air attack, later regarded, along with the atomic bomb and radar, as one of the three greatest technology contributions to U.S. victory in World War II. Based on this initial success, APL's programs, budget and facilities have been expanding ever since. The Tomahawk cruise missile, Aegis missile defense and one-of-a-kind spacecraft are among the many advanced weapons and space systems developed for the Defense Department and NASA by APL in recent decades.

In addition to weapons and space exploration, there has always been a strong intellectual and strategic side to what the Applied Physics Laboratory does for the military. Preeminent among these more abstract functions is the lab's Warfare Analysis Laboratory, one of the leading venues for war games and strategic planning in the country. The lab's proximity to Washington, D.C., makes it a favorite for war-fighting simulations and it has played host to many such games over the decades. It was for this purpose, the conduct of a war game sponsored by the Pentagon, that about sixty experts from the military, intelligence and academic communities arrived at APL on a rainy morning in the late winter of 2009. This war game was to be different from any other that had ever been conducted by the military. The rules of engagement prohibited what the military calls kinetic methods—things that shoot or explode. There would be no amphibious invasions, no special forces, no armored flanking maneuvers. Instead the only weapons allowed would be financial—currencies, stocks, bonds and derivatives. The Pentagon was about to launch a global financial war using currencies and capital markets instead of ships and planes.

At the dawn of the twenty-first century, U.S. military dominance in conventional and advanced high-tech weapons systems and in what the military calls 4CI, for command, control, communications, computers and intelligence, had become so great that no rival nation would dare confront her. This does not mean wars are impossible. A rogue nation such as North Korea might escalate an incident into a major attack without heed to the consequences. The United

States might be drawn into a war involving others such as Iran and Israel if U.S. national interests were affected. Apart from these special situations, a conventional military confrontation with the United States seems highly unlikely because of the United States' ability to suppress and ultimately decimate the opposing side. As a result, rival nations and transnational actors such as jihadists have increasingly developed capabilities in unconventional warfare, which can include cyberwarfare, biological or chemical weapons, other weapons of mass destruction or now, in the most unexpected twist of all, financial weapons. The financial war game was the Pentagon's first effort to see how an actual financial war might evolve and to see what lessons might be learned.

The war game had been many months in the making, and I had been part of the strategy sessions and game design that preceded the actual game. Although a well-designed war game will try to achieve unexpected results and simulate the fog of real war, it nevertheless requires some starting place and a set of rules in order to avoid descending into chaos. APL's game design team was among the best in the world at this, but a financial game required some completely new approaches, including access to Wall Street expertise, which the typical physicist or military planner does not have. My role was to fill that gap.

My association with the lab started in December 2006 in Omaha, Nebraska, where I was attending a strategy forum hosted by U.S. Strategic Command, or STRATCOM. I presented a paper on the new science of market intelligence, or what intelligence experts call MARKINT, which involves analyzing capital markets to find actionable intelligence on the intentions of market participants. Hedge funds and investment banks had been using these methods for years to gain information advantage on takeovers and government policy shifts. Now, along with my partners, Chris Ray, a seasoned options trader and risk manager, and Randy Tauss, recently retired after thirty-five years with the CIA, we had developed new ways to use these techniques in the national security realm to identify potential terrorist attacks in advance and to gain early warning of attacks on the U.S. dollar. Several members of the APL Warfare Analysis Lab had been in attendance at the Omaha event and later contacted me about ways we might work together to integrate MARKINT concepts with their own research.

So it was not a surprise when I received a call in the summer of 2008 to join a global financial seminar sponsored by the Office of the Secretary of Defense and hosted by APL. It was scheduled for that September, its stated purpose to "examine the impact of global financial activities on national security issues." This was one of a series of such seminars planned by the Defense Department to be held throughout the late summer and fall of that year as preparation for the financial war game itself. Defense wanted to know if such a game was even possible—if it made sense. They needed to think about the appropriate "teams." Would they be countries, sovereign wealth funds, banks or some combination? They also needed to think about remote but still plausible scenarios for the players to enact. A list of expert participants had to be developed and some recruitment might be needed to reach out to those who had not been involved with war games before. Finally, rules had to be established for the actual play.

To protect the top secret work that goes on inside the lab, the security procedures for visitors there are as strict as at any U.S. government defense or intelligence installation, starting with advance clearance and background checks. Upon arrival, visitors are quickly sorted into two categories, "No Escort" or "Escort Required," reflected in different-colored badges. The practical impact of this has mainly to do with trips to the coffee machine, but the implicit understanding is that those with the No Escort badges hold current high-security clearances from their home directorates or government contractors. BlackBerrys, iPhones and other digital devices have to be deposited at the security desk to be retrieved upon departure. X-ray scanners, metal detectors, multiple security perimeters and armed guards are routine. Once inside, you are truly in the bubble of the military-intelligence complex.

At the September meeting, there were about forty attendees in total, including a number of distinguished academics, think tank experts, intelligence officials and uniformed military. I was one of five asked to give a formal presentation that day, and my topic was sovereign wealth funds, or SWFs. Sovereign wealth funds are huge investment pools established by governments to invest their excess reserves, many with assets in the hundred-billion-dollar range or higher. The reserves are basically hard currency surpluses, mostly dollars, which governments have earned by exporting natural resources or manufactured goods. The largest reserves are held by oil-producing countries such as Norway or Arab states and by manufacturing export powerhouses such as China or Taiwan. Traditionally these reserves were managed by the central banks of those countries in a highly conservative manner; investments were limited to low-risk, liquid instruments such as U.S. Treasury bills. This strategy offered liquidity but did not provide much income, and it tended to concentrate a large amount of the portfolio in just one type of investment. In effect, the surplus countries were placing all their eggs in one basket and not getting very much in return. Because of the drastic increase in the size of reserves beginning in the 1990s, partly as the result of globalization, surplus countries began to seek out ways of getting higher returns on their investments. Central banks were not well equipped to do this because they lacked the investment staff and portfolio managers needed to select stocks, commodities, private equity, real estate and hedge funds, which were the key to higher returns. So the sovereign wealth funds began to emerge to better manage these investments; the earliest SWFs were created some decades ago, but most have come into being in the past ten years, with their government sponsors giving them enormous allocations from their central bank reserves with a mandate to build diversified portfolios of investments from around the world.

In their basic form, sovereign wealth funds do make economic sense. Most assets are invested professionally and contain no hidden political agenda, but this is not always the case. Some purchases are vanity projects, such as Middle Eastern investments in the McLaren, Aston Martin and Ferrari Formula 1 racing teams, while other investments are far more politically and economically consequential. During the first part of the depression that began in 2007, sovereign wealth funds were the primary source of bailout money. In late 2007 and early 2008, SWFs invested over $58 billion to prop up Citigroup, Merrill Lynch, UBS and Morgan Stanley. China was considering an additional $1 billion investment in Bear Stearns in early 2008 that was abandoned only when Bear Stearns neared collapse in March of that year. When these investments were decimated in the Panic of 2008 the U.S. government had to step in with taxpayer money to continue the bailouts. The sovereign wealth funds lost vast fortunes on these early investments, yet the stock positions and the influence that came with them remained.

My presentation focused on the dark side of SWF investments, how they could operate through what intelligence analysts call cutouts, or front companies, such as trusts, managed accounts, private Swiss banks and hedge funds. With these fronts in place, sovereign wealth funds could then be used to exercise malign influence over target companies in order to steal technology, sabotage new projects, stifle competition, engage in bid rigging, recruit agents or manipulate markets. I did not assert that such activities were common, let alone the norm, but rather that such activities were possible and the United States needed to develop a stronger watch function to protect its national security interests. Along with these specific threats, I suggested an even greater threat: a full-scale attack on Western capital markets to disable the engine of capitalist society. My presentation included metrics and system specifications to monitor sovereign wealth fund behavior, to look for behind-the-scenes malign acts and to identify financial choke points—the information age equivalents of the Suez Canal or the Strait of Hormuz—which could be monitored to prevent or fight off future financial attacks.

By the end of the two-day event, the Defense Department officials in attendance seemed satisfied that the lab had developed a solid core of experts, subjects and threat analysis with which to take the war game to the next level.

The core group of experts met again at the lab the following month to continue developing the financial war game. In addition to the APL hosts and our sponsors from the Department of Defense, there were representatives from other cabinet-level departments, including Commerce and Energy; several major universities, including the Naval War College; think tanks, including the Peterson Institute and RAND Corporation; other physics labs, including Los Alamos; and senior military officers from the staff of the Joint Chiefs.

At this point I noticed the absence of representatives with any actual capital markets experience. I was the only one in the room with a lengthy career on Wall Street that included time at investment banks, hedge funds and exchanges. If we were going to conduct a financial war, we needed people who knew how to use financial weapons—such as front running, inside information, rumors, "painting the tape" with misleading price quotes, short squeezes and the rest of the tricks on which Wall Street thrives. We needed people who, in the immortal words of legendary banker John Gutfreund, were ready "to bite the ass off a bear" when it came to trading currencies, stocks and derivatives. There was no lack of testosterone among the uniformed military or the spies in the room, but they knew no more about destroying a country with credit default swaps than the average stock trader knew about the firing sequence for an ICBM. If this project was going to succeed, I had to persuade Defense to let me recruit some of my peers to make the game more realistic and more valuable for them.

At the October session, I gave a presentation on futures and derivatives to explain how these leveraged instruments could be used to manipulate underlying physical markets, including those in strategic commodities such as oil, uranium, copper and gold. I also explained how the prohibition of derivatives regulation in the Commodity Futures Modernization Act, legislation led by Senator Phil Gramm and signed by President Clinton in 2000, had opened the door to exponentially greater size and variety in these instruments that were now hidden off the balance sheets of the major banks, making them almost impossible to monitor. I finished with a picture of how cutouts, sovereign wealth funds and derivatives leverage could be combined to launch a financial Pearl Harbor for which the United States was completely unprepared. The pregame seminars were beginning to achieve their purpose; the military, intelligence and diplomatic experts were now on the same page as the financial types. The threat of financial warfare was becoming clearer.

Our third group planning session took place in mid-November; this time there were a few new faces, including senior officials from the intelligence community. We were no longer contemplating the feasibility of a financial war game; by now it was game on and we were specifically focused on game design. I presented detailed financial warfare scenarios and made a pitch that the game design should incorporate unpredictable outcomes that would surprise both attackers and defenders due to the complex dynamics of capital markets. By the conclusion, the Defense Department and the APL game design team had received enough input from the experts to complete the final design. All that remained was to select the participants, set the date and let the game begin.

After some delays and uncertainty during the changeover of administrations, the Obama administration gave the go-ahead to proceed as planned. The formal invitations went out in late January 2009. The war game would be played over two days, March 17 and 18, at the APL Warfare Analysis Laboratory inside the imposing war room it had used in many past simulations.

All war games have certain elements in common. They involve two or more teams, or cells, which are customarily designated either by the names of countries involved or by colors. A typical game might involve a red cell, usually bad guys, versus a blue cell, the good guys, although some games have multiple sides. One critical cell is the white cell, which consists of a game director and participants designated as umpires or referees. The white cell decides if a particular game move is allowed and also determines who wins or loses during each round of the game. Generally the game designers attribute specific goals or objectives to each cell; thereafter the players are expected to make moves that logically advance those objectives rather than move off in unexplained directions. The game design team will also use political scientists, military strategists and other analysts to describe the initial conditions affecting all the players—in effect, they determine the starting line. Finally, some system of power metrics is devised so that the relative strength of each cell can be established at the beginning of the game, in the same way that some armies are larger than others or some economies have greater industrial potential at the start of any war.

Once in play, the participants will then direct the moves for each cell, with the white cell adding or subtracting points from each competing cell based on its assessment of the success or failure of each move. Other design features include specifying the number of days over which the game will be conducted and the number of moves on each day. This is an important practical constraint, because many of the outside experts find it difficult to be away from their other professional duties for more than two or three days at a time.

I was not a war game expert but I was the designated Wall Street expert, so I worked side by side with the game designers to fit the world I knew into the categories, timelines, rules and budgets that they had within their parameters. One of my main goals was to make sure that the game design allowed for unconventional scenarios. I knew that a real financial attack would not involve anything as obvious as dumping Treasury notes on the open market, because the president has near dictatorial powers to freeze any accounts that try to disrupt the market in that way. An attack would almost certainly involve hard-to-identify cutouts and hard-to-track derivatives. Above all, a financial attack would almost certainly involve the dollar itself. Destroying confidence in the dollar would be far more effective than dumping any particular dollar-denominated instrument. If the dollar collapsed, all dollar-denominated markets would collapse with it and the president's powers to freeze accounts would be moot. I wanted to make sure the game design would allow for a true currency war and not just a war of stocks, bonds and commodities.

The final pieces were falling into place. The team decided we would definitely play a U.S. cell, a Russia cell and a China cell. In addition, there would be a Pacific Rim cell, which would include Japan, South Korea, Taiwan and Vietnam, among others. This was not ideal because as separate states South Korea and Taiwan, for instance, could take very different positions depending on the issue involved, but these kinds of compromises were necessary to stick to our budget and get the game off the ground. There would also be a gray cell, to represent the rest of the world. (I was not sure how pleased real Europeans would be to learn that they did not get their own cell and would have to share their platform with the IMF, hedge funds and the Cayman Islands.) Finally, of course, was the all-powerful white cell, directing course and calling the shots as the game played out.

The game would have three moves played over two days. Two moves would be played on day one and one additional move on day two, with time at the end for debriefing. The cells would have private facilities to use as their "capitals" for deciding each move, and there would be plenary sessions in the war room, where the cells would make their moves and their opponents would respond. The white cell would preside over the plenary sessions and award or subtract power points to each cell's "national power index." Cells could conduct bilateral summits or negotiations with other cells at designated locations while each turn was being played.

Most intriguingly, each cell would have a set of wild cards that allowed for actions and responses not included in the opening set of scenarios for each turn. Although this was being conducted for the first time on a tight budget and the results were far from clear at the outset, the combination of summit conferences and wild cards was enough to suggest that we might show the Pentagon how real unconventional financial warfare could occur.

As we completed our overview, I again pointed out that we were top-heavy with military, intelligence and think tank participants but didn't have anyone from Wall Street except me. I knew we were going to get very predictable action-response functions by inviting the usual suspects. These people are brilliant on macroeconomics and strategy, but none of them really understands how capital markets function in the trenches. I told them I wanted to recruit some investment bankers and hedge fund people to join us. There was room in the budget for two more participants, they said, and I could have my pick.

My first recruit was Steve Halliwell, a seasoned banker and private equity investor. Steve is trim, dapper, animated and highly recognizable with his thick-framed glasses and shaved head. He is the epitome of the Old Russia Hand, having made his first trip to Russia in 1963 during the Kennedy-Khrushchev era as an early exchange student while an undergraduate at Wesleyan. He later went to grad school at Columbia and had a long career at Citibank, where he was involved in opening Citibank's Moscow branch, before he launched one of the first U.S.–Russia investment funds in the 1990s. Steve's supply of Russian anecdotes is inexhaustible and he tells each one in vivid detail with a strong sense of humor. He speaks Russian like a native and has a dense network of connections in that country as a result of his banking and investment activities. Steve and I had spent a week in Moscow in the winter of 2008 doing market research for some hedge fund clients of mine. The trip was memorable for the beauty of the nighttime snowfall on Red Square and copious amounts of vodka and caviar consumed with our Russian hosts. I knew he'd be perfect to play the Russian side in the Pentagon's financial game. He readily agreed to come on board.

Now I had one more recruitment to make. Since Steve was a private equity fund guy and a more long-term investor, I wanted someone closer to the day-to-day action of the markets, someone who understood what are called "technicals"—that is, short-term supply and demand imbalances that could push security prices away from their fundamental values and catch supposedly rational investors off guard. I needed someone who knew every trick in the book when it came to handling the kind of huge orders that could push markets around and steamroll the unsuspecting. I called a friend who had been in the trenches for over thirty years and was known on the Street as "O.D."

I had known Bill O'Donnell for decades, going back to our days at Greenwich Capital, the primary dealer in government bonds. Bill is one of the smartest salespeople around and always has a smile— except when he's working hard on an order for a customer. He's never in a bad mood and never loses his temper, which is unusual on a trading floor. Sporting wavy salt-and-pepper hair, preppy clothes and good looks, Bill has an easygoing demeanor that makes him one of the most well-liked people in the bond business, otherwise known for its share of off-putting type A personalities. He loves the business and has seen it all, from the beginning of the bull market in 1982 through the housing bubble years beginning in 2002. When I called him in 2009, he was working as head of interest rate strategy for banking giant UBS at their North American headquarters in Stamford, Connecticut.

As with a lot of Wall Street folks I had recruited for help on national security projects, he grasped the situation immediately and could not wait to volunteer. After running it by his bosses at UBS, he called me back a few days later. "I'm in," he said. "Just tell me where I need to be. This'll be great to mix things up with the generals and intelligence people. Can't wait." And that was that.

Steve was assigned to the Russia cell, of course. O.D. was assigned to the gray cell, representing the hedge funds and Swiss banks—another appropriate assignment. I was put in the China cell, along with a well-known Harvard academic, a highly cerebral RAND Corporation analyst and two other area experts.

The financial war was just a few weeks away and it was time to lay some traps—something the military calls "conditioning the battle space." I knew that Russia would begin the game with significantly less national power than the United States or even China. In fact, the national power assessment showed Russia having about only two-thirds the strength of the United States, with China somewhere between the two. As far as I was concerned, this just meant that Russia would have to play smarter and harder and do something unconventional to set the United States back on its heels. As an American concerned about the economic course we were on and our vulnerabilities to financial attack, I wanted the United States to suffer some kind of shock or setback in the game environment. That seemed like the best way to do our jobs for America and open some eyes at the Defense Department and in the intelligence community before a serious setback took place in the real world. The fact that Steve, O.D. and I were playing non-U.S. teams left us in a position to deliver a shock. The fact that we had less national power to start with just meant that we would have to be more creative—and more stealthy.

Ten Twenty Post is a popular bistro in Darien, Connecticut, near where I live and not far from Steve's home in Westchester County, New York. It's also become a hangout for investment bankers from RBS and UBS in nearby Stamford. With its mahogany bar, brass fixtures, glass chandeliers and white tablecloths, it conjures up the look and feel of a classic French original. I suggested to Steve that we meet there for dinner one week before the game to work out a scheme to put the United States on the defensive.

Over oysters, white wine and vodka toasts of *Na zdrovyeh!*, we reminisced a little about our Moscow adventures and then got down to business. I handed Steve a mock press release from the Russian Central Bank, something I had written earlier and used in a few articles and lectures. It said that Russia was moving its gold to Switzerland and starting a new bank in London. The bank would issue a new form of gold-backed currency supported by gold in the Swiss vaults. Initially Russia would own all of the new currency. But everyone would be free to deposit gold and receive similar currency. It had other technical features to make the plan feasible, such as lending and clearing facilities. The kicker was that, from now on, any Russian exports of oil or natural gas would have to be paid for in the new currency. U.S. dollars would no longer be welcome.

"Jim, I'm worried about you—you're starting to think like a Russian," Steve said.

"Coming from you, that's high praise," I replied.

"Why are you using Switzerland and London in this?"

"No one trusts the Russians not to steal the gold," I said. "But they trust the Swiss and Brits, so if you do everything under their legal systems, people won't be afraid to deposit gold."

"Right. Russia has been looking for a way out of the dollar system for years. They try to play by our rules and get screwed every time," said Steve. "This is perfect for them."

"Now here's the deal," I said, leaning toward Steve. "If you play this move for Russia, I'll get the Chinese team to go along. If you can't get Russia to make the move, I'll launch this idea from China myself. Either way we'll work this into the game and try to sink the dollar. That will be a shock to the U.S. The Pentagon is paying to learn something from this. Let's give them their money's worth."

Steve took the mock press release, folded it and tucked it inside his jacket to study in detail at home. We finished our vodka and left ready to spring our sneak attack on the dollar.

Now Steve, O.D. and the rest of us were ready to start the war. Over those two days, the game would quickly take on a life of its own and open a lot of eyes to how markets work and how financially vulnerable nations actually are.

CHAPTER 2

Financial War

> "The primary near-term security concern of the United States is the global economic crisis and its geopolitical implications. . . . Indeed, policies . . . such as competitive currency devaluations . . . risk unleashing a wave of destructive protectionism."
>
> Dennis C. Blair,
> U.S. Director of National Intelligence,
> February 2009

■ Day One

As we arrived at the lab that rainy March morning for the war game, the first thing I noticed in the parking lot were rows of high-performance motorcycles—Kawasakis, Suzukis and the like. I guess physicists working on weapons design have their wild sides too, I thought. We were headed to Building 26, a new venue for us. We parked nearby and walked to the main entrance. Once inside, we cleared security, got our badges, dropped off our cell phones and headed upstairs. After months of meeting in seminar rooms and offices, we were being admitted to the Warfare Analysis Lab war room. The scene did not disappoint. Growing up in the Cold War, I routinely entertained visions of the war rooms used for nuclear war fighting from the classic films *Dr. Strangelove* and *Fail-Safe*. Now we were entering something similar, but would be fighting not with B-52s, but with currencies.

The APL war room is large, with electronic battle stations and observation posts for about a hundred participants and observers.

The rectangular room has four wall-sized screens at the front end and banks of smaller fifty-inch plasma video screens mounted on the walls along both sides to patch in additional participants from remote locations or to display additional graphics. The seating is tiered with a central trapezoid-shaped table for twelve on the lowest level closest to the wall screens; the trapezoid is flanked by four banks of long tables, two on each side, at a slightly higher level laid out in a chevron pattern around the center. In the rear, on an even higher mezzanine level, are rows of additional observer stations laid out across the room perpendicular to the main tables below. Finally, at the back of the room, opposite the large screens, are tinted glass windows hiding a separate chamber with five additional battle stations and some standing room. I discovered later that this separate chamber was used by senior military observers who wanted to watch the game in progress unbeknownst to the other players.

There was a podium and microphone at the front to the right side of the screens, where representatives of each cell could announce their moves and respond to moves of other cells. Every battle station was equipped with a laptop linked to groupware that enabled each player to provide continuous silent commentary on game progress even while others were describing their moves and motives. Adjacent to the war room was a technical support room that controlled the screen projections and monitored the groupware supporting the running commentary.

Down a corridor from the war room were separate large meeting rooms that had been outfitted as the "capitals" of the warring states. These were equipped with a single wall screen each and separate groupware shared only by the members of each team and accessed through additional sets of laptops for the team members. Other rooms had been set aside for summit conferences and bilateral negotiations if cells wanted to conduct private meetings away from the war room. All of the facilities—the war room, the capitals and the summit conference venues—were equipped with workstations for lab staff acting as facilitators, analysts and neutral observers of the proceedings. Although we were autonomous actors, it was hard to shake the feeling that we were also lab rats in the purview of APL's larger mission.

We had a chance to get acquainted with the other players at a buffet-style breakfast served up by the lab. Then we filed into the war room and took our assigned places. The members of the white cell, the referees, were seated at the large trapezoid in the center. The five combatant teams, Russia Cell, U.S. Cell, Pacific Rim Cell, China Cell and Gray Cell (the "all other" group), and some Pentagon and intelligence community observers were seated in the chevron layout around the white cell.

Thanks to the secure Warfare Analysis Lab website, codenamed WALRUS, we had all been supplied in advance with thick packets of briefing books. One was the game overview, which provided the relative "national strength" of each team with a detailed rationale behind it. The overview included the instruction that "player cells may select actions from game menu and/or 'innovate' their own actions." I was all for the innovation.

We also received "Baseline Scenario" briefing books, which described the near future economic world of 2012, in which we would be playing the game, and a "Mechanics" book, which was basically a rulebook. I recalled how my brothers and I used to fight over the rules in Risk as kids and often had to dig the Parker Brothers rulebook out of the game box to settle disputes. Now we had a war game rulebook, but this would go quite differently. I wanted to break as many rules as I could to help the Pentagon understand how capital markets really work in an age of greed, deregulation and bad intent. Wall Street was like the Wild West in the best of times, but with globalization and too-big-to-fail government backing, it was now even more out of control.

After a few hours of instruction, orientation and snap training on the groupware, we broke out to our separate capitals to work on move one. This broadly involved a long-term trade agreement between Russia and Japan that would reduce the availability of Russian oil and natural gas to the rest of the world. The big idea in move one was that Russia would leverage its natural resources to improve its foreign currency reserve position. Of course, there was no coordination between the scenario the lab had produced and the wild card Steve and I were secretly ready to play, but this was a pretty good fit. Russia could exempt Japan from its gold currency deal and still placate China by inviting it to join in its plan to sideline the dollar. I sat in our simulated Chinese capital listening to my Harvard and RAND teammates discussing how to punish Japan for deviating from the Washington Consensus free trade paradigm, but my mind was elsewhere, literally waiting for the phone to ring. A few minutes later, our lab observers informed us that a communiqué had come in from Russia requesting a summit conference. This was good news; it meant Steve had convinced his teammates to let him play the gold wild card.

Before my team could digest the news, I offered, "Hey, guys. My friend Steve Halliwell is playing the Russian cell—I'm guessing he's behind this. Okay if I attend the summit from our side?"

They quickly agreed and off I went down the hall to one of the designated summit conference rooms, where Steve was waiting. A lab facilitator was there, so I had to play dumb even though I knew what Steve was going to propose.

"Jim, we expect U.S. pushback on our deal with Japan, and frankly we're tired of the U.S. using its dominant position in the dollar-based trading system to call the shots. There's a better way. None of our currencies is ready to replace the dollar—we all know that. But gold has always been money good. It's just a matter of time before the world gets to some kind of gold standard. There's a huge first-mover advantage here. The first country that moves to gold will have the only currency anyone wants. Here's our proposal."

Steve handed me a reworked copy of the mock press release I had given him at the Darien bistro the week before. It was all there: the new gold-based currency, a London bank of issue, the ability to expand the new money supply by depositing gold, the English and Swiss rule of law, clearance and settlement facilities and a true market price. Russia would demand payment in the new currency for natural resource exports going forward. The dollar would be pushed to one side.

"We can do this alone," Steve continued, "but it works much better with China and maybe others. The more of us who join in, the harder it will be for the U.S. to fight it. You can do the same thing with your manufactured goods that we're doing with oil and natural gas. Are you with us?"

"Look, let me go back to China and I'll let you know," I said. "I'm not authorized to agree to anything; I just came to get the message. We'll discuss it and I'll call you with our answer."

Back in the Chinese capital, my teammates had been diligently working out a response to the scenario we had been presented. The overall sense was to do nothing. The Russia-Japan natural resources deal affected not only those two parties but also Europe, to the extent it might lead to reduced supplies of Russian natural gas. The United States would have to coordinate the response because it was in the best position to pressure Japan. China's posture would be to keep its head down and let the others work things out.

Then I played the Russian wild card by briefing my teammates on Steve's proposal.

It's difficult to describe their reaction. "Nonplussed" is probably the best word. They had difficulty processing any economic scenario that had the word "gold" in it.

"That's ridiculous," our Harvard guy said. "It has nothing to do with the scenario we were given and it makes no sense anyway. Gold is irrelevant to trade and international monetary policy. It's just a dumb idea and a waste of time."

The RAND guy was a little more intrigued and asked a few questions but clearly was not prepared to move in the Russian direction. I urged my teammates to take the plunge with Russia and set the United States back on its heels, but they were not persuaded. They were soon back to drafting their noncommittal communiqué on the original problem.

"Okay," I said. "I have to get back to Russia on this. Can I call a summit to give them our answer?"

"Sure, go ahead," said Harvard. "We'll keep working on the scenario."

Pretty soon Steve and I were back in the summit conference room.

"Look, Steve, I can't get my guys to go along. I'll keep working on this over the next few rounds, but you're on your own for now. I can't blame you if you pull the plug on this; I really thought China would see the benefits and we'd do this together."

"It's fine," he said. "The Russia team really likes this. They think it's about time someone stood up and showed what a scam the dollar system is. Too bad you can't join us, but we'll go ahead anyway. Let's see what happens."

By the time I got back to China, our team had finished drafting the statement representing our move for this turn of the game. It boiled down to saying nothing and doing nothing. It was the perfect academic solution and would teach the Pentagon exactly nothing. Now it was time to go back to the war room to announce our moves along with the other cells.

War room meetings were plenary sessions, what in Pentagonese are called "brief backs," with all the teams and observers gathered together. One representative of each cell would take the podium, describe his cell's policy response and the rationale behind it, answer some questions from the other cells, and turn the podium over to the next cell. The lab staff had assisted each cell in the instant preparation of slides with maps, bullet points or other illustrations to throw up on the wall screens. The groupware chat functions were going full bore with twenty or more simultaneous and overlapping discussions, only some of which were responsive to others and all of which came scrolling across the screens in front of each player. It was like Twitter without the avatars and virtual wallpaper. If you felt someone was making a brilliant move or a ridiculous move, or you wanted to pose a question, you just said so. Each player could participate as much or as little as she liked while the entire stream-of-consciousness digital scroll was preserved for future evaluation by Pentagon planners.

The China brief was predictably boring given the proclivities of the team and my failure to excite much interest in gold-backed currency. We meekly accepted the scripted Russia-Japan energy deal but made some comment about accelerating China's efforts to increase energy diversification.

Russia went next. The brief started with some happy talk about continuing to work with China on a joint venture pipeline, but then veered into the announcement about demanding gold-backed currency for future energy shipments. An official summary of the war game prepared much later referred to this move as "aggressive" and "threatening," but the immediate response was more in keeping with the absurd style of *Dr. Strangelove*. The white cell asked for time to caucus once the Russian presentation was complete. From their position at the center of the room, they made a ruling that the Russian currency move was "illegal" and would have to be struck from the game record. Steve and I were incredulous, as were Steve's Russian teammates who had endorsed the idea.

"What do you mean, 'illegal'?" Steve demanded. "This is war! How can something be illegal!"

It was exactly what I had feared. Not only did the player selection discourage out-of-the-box thinking, but even when we could inject an unconventional move we were ruled out of bounds. I felt compelled to add my voice to Steve's even though I was playing a different cell.

"You know," I began from my seat in the China cell, "it's not like there's a Geneva Convention here. Russia's move is not far-fetched. The United States was on a gold standard until 1971 and a lot of people in this room remember it. Russia's being provocative but they're always provocative. Let's go ahead and see how this plays out."

The white cell seemed a little stung. Steve was like a batter who gets called out on a close play at first base and I was like the first-base coach trying to protect his player from being ejected. The digital chat room had erupted with the equivalent of "Kill the ump!" The white cell asked for another caucus to consider their ruling. Finally the white cell leader took the microphone. At this point I was half expecting to hear, "Upon further review . . . ," but in suitably bland bureaucratic language he confirmed Russia's move would be allowed. The white cell clarified that the move was not "illegal" but "ill-advised." I knew this was a polite way of saying Russia had done something stupid, but that was fine with me. Gold currency was now in the game; we would see how this evolved over the next two days.

The rest of the moves made were announced in fine multilateral fashion. The United States made the obligatory announcement in support of free trade and the need to think about green energy alternatives. The Pacific Rim announced that Japan would provide aid to any Asian nations suffering short-term hardships in energy costs and also pledged to seek alternative sources of energy. The gray cell, wearing its IMF hat, announced financial support to any former Soviet bloc nations suffering as a result of the Russia-Japan deal. None of the teams had anything to say about the new gold currency on the scene. It was just there, a newborn eight-hundred-pound gorilla sitting in the war room waiting for someone to notice.

At the end of move one, the white cell gave us the score. The United States had lost a small amount of power because it appeared that Japan had moved somewhat out of the U.S. orbit and the United States had not mustered an effective response. China gained a small amount of power essentially for doing nothing. Russia was heavily penalized for making what the white cell clearly regarded as a hostile move that showed a lack of cooperation with the rest of the world and had no immediate payoff. Net/net, Steve and I had collectively cost our teams some national power at the end of round one. However, we were playing what Russian Grandmasters call a deep game. There would be more moves to come.

Now it was on to move two. This baseline scenario did not mesh with my ideas about currency wars as well as the scenario used in the first move. This move had to do with an economic collapse in North Korea and the global reaction, which was intended to combine both geopolitical and humanitarian motives. It was a plausible scenario, but a strange choice for a financial war game. North Korea was about as unconnected to the global financial system as one country could get. It was difficult at first to see how to work the gold and currency angle into the North Korea scenario.

Sitting in our Chinese capital, I listened to my teammates earnestly discuss whether the United States might refuse to aid North Korea in order to let the situation deteriorate as a prelude to Korean unification. Since this was a risk-averse crew, they settled on a package of humanitarian aid coupled with some indication that China might support reunification at some future date on nonconfrontational terms.

At an appropriate lull in the conversation, I turned to Harvard and said, "Look, it's not too late to revisit this gold currency thing. We could announce some support for the Russian initiative combined with some intention to study it and possibly join in the future."

At this point Harvard began to lose patience. He clearly thought the issue had been buried and could be safely ignored. If China joined the Russian system, it would be swapping its dollar reserves for physical gold in order to back the new currency. Among other objections, Harvard thought the Russians had set the price too high. "Look," he snapped back, "this whole thing makes no sense. Gold is not part of the monetary system and it's not coming back no matter what the Russians do. They're on their own. You want to use hard currency to buy gold at an inflated price; I'd rather keep the dollars—they're much more valuable. Now let's get back to North Korea."

As a renowned Asia expert, Harvard clearly relished the chance to dig in on complicated bilateral East Asian problems rather than pursue what he thought of as a pointless conversation about currencies and gold. Yet I had been trained since law school to argue both sides of an issue without pausing for breath, so I quickly turned his argument back on him just to keep the idea alive.

"You think we'd be paying too much for the gold?" I asked.

"Right," he said. "Way too much."

"So why don't we sell our gold to Russia?"

This was not just the lawyer's instinct but also the trader's. Every market has a bid side where someone is willing to buy and an offer side where someone is willing to sell. Market making is the art of price discovery between the bid and the offer. Someone may start out as a buyer, but if something is really priced too high she immediately becomes a seller. It was just this kind of dispassionate ice-water-in-the-veins mentality that typified the best traders I had ever met. I was calling Harvard's bluff. If the price was too high to buy, then we should sell. I waited to see if he would take the bait.

"Fine," he said. "Let's dump it all, sell all the gold to Russia for dollars and euros and diversify our foreign exchange position."

He may have said this just to shut me up, but it was fine with me. We had just tightened the noose around the U.S. dollar's neck. The rest of the team quickly concurred and I promptly convened a summit with Russia to give them our offer. Steve and I met for the third time and, as I expected, Russia agreed to buy all of China's gold, about one thousand metric tons, in exchange for currency from Russia's foreign exchange reserves. This trade was ideal from Russia's perspective because it was a huge purchase with minimal market impact. In ordinary gold trading, a large bloc trade of as little as ten tons would have to be arranged in utmost secrecy in order not to send the market price through the roof, but now Russia had pulled off the largest single gold purchase in history with no immediate adverse market impact at all. I was sorry to see China out of the gold game, but I was pleased to see Russia moving the ball down the field.

Now it was back to the war room and our third plenary session. We went around the room, with each team spokesperson reporting its response to the North Korean scenario. As expected, the United States and the Pacific Rim pledged humanitarian aid, as did China, which furthermore made some conciliatory noises about potential reunification since the North Korean regime was clearly on its last legs at this point. Russia joined in the humanitarian aid chorus but also took a harder line by sealing its border with North Korea. Then, almost in passing, Russia announced that it had acquired all of China's gold and was adding this to its own preexisting hoard in support of the new gold-backed currency.

The white cell was visibly perturbed. Russia was playing its own game by its own rules. As far as Steve and I were concerned, Russia had been playing by its own rules for a thousand years, so this was a typically Russian course of action. At this point, the eight-hundred-pound gorilla could no longer be ignored and the adjudication came quickly. There was very little change in the national power of China, the United States or the Pacific Rim as a result of round two. This made sense because North Korea, while volatile and dangerous, was isolated, so no one gained or lost much relative power when the North Koreans decided to rock the boat—it was everyone's problem. But the white cell then reported, sheepishly, "It appears Russia has taken concrete steps toward launching a credible alternative to the dollar in international trade. Its prospects are highly uncertain, but we have decided to award Russia additional points for its currency-related moves." Steve and I looked at each other from across the war room. This was far from vindication, but it was hard to resist a slight smile.

It was now the end of day one. We were having a good war so far, but it had been a long day. We decided to find a local restaurant, have a few drinks and dinner, and then head back to our hotel early to catch up on the news and get ready for day two. It is one of the paradoxes of working inside a secure location that you have no idea what is going on in the outside world. Someone may be in the nerve center of intelligence analysis or weapons development, but, because of limited access to cell phones, news apps and the desiderata of twenty-first-century connectedness, he would be the last one to know if stock markets were collapsing. As market participants and news junkies, we were now as hungry for information as we were for food. We got directions to a not too fancy place nearby that the lab staff had recommended, and Steve and O.D. chatted and tapped on their BlackBerrys while I drove in the general direction of Fort Meade, Maryland. We found the place without too much difficulty but were surprised to find the parking lot full and people jamming the second-story balcony outside the restaurant at 5:30 on a Tuesday afternoon.

"Ah," said O.D., drawing on his O'Donnell family roots and putting on an Irish accent for the occasion. "It's Saint Paddy's Day—the place has probably been packed since noon."

In our quest to shake the world financial system to its core, we had completely forgotten about Saint Patrick's. I'm part Irish; my mother's side are Thorntons. With that as my pedigree, O.D. and I dubbed Steve an honorary Irishman and we made our way up the outdoor stairs, through the crowd on the balcony and pushed inside the equally crowded dining room to find a table by a window with a nice view of the surrounding Maryland countryside. We sat down, ordered three pints of Guinness and some entrées and started our own "brief back," as the Pentagon would put it.

"You know the problem with this game?" asked O.D.

"What's that?" I said.

"There's no market. I mean the white cell can tell us if we gained or lost ground, but there's no price system to measure the impact of what we're doing."

O.D. was right. A trader could have the best trading idea ever, but losing money on a trade is nature's way of telling you something's wrong. The best traders always got out of a losing trade, cut their losses and sat back looking for the next good opportunity. It would always come around eventually. Bad traders would rationalize the loss, assume the market didn't understand how smart they were, put on more of the trade in larger size, in effect doubling down, and usually go on to lose more money until some senior risk manager forced them out of the position. Whatever the strategy, it was the price signals that kept traders honest and gave traders the market feedback needed to validate their theories.

Still, it was hard to be too upset about what we didn't have. This was the first time the Department of Defense had ever run a financial war game and they were getting it done over some internal opposition. I was glad they were doing as much as they were. At least they were forward leaning, which was more than I could say about some of the civilian agencies. When I'd warned other government officials about the dangers of financial warfare launched by adversaries, the typical response was along the lines of "Oh, they would never do that—it would cost them money and they'd be shooting themselves in the foot." They said this as if military hardware didn't cost money, as if aircraft carriers were free. These officials failed to grasp the fact that the costs of a financial war might be far less than the costs of an arms race and possibly be much more effective at undermining U.S. power than a military confrontation. The Pentagon deserved a lot of credit for taking this as far as it had. There would be time to add bells and whistles later in some future game.

We ordered another round of Guinness, finished our meal and then headed back to Columbia, Maryland, where we were staying. It had been a long day and we had a 7:30 a.m. start on day two. We agreed to meet in the lobby in the morning and drifted off to our rooms.

■ Day Two

I woke up at 6:30 a.m. feeling a little groggy from the Guinness, but it was nothing two cups of coffee couldn't cure. I packed quickly and decided to check the news online before I stowed my laptop away. There was no time to get through the stack of e-mails that awaited me each morning, so I decided just to check the Drudge Report for a quick headline fix. Since I had been news deprived the day before and would be again today, it was a fast way to catch up with the world.

I clicked on the Drudge bookmark, waited a few seconds for the page to come up and then stared in complete disbelief at what I saw. In typical Drudge style, there was a huge headshot of a single individual dominating the center of the page. This morning it was Vladimir Putin. The banner headline underneath declared that Russia was calling for an end to the dollar and was looking for some alternative reserve currency, one possibly backed by tangible goods including gold.

These types of headlines have become commonplace in the past year, but in March 2009 it was still a new idea and one that a lot of people were just hearing about for the first time. It was easy to ridicule Putin as a chauvinist or headline seeker, but I knew that work on a dollar replacement had already been discussed in Europe and China and at the IMF. This was just Putin getting out ahead of the crowd and making known Russia's displeasure with the dollar-based hegemony imposed on the world by the United States—exactly what Steve and I had discussed over oysters and white wine the week before. There could not have been a better validation of our game moves if we had written the Drudge article ourselves.

I threw my laptop in my briefcase and ran down to the lobby, trying to get the same Drudge banner on my BlackBerry screen. Steve and O.D. were waiting for me.

"Hey, guys, have you seen Drudge this morning?" I yelled out from a distance. "You won't believe it."

I handed the BlackBerry to Steve, who studied the screen and passed it to O.D.

"Amazing," said Steve. "Those guys at the lab will think we planned the whole thing, like we had inside information. Let's get over there and show them what's going on in the world."

We arrived at the lab, rushed through security as quickly as possible and raced up the stairs of Building 26 to the war room.

Folks were having coffee and quietly chatting about events from the day before. I was fairly certain that the serious military and academic types around us had more important things to do each morning than read Drudge, so our scoop was still under wraps for the moment. I went into the technical support room adjacent to the main war room. The tech room had its own wall-sized screen to preview or troubleshoot what was going on in the war room. I asked the video tech if he could put the Internet up on the big screen and gave him the Web address for Drudge. Within a few seconds our friend Putin was on the screen, larger than life, throwing down the gauntlet at U.S. dollar hegemony. With a few more clicks on the control panel, the Drudge banner now appeared in the war room itself, while the lab staff helpfully printed out the story behind the headline and made sure a copy was placed among the rulebooks and scenarios sitting at every battle station.

Harvard was not amused. He thought Steve and I were being ridiculous and now he thought pretty much the same thing about Putin. But most of the participants were kind enough to give us some kudos for driving the game toward the next big thing before it happened.

Once the Putin buzz died down, it was back to the war game and move three, the final move in the game. This scenario involved the election of a proindependence candidate in Taiwan and an effort to reverse Taiwan's increasing economic integration with mainland China. There was not much left to do on the gold currency front by now. Russia had made its move, China had refused to go along and the United States acted indifferent, although this seemed strange because in the real world any move toward gold by Russia would have been met with a much more robust reaction by the United States. The U.S. cell was composed entirely of academics, think-tankers and uniformed military, and had no market experience at all, so I had to assume they just didn't get it when it came to an assault on the dollar. Like most experts I'd spoken to, they probably assumed the dollar would always remain dominant and did not think much about alternative scenarios.

We set about preparing our responses to the problem at hand. China reiterated its "One China" policy and warned other nations not to support the Taiwanese initiative. Japan tried to promote an Asian Free Trade Area that would welcome both China and Taiwan as a way to obviate their divisions. The United States emphasized military cooperation with Taiwan but urged that such cooperation in the future would be conditioned on Taiwan's reducing its confrontational stance. Only Russia continued to play the alternative currency wild card by trying to woo OPEC members in the gray cell to join its gold plan and by suggesting to China that it would be more inclined to take their side in the Taiwan dispute if China supported the new currency. I had to hand it to Steve and his teammates; they played their cards for all they were worth even if no one else was particularly paying attention.

Just when it looked like the game would wind down anticlimactically, O.D. played a wild card of his own. Speaking on behalf of the gray cell, he announced that the Japanese coast guard had interdicted large shipments of nearly perfect counterfeit hundred-dollar bills, called supernotes by U.S. Treasury officials. Supernotes are produced by North Korea's infamous Bureau 39, the state-sponsored racketeering agency set up in 1974 by Kim Il Sung to conduct money laundering, counterfeiting, drug smuggling and other acts usually perpetrated by criminal groups, in order to raise hard currency for the regime. O.D.'s move had a nice historical resonance with countries that had engaged in financial warfare by counterfeiting the currency of their enemies and flooding enemy territory with the counterfeits in order to cause distrust of legitimate bills and contribute to an economic collapse. During the U.S. Civil War, a Union sympathizer and Philadelphia stationery shop owner named Samuel Upham printed over $15 million in counterfeit Confederate bills, about 3 percent of the total amount in circulation. Many of these were carried south by Union soldiers and did undermine confidence in the real Confederate currency. O.D.'s counterfeit dollar discovery was a distant echo of this earlier episode of currency warfare.

O.D. also reported that Swiss banks had been scammed by deposits of these supernotes, which seemed to be flooding in from all over the world. The Swiss banking losses and the large size of the interdicted shipment were enough to cast doubt on the value of U.S. currency held abroad, mostly in the form of one-hundred-dollar bills. Dollars were now reported to trade on the black markets at a discount to their face value on world currency markets. The cash portion of total dollar holdings is small relative to the much larger amounts held in electronic form in banks, so the effect of the proliferating supernotes was not catastrophic. Still, it was one more swipe at the dollar and a nice parting shot from O.D.

Finally, the white cell seemed to be impressed with Russia's tenacity on the alternative currency, especially its overture to OPEC, and awarded the country additional national power points. This was a complete turnaround from day one, when Russia's play had been ridiculed. China was awarded more points mostly for doing nothing. It was a case study in how to win a zero-sum game just by keeping your head down while everyone else blundered around. The United States lost national power, partly because of Russia's dollar assault, but also because it appeared that East Asia was coalescing around a China-Japan bloc that would eventually include most of the region and exclude the United States from its key decisions on trade and capital flows. In the end, China gained the most by doing the least while Russia and East Asia gained slightly and the United States was the biggest loser.

The rest of the session was taken up with debriefings. It had been a fascinating two days on top of all the work that had gone into the preparation. It is genuinely helpful to U.S. national security when so many experts, with varied perspectives and some from distant locations, gather under one roof to exchange ideas and give the military new ways of understanding potential threats. When the Treasury and Fed did scenarios, they usually thought about bursting bubbles and market crashes, not state-sponsored financial wars. Former Fed chairman Alan Greenspan liked to say that the Fed had no expertise in stopping bubbles and that its resources were better utilized cleaning up the mess after a bubble had burst. That Greenspan view works only for messes of a certain size. For the really big messes—those involving civil unrest, food riots, looting, refugees and general collapse—the Fed has no answer and societies inevitably turn to the military for solutions. So the military had a large stake in understanding the potential for economic catastrophes. We had at least given the Pentagon some framework for thinking about an economic surprise attack. My hope was that they would not need it; my concern was that they would.

Over the next few weeks, with the recollections of the financial game fresh in my mind, I couldn't help but be reminded that a real currency war had already broken out and was being fought hard around the world. In March 2009, no one was yet using the term "currency war"—that would come later—but still all the signs were there. The Federal Reserve's first quantitative easing program, so-called QE, had begun in November 2008 with the not so hidden goal of weakening the dollar on foreign exchange markets. The Fed's cheap-dollar policies were having their intended effects.

Over the two years following the war game, stocks and gold both rose over 85 percent. Some analysts were initially baffled by the positive correlation of stocks and gold until they realized that exactly the same thing had happened in April 1933 when FDR smashed the dollar against sterling during the "beggar-thy-neighbor" currency wars of the Great Depression. The massive price gains in stocks and gold in 1933 and 2010 were just the flip side of trashing the dollar. The assets weren't worth more intrinsically—it just took more dollars to buy them because the dollar had been devalued.

In the world outside the war room, trashing the dollar was the easy part. The hard part was calculating what would come next, when exporters like China, Russia and Saudi Arabia tried to protect their interests by raising prices or avoiding U.S. dollar paper assets.

That's when the currency wars would really heat up, yet that was still in the future from the perspective of the war game in 2009.

One lesson of the war game for the Pentagon was that, even if the dollar collapsed altogether, the United States still had massive gold reserves to fall back on. It is an intriguing fact that almost all of the U.S. gold hoard is located not in civilian bank vaults but on military bases—Fort Knox in Kentucky and West Point along the Hudson River in New York. That says something about the connection of national wealth and national security.

The 1930s currency devaluations led quickly to Japan's invasions in Asia and Germany's attacks in Europe. The 1970s currency devaluations led quickly to the worst period of inflation in modern history. The United States was now entering a period of financial danger, similar to the 1930s and the 1970s. The Pentagon's financial war game was ahead of its time, but only slightly, and seemed like part of the preparation for more dire days ahead—more of a beginning than the end to a new world of financial threats.

PART TWO

CURRENCY WARS

CHAPTER 3

Reflections on a Golden Age

"We're in the midst of an international currency war."
Guido Mantega, Finance Minister of Brazil,
September 27, 2010

"I don't like the expression . . . currency war."
Dominique Strauss-Kahn, Managing Director, IMF,
November 18, 2010

A currency war, fought by one country through competitive devaluations of its currency against others, is one of the most destructive and feared outcomes in international economics. It revives ghosts of the Great Depression, when nations engaged in beggar-thy-neighbor devaluations and imposed tariffs that collapsed world trade. It recalls the 1970s, when the dollar price of oil quadrupled because of U.S. efforts to weaken the dollar by breaking its link to gold. Finally, it reminds one of crises in UK pounds sterling in 1992, Mexican pesos in 1994 and the Russian ruble in 1998, among other disruptions. Whether prolonged or acute, these and other currency crises are associated with stagnation, inflation, austerity, financial panic and other painful economic outcomes. Nothing positive ever comes from a currency war.

So it was shocking and disturbing to global financial elites to hear the Brazilian finance minister, Guido Mantega, flatly declare in late September 2010 that a new currency war had begun. Of course, the events and pressures that gave rise to Mantega's declaration were not new or unknown to these elites. International tension on exchange rate policy and, by extension, interest rates and fiscal policy had been building even before the depression that began in late 2007. China had been repeatedly accused by its major trading partners of manipulating its currency, the yuan, to an artificially low level and of accumulating excess reserves of U.S. Treasury debt in the process. The Panic of 2008, however, cast the exchange rate disputes in a new light. Suddenly, instead of expanding, the economic pie began to shrink and countries formerly content with their share of a growing pie began to fight over the crumbs.

Despite the obvious global financial pressures that had built up by 2010, it was still considered taboo in elite circles to mention currency wars. Instead international monetary experts used phrases like "rebalancing" and "adjustment" to describe their efforts to realign exchange rates to achieve what were thought by some to be desired goals. Employing euphemisms did not abate the tension in the system.

At the heart of every currency war is a paradox. While currency wars are fought internationally, they are driven by domestic distress. Currency wars begin in an atmosphere of insufficient internal growth. The country that starts down this road typically finds itself with high unemployment, low or declining growth, a weak banking sector and deteriorating public finances. In these circumstances it is difficult to generate growth through purely internal means and the promotion of exports through a devalued currency becomes the growth engine of last resort. To see why, it is useful to recall the four basic components of growth in gross domestic product, GDP. These components are consumption (C), investment (I), government spending (G) and net exports, consisting of exports (X) minus imports (M). This overall growth definition is expressed in the following equation:

$$GDP = C + I + G + (X - M)$$

An economy that is in distress will find that consumption (C) is either stagnant or in decline because of unemployment, an excessive debt burden or both. Investment (I) in business plant and equipment and housing is measured independently of consumption but is nevertheless tied closely to it. A business will not invest in expanded capacity unless it expects consumers to buy the output either immediately or in the near future. Thus, when consumption lags, business investment tends to lag also. Government spending (G) can be expanded independently when consumption and investment are weak. Indeed, this is exactly what Keynesian-style economics recommends in order to keep an economy growing even when individuals and businesses move to the sidelines. The problem is that governments rely on taxes or borrowing to increase spending in a recession and voters are often unwilling to support either at a time when the burden of taxation is already high and citizens are tightening their own belts. In democracies, there are serious political constraints on the ability of governments to increase government spending in times of economic hardship even if some economists recommend exactly that.

In an economy where individuals and businesses will not expand and where government spending is constrained, the only remaining way to grow the economy is to increase net exports (X – M) and the fastest, easiest way to do that is to cheapen one's currency. An example makes the point. Assume a German car is priced in euros at €30,000. Further assume that €1 = $1.40. This means that the dollar price of the German car is $42,000 (i.e., €30,000 × $1.40/€1 = $42,000). Next assume the euro declines to $1.10. Now the same €30,000 car when priced in dollars will cost only $33,000 (i.e., €30,000 × $1.10/€1 = $33,000). This drop in the dollar price from $42,000 to $33,000 means that the car will be much more attractive to U.S. buyers and will sell correspondingly more units. The revenue to the German manufacturer of €30,000 per car is the same in both cases. Through the devaluation of the euro, the German auto company can sell more cars in the United States with no drop in the euro price per car. This will increase the German GDP and create jobs in Germany to keep up with the demand for new cars in the United States.

Imagine this dynamic applied not just to Germany but also to

France, Italy, Belgium and the other countries using the euro. Imagine the impact not just on automobiles but also French wine, Italian fashion and Belgian chocolates. Think of the impact not just on tangible goods but also intangibles such as computer software and consulting services. Finally, consider that this impact is not limited solely to goods shipped abroad but also affects tourism and travel. A decline in the dollar value of a euro from $1.40 to $1.10 can lower the price of a €100 dinner in Paris from $140 to $110 and make it more affordable for U.S. visitors. Take the impact of a decline in the dollar value of the euro of this magnitude and apply it to all tangible and intangible traded goods and services as well as tourism spread over the entire continent of Europe, and one begins to see the extent to which devaluation can be a powerful engine of growth, job creation and profitability. The lure of currency devaluation in a difficult economic environment can seem irresistible.

However, the problems and unintended consequences of these actions appear almost immediately. To begin with, very few goods are made from start to finish in a single country. In today's globalized world a particular product may involve U.S. technology, Italian design, Australian raw materials, Chinese assembly, Taiwanese components and Swiss-based global distribution before the product reaches consumers in Brazil. Each part of this supply and innovation chain will earn some portion of the overall profit based on its contribution to the whole. The point is that the exchange rate aspects of global business involve not only the currency of the final sale but also the currencies of all the intermediate inputs and supply chain transactions. A country that cheapens its currency may make final sales look cheaper when viewed from abroad but may hurt itself as more of its cheap currency is needed to purchase various inputs. When a manufacturing country has both large foreign export sales and also large purchases from abroad to obtain raw materials and components to build those exports, its currency may be almost irrelevant to net exports compared to other contributions such as labor costs, low taxes and good infrastructure.

Higher input costs are not the only downside of devaluation. A bigger immediate concern may be competitive, tit-for-tat devaluations. Consider the earlier case of the €30,000 German car whose U.S. dollar price drops from $42,000 to $33,000 when the euro is devalued from $1.40 to $1.10. How confident is the German manufacturer that the euro will stay down at $1.10? The United States may defend its domestic auto sector by cheapening the dollar against the euro, pushing the euro back up from $1.10 to some higher level, even back up to $1.40. The United States can do this by lowering interest rates—making the dollar less attractive to international investors—or printing money to debase the dollar. Finally, the United States can intervene directly in currency markets by selling dollars and buying euros to manipulate the euro back up to the desired level. In short, while devaluing the euro may have some immediate and short-term benefit, that policy can be reversed quickly if a powerful competitor such as the United States decides to engage in its own form of devaluation.

Sometimes these competitive devaluations are inconclusive, with each side gaining a temporary edge but neither side ceding permanent advantage. In such cases, a more blunt instrument may be required to help local manufacturers. That instrument is protectionism, which comes in the form of tariffs, embargoes and other barriers to free trade. Using the automobile example again, the United States could simply impose a $9,000 duty on each imported German car. This would push the U.S. price back up from $33,000 to $42,000 even though the euro remained cheap at $1.10. In effect, the United States would offset the benefit of the euro devaluation for the Germans with a tariff roughly equal to the dollar value of that benefit, thereby eliminating the euro's edge in the U.S. market. From the perspective of an American autoworker, this might be the best outcome since it protects U.S. industry while allowing the autoworker to take an affordable European holiday.

Protectionism is not limited to the imposition of tariffs but may include more severe trade sanctions, including embargoes. A notable recent case involving China and Japan amounted to a currency war skirmish. China controls almost all of the supply of certain so-called rare earths, which are exotic, hard-to-mine metals crucial in the manufacture of electronics, hybrid automobiles and other high-tech and green technology applications. While the rare earths come from China, many of their uses are in Japanese-made electronics and automobiles. In July 2010, China announced a 72 percent reduction in rare earth exports, which had the effect of slowing manufacturing in Japan and other countries that depend on Chinese rare earth supplies.

On September 7, 2010, a Chinese trawler collided with a Japanese patrol ship in a remote island group in the East China Sea claimed by both Japan and China. The trawler captain was taken into custody by the Japanese patrol while China protested furiously, demanding the captain's release and a full apology from Japan. When the release and apology were not immediately forthcoming, China went beyond the July reduction in exports and halted *all* rare earth shipments to Japan, crippling Japanese manufacturers. On September 14, 2010, Japan counterattacked by engineering a sudden devaluation of the Japanese yen in international currency markets. The yen fell about 3 percent in three days against the Chinese yuan. Persistence by Japan in that course of devaluation could have hurt Chinese exports to Japan relative to exports from lower-cost producers such as Indonesia and Vietnam.

China had attacked Japan with an embargo and Japan fought back with a currency devaluation while both sides postured over a remote group of uninhabited rocks and the fate of the imprisoned trawler captain. Over the next few weeks the situation stabilized, the captain was released, Japan issued a pro forma apology, the yen began to strengthen again and the flow of rare earths resumed. A much worse outcome had been avoided, but lessons had been learned and knives sharpened for the next battle.

A prospective currency warrior always faces the law of unintended consequences. Assume that a currency devaluation, such as one in Europe, succeeds in its intended purpose and European goods are cheaper to the world and exports become a significant contributor to growth as a result. That may be fine for Europe, but over time manufacturing in other countries may begin to suffer from lost markets leading to plant closures, layoffs, bankruptcy and recession. The wider recession may lead to declining sales by Europeans as well, not because of the exchange rate, but because foreign workers can no longer afford to buy Europe's exports even at the cheaper prices. This kind of global depressing effect of currency wars may take longer to evolve, but may be the most pernicious effect of all.

So currency devaluation as a path to increased exports is not a simple matter. It may lead to higher input costs, competitive devaluations, tariffs, embargoes and global recession sooner rather than later. Given these adverse outcomes and unintended consequences, one wonders why currency wars begin at all. They are mutually destructive while they last and impossible to win in the end.

As with any policy challenge, some history is instructive. The twentieth century was marked by two great currency wars. The first, Currency War I, ran from 1921 to 1936, almost the entire period between World War I and World War II including the Great Depression, with which it is closely associated. The second, Currency War II, ran from 1967 to 1987 and was finally settled by two global agreements, the Plaza Accord in 1985 and the Louvre Accord in 1987, without descending into military conflict.

Currency wars resemble most wars in the sense that they have identifiable antecedents. The three most powerful antecedents of CWI were the classical gold standard from 1870 to 1914, the creation of the Federal Reserve from 1907 to 1913, and World War I and the Treaty of Versailles from 1914 to 1919. A brief survey of these three periods helps one to understand the economic conflicts that followed.

■ The Classical Gold Standard—1870 to 1914

Gold has served as an international currency since at least the sixth century BC reign of King Croesus of Lydia, in what is modern-day Turkey. More recently, England established a gold-backed paper currency at a fixed exchange rate in 1717, which continued in various forms with periodic wartime suspensions until 1931. These and other monetary regimes may all go by the name "gold standard"; however, that term does not have a single defined meaning. A gold standard may include everything from the use of actual gold coins to the use of paper money backed by gold in various amounts. Historically the amount of gold backing for paper money has ranged from 20 percent up to 100 percent, and sometimes higher in rare cases where the value of official gold is greater than the money supply.

The classical gold standard of 1870 to 1914 has a unique place in the history of gold as money. It was a period of almost no inflation—in fact, a benign deflation prevailed in the more advanced economies as the result of technological innovation that increased productivity and raised living standards without increasing unemployment. This period is best understood as the first age of globalization, and it shares many characteristics with the more recent, second age of globalization that started in 1989 with the end of the Cold War.

The first age of globalization was characterized by technological improvements in communication and transportation, so that bankers in New York could speak on the phone to their partners in London and travel time between the two financial hubs could be as short as seven days. These improvements may not have been widespread, but they did facilitate global commerce and banking. Bonds issued in Argentina, underwritten in London and purchased in New York created a dense web of interconnected assets and debts of a kind quite familiar to bankers today. Behind this international growth and commerce was gold.

The classical gold standard was not devised at an international conference like its twentieth-century successors, nor was it imposed top-down by a multilateral organization. It was more like a club that member nations joined voluntarily. Once in the club, those members behaved according to well-understood rules of the game, although there was no written rulebook. Not every major nation joined, but many did, and among those who joined, capital accounts were open, free market forces prevailed, government interventions were minimal and currency exchange rates were stable against one another.

Some nations had been on a gold standard since well before 1870, including England in 1717 and the Netherlands in 1818, but it was in the period after 1870 that a flood of nations rushed to join them and the gold club took on its distinctive character. These new members included Germany and Japan in 1871, France and Spain in 1876, Austria in 1879, Argentina in 1881, Russia in 1893 and India in 1898. While the United States had been on a de facto gold standard since 1832, when it began minting one-troy-ounce gold coins worth about twenty dollars at the time, it did not legally adopt a gold standard for the conversion of paper money until the Gold Standard Act of 1900, making the United States one of the last major nations to join the classical gold system.

Economists are nearly unanimous in pointing out the beneficial economic results of this period. Giulio M. Gallarotti, the leading theorist and economic historian of the classical gold standard period, summarizes this neatly in *The Anatomy of an International Monetary Regime:*

> Among that group of nations that eventually gravitated to gold standards in the latter third of the 19th century (i.e., the gold club), abnormal capital movements (i.e., hot money flows) were uncommon, competitive manipulation of exchange rates was rare, international trade showed record growth rates, balance-of-payments problems were few, capital mobility was high (as was mobility of factors and people), few nations that ever adopted gold standards ever suspended convertibility (and of those that did, the most important returned), exchange rates stayed within their respective gold points (i.e., were extremely stable), there were few policy conflicts among nations, speculation was stabilizing (i.e., investment behavior tended to bring currencies back to equilibrium after being displaced), adjustment was quick, liquidity was abundant, public and private confidence in the international monetary system remained high, nations experienced long-term price stability (predictability) at low levels of inflation, long-term trends in industrial production and income growth were favorable and unemployment remained fairly low.

This highly positive assessment by Gallarotti is echoed by a study published by the Federal Reserve Bank of St. Louis, which concludes, "Economic performance in the United States and the United Kingdom was superior under the classical gold standard to that of the subsequent period of managed fiduciary money." The period from 1870 to 1914 was a golden age in terms of noninflationary growth coupled with increasing wealth and productivity in the industrialized and commodity-producing world.

A great part of the attraction of the classical gold standard was its simplicity. While a central bank might perform certain functions, no central bank was required; indeed the United States did not have a central bank during the entire period of the classical gold standard. A country joining the club merely declared its paper currency to be worth a certain amount in gold and then stood ready to buy or sell gold at that price in exchange for currency in any quantity from another member. The process of buying and selling gold near a target price in order to maintain that price is known today as an open market operation. It can be performed by a central bank, but that is not strictly necessary; it can just as well be performed by a government operating directly or indirectly through fiscal agents such as banks or dealers. Each authorized dealer requires access to a reasonable supply of gold with the understanding that in a panic more gold could readily be obtained. Although government intervention is involved, it is conducted transparently and can be seen as stabilizing rather than manipulating.

The benefit of this system in international finance is that when two currencies become anchored to a standard weight of gold, they also became anchored to each other. This type of anchoring does not require facilitation by institutions such as the IMF or the G20. In the classical gold standard period, the world had all the benefits of currency stability and price stability without the costs of multilateral overseers and central bank planning.

Another benefit of the classical gold standard was its self-equilibrating nature not only in terms of day-to-day open market operations but also in relation to larger events such as gold mining production swings. If gold supply increased more quickly than productivity, which happened on occasions such as the spectacular discoveries in South Africa, Australia and the Yukon between 1886 and

1896, then the price level for goods would go up temporarily. However, this would lead to increased costs for gold producers that would eventually lower production and reestablish the long-term trend of price stability. Conversely, if economic productivity increased due to technology, the price level would fall temporarily, which meant the purchasing power of money would go up. This would cause holders of gold jewelry to sell and would increase gold mining efforts, leading eventually to increased gold supply and a restoration of price stability. In both cases, the temporary supply and demand shocks in gold led to changes in behavior that restored long-term price stability.

In international trade, these supply and demand factors equilibrated in the same way. A nation with improving terms of trade—an increasing ratio of export prices versus import prices—would begin to run a trade surplus. This surplus in one country would be mirrored by deficits in others whose terms of trade were not as favorable. The deficit nation would settle with the surplus nation in gold. This caused money supply in the deficit nation to shrink and money supply in the surplus nation to expand. The surplus nation with the expanding money supply experienced inflation while the deficit nation with the decreasing money supply experienced deflation. This inflation and deflation in the trading partners would soon reverse the initial terms of trade. Exports from the original surplus nation would begin to get more expensive, while exports from the original deficit nation would begin to get less expensive. Eventually the surplus nation would go to a trade deficit and the deficit nation would go to a surplus. Now gold would start to flow back to the nation that had originally lost it. Economists called this the price-specie-flow mechanism (also the price-gold-flow mechanism).

This rebalancing worked naturally without central bank intervention. It was facilitated by arbitrageurs who would buy "cheap" gold in one country and sell it as "expensive" gold in another country once exchange rates, the time value of money, transportation costs and bullion refining costs were taken into account. It was done in accordance with the rules of the game, which were well-understood customs and practices based on mutual advantage, common sense and the profits of arbitrage.

Not every claim had to be settled in gold immediately. Most international trade was financed by short-term trade bills and letters of credit that were self-liquidating when the imported goods were received by the buyer and resold for cash without any gold transfers. The gold stock was an anchor or foundation for the overall system rather than the sole medium of exchange. Yet it was an efficient anchor because it obviated currency hedging and gave merchants greater certainty as to the ultimate value of their transactions.

The classical gold standard epitomized a period of prosperity before the Great War of 1914 to 1918. The subsequent and much maligned gold exchange standard of the 1920s was, in the minds of many, an effort to return to a halcyon prewar age. However, efforts in the 1920s to use the prewar gold price were doomed by a mountain of debt and policy blunders that turned the gold exchange standard into a deflationary juggernaut. The world has not seen the operation of a pure gold standard in international finance since 1914.

■ The Creation of the Federal Reserve—1907 to 1913

The second of the currency war antecedents was the creation of the Federal Reserve System in 1913. That story has antecedents of its own, and for those one must look back even further, to the Panic of 1907. This panic began amid a failed attempt by several New York banks, including one of its largest, the Knickerbocker Trust, to corner the copper market. When Knickerbocker's involvement in the scheme came to light, a classic run on the bank commenced. If the Knickerbocker revelations had occurred in calmer markets, they might not have triggered such a panicked response, but the market was already nervous and volatile after massive losses caused by the 1906 San Francisco earthquake.

The failure of the Knickerbocker Trust was just the beginning of a more general loss of confidence, which led to another stock market crash, even further bank runs, and finally a full-scale liquidity crisis and threat to the stability of the financial system as a whole. This threat was stemmed only by collective action of the leading bankers of the day in the form of a private financial rescue organized by J. P. Morgan. In one of the most famous episodes in U.S. financial history, Morgan summoned the financiers to his town house in the Murray Hill neighborhood of Manhattan and would not allow them to leave until they had hammered out a rescue plan involving specific financial commitments by each one intended to calm the markets. The plan worked, but not before massive financial losses and dislocations had been sustained.

The immediate result of the Panic of 1907 was a determination by the bankers involved in the rescue that the United States needed a central bank—a government-established bank with the ability to issue newly created funds to bail out the private banking system when called upon. The bankers wanted a government-sponsored facility that could lend them unlimited amounts of cash against a broad range of collateral. The bankers realized that J. P. Morgan would not always be around to provide leadership, and some future panic could call for solutions that exceeded even the resources and talents of the great Morgan himself. A central bank to act as an unlimited lender of last resort to private banks was needed before the next panic arose.

America had a long history of antipathy to central banks. There had been two efforts at something like a central bank in U.S. history prior to 1913. The first of these, the Bank of the United States, was chartered by Congress at the urging of Alexander Hamilton in 1791, but its charter expired in 1811 during the presidency of James Madison and a bill to recharter the bank failed by a single vote. Five years later, Madison steered the chartering of a Second Bank of the United States through Congress. But this second charter had a limited life of twenty years and would be up for renewal in 1836.

When the time for renewal came, the Second Bank ran into opposition not only in Congress but from the White House. President Andrew Jackson had based part of his 1832 presidential campaign on a platform of abolishing the bank. After a contentious national debate, which included Jackson pulling all U.S. Treasury deposits out of the Second Bank of the United States and placing them in state-chartered banks, the rechartering did pass Congress. Jackson vetoed it, and the charter was not renewed.

The political opposition to both national banks was based on a general distrust of concentrated financial power and a belief that the issuance of national banknotes contributed to asset bubbles that were inflated away by easy bank credit. From 1836 to 1913, an almost eighty-year period of unprecedented prosperity, innovation and strong economic growth, the United States had no central bank.

Now, literally in the rubble of the 1906 San Francisco earthquake and the financial rubble of the Panic of 1907, a concerted effort began to create a new central bank. Given the popular distrust of the idea of central banking, the bank sponsors, led by representatives of J. P. Morgan, John D. Rockefeller, Jr., and Jacob H. Schiff of the Wall Street firm Kuhn, Loeb & Company, knew that an education campaign to build popular support would need to be conducted. Their political patron, Senator Nelson W. Aldrich, Republican of Rhode Island, who was head of the Senate Finance Committee, sponsored legislation in 1908 creating the National Monetary Commission. Over the next several years, the National Monetary Commission was the platform for numerous research studies, sponsored events, speeches and affiliations with prestigious professional associations of economists and political scientists, all with a view to promoting the idea of a powerful central bank.

In September 1909, President William H. Taft publicly urged the country to consider supporting a central bank. That same month, the *Wall Street Journal* launched a series of editorials favoring the central bank under the heading "A Central Bank of Issue." By the summer of the following year, the popular and political foundations had been laid and it was now time to move toward a concrete plan for the new bank. What followed was one of the most bizarre episodes in the history of finance. Senator Aldrich was to be the primary sponsor of the legislation setting up the bank, but it would have to be drafted in accordance with a plan that satisfied the wishes of New York bankers still reeling from the Panic of 1907 and still searching for a lender of last resort to bail them out the next time a panic arose. A committee of bankers was needed to draft the plan for the central bank.

In November 1910, Aldrich convened a meeting to be attended by himself, several Wall Street bankers and Abram Piatt Andrew, the recently appointed assistant secretary of the Treasury. The bankers included Paul Warburg of Kuhn, Loeb; Frank A. Vanderlip of the Rockefeller-controlled National City Bank of New York; Charles D. Norton of the Morgan-controlled First National Bank of New York; and Henry P. Davison, the most senior and powerful partner at J. P. Morgan & Company after Morgan himself. Andrew was a Harvard economist who would act as technical adviser to this carefully balanced group of Morgan and Rockefeller interests.

Aldrich instructed his delegation to meet under cover of darkness at an isolated railway siding in Hoboken, New Jersey, where a private railroad car would be waiting. The men were told to come singly and to avoid reporters at all costs. Once aboard the train, they used first names only so that porters could not identify them to friends or reporters once they left the train; some of the men adopted code names as an extra layer of security. After traveling for two days, they arrived in Brunswick, Georgia, along the Atlantic coast about halfway between Savannah and Jacksonville, Florida. From there they took a launch to Jekyll Island and checked into the exclusive Jekyll Island Club, partly owned by J. P. Morgan. The group worked for over a week to hammer out the Aldrich bill, which would become the blueprint for the Federal Reserve System.

It still took over three years to pass the Federal Reserve Act, the formal name given to the Aldrich bill based on the Jekyll Island plan. The Federal Reserve Act finally passed with large majorities on December 23, 1913, and went into effect in November 1914.

The Federal Reserve Act of 1913 contained many features promoted by Aldrich and Warburg designed to overcome traditional objections to a U.S. central bank. The new entity would not be called a central bank but rather the Federal Reserve System. It would not be a single entity but rather a collection of regional reserve banks guided by a Federal Reserve Board whose members would not be picked by bankers but rather by the president and subject to Senate confirmation.

On the whole, it looked decentralized and under the control of democratically elected officials. Inside the plan, however, was a de facto mechanism much more in line with the true intent of the Aldrich party on Jekyll Island. Actual monetary policy, conducted through open market operations, would be dominated by the Federal Reserve Bank of New York since New York was the location of the major banks and dealers with whom the Fed would do business. The Federal Reserve Bank of New York was run by a board of directors and governor, not selected by politicians but selected by its stockholders, who were dominated by the large New York banks. The result was a "Fed within the Fed," run by the New York banks and amenable to their goals, including easy credit for bailouts as needed.

Some of these features were changed by subsequent legislation in the 1930s, which centralized power in the Board of Governors of the Federal Reserve in Washington, D.C., where it resides today. In more recent years the board has been dominated not by bankers but by academic economists and lawyers who ironically seem even more favorably disposed toward easy money and bailouts than the bankers. Yet, at least through the 1920s, the Fed "system" was dominated by the New York Fed under the firm hand of its first governor, Benjamin Strong, who ran the bank from 1914 until he died in 1928. Strong was a protégé of Morgan partner Henry Davison as well as of J. P. Morgan himself. Thus the circle of Morgan influence on the new central bank of the United States was complete.

History has its echoes. Decades after the Jekyll Island meeting, Frank Vanderlip's National City Bank and Charles Norton's First National Bank merged to become the First National City Bank of New York, which later shortened its name to Citibank. In 2008, Citibank was the recipient of the largest bank bailout in history, conducted by the U.S. Federal Reserve. The foundation laid by Vanderlip and Norton and their associates on Jekyll Island in 1910 would prove durable enough to bail out their respective banks almost one hundred years later exactly as intended.

■ World War I and the Treaty of Versailles—1914 to 1919

The last of the antecedents of Currency War I was the sequence of the Great War, the Paris Peace Conference and the Treaty of Versailles.

World War I ended not with surrender but with an armistice, an agreement to stop fighting. With any armistice, the expectation is that the cessation of hostilities will allow the parties to negotiate a peace treaty, but in some cases the negotiations break down and fighting resumes. Negotiation of a lasting peace was the objective of the Paris Peace Conference of 1919. England and France were well aware that the financial bill for the war was about to be presented. They saw the Paris Peace Conference as an opportunity to impose these adjustment costs on the defeated Germans and Austrians.

However, a successful negotiation in Paris was by no means a foregone conclusion. Although the German army and navy were definitely beaten by November 1918, as of the spring of 1919 no peace treaty had been concluded and it seemed increasingly unlikely that the Allies would be willing or able to resume the war. Therefore the reparations negotiations were just that: negotiations. The Allied ability to dictate terms had withered between November 1918 and March 1919, when the subject was taken up. Now Germany would have to be prevailed upon to agree to any plan the Allies devised.

The size and nature of German reparations were among the most vexing questions facing the Paris Peace Conference. On the one hand, Germany would be asked to cede territory and some industrial capacity. On the other hand, the more Germany gave up, the less able it would be to pay financial reparations that were also being demanded. France had its eye on German gold, which in 1915 had amounted to over 876 metric tons, the fourth largest hoard in the world after the United States, Russia and France.

While these reparations are often thought of solely in terms of how much Germany could afford to pay the Allies, the picture was considerably more complicated, as both the winners and the losers were in debt. As Margaret MacMillan writes in her book *Paris 1919*, both Britain and France had loaned vast amounts to Russia, which defaulted in the wake of the Russian Revolution. Other debtors, such as Italy, were unable to repay. Yet Britain owed $4.7 billion to the United States, while France owed $4 billion to the United States and another $3 billion to Britain. Virtually none of the debtor nations could afford to repay. The entire mechanism of credit and trade was frozen.

The issue was not just one of German reparations to the Allies but of a complex web of inter-Allied loans. Something was needed to reprime the pump and get credit, commerce and trade moving again. The optimal approach was to have the strongest financial power, the United States, begin the process with new loans and guarantees on top of those already provided. This new liquidity, combined with a free trade area, might have encouraged the growth needed to deal with the debt burdens. Another approach, also with much to recommend it, was to forgive all the debts and start the game over. While it would be difficult for France to forgive Germany, it would be a relief for France to be forgiven by the United States: the net effect on France would have been positive because the United States was more persistent as a creditor than Germany was reliable as a debtor. In fact, none of these things happened. Instead the stronger, led by England and France, prevailed upon the weaker, primarily Germany, to pay punitive reparations in cash, in kind and in gold.

Calculation of the reparations and agreement on a mechanism by which reparations would be paid was a nearly impossible task. France, Belgium and England wanted to base reparations on actual war damages, while the United States was more inclined to consider Germany's ability to pay. The German statistics, however, were abysmal and no reliable calculation of their ability to pay could be made. The assessment of damages was also impossible in the short run. Many areas were barely accessible, let alone amenable to some sort of appraisal of needed reconstruction.

The Allies argued as much among themselves as they did with German representatives about whether reparations should be limited to actual damages, which favored France and Belgium, or should include purely financial costs such as pensions and soldiers' salaries, which would favor England. In the end, no exact amount of reparations was specified in the Treaty of Versailles. This was the result of the technical impossibility of calculating a number and the political impossibility of agreeing to one. Any figure high enough to enjoy domestic approval in England and France might have been too high for the Germans to agree to and vice versa. American admonitions for moderation and practicality were largely ignored. Domestic politics triumphed over international economic needs. Instead of a specific number, expert panels were empowered to continue studying the question and make specific findings in the years ahead, which would form the basis for actual reparations. This bought time, but the hard issues on reparations were put off only to become entangled during the 1920s with the gold exchange standard and efforts to restart the international monetary system. Reparations were like an albatross hung around the neck of the international financial system for the next fifteen years.

■ Conclusion

By 1921, the table was set for the first modern currency war. The classical gold standard had acted as an intellectual magnet, a monetary North Star that framed the debate over what kind of system was needed in the 1920s to restart international capital flows and world trade. World War I and the Treaty of Versailles introduced a new element, not predominant in the gold standard age, of massive, interlocking and unpayable sovereign debts, which imposed an insurmountable obstacle to normalized capital flows. The creation of the Federal Reserve System and the role of the New York Fed in particular heralded the arrival of the United States on the international monetary scene as the dominant player and not just another participant. The potential for the Fed to reliquify the system through its own money printing efforts was just coming into full view. By the early 1920s, nostalgic affection for the prewar classical gold standard, tension over unpayable reparations and uncertainty about the money power of the Federal Reserve all conditioned the creation of a new international monetary system and the course of Currency War I.

CHAPTER 4

Currency War I (1921–1936)

> "There is hardly a part of the United States where men are not aware that secret private purposes and interests have been running the government."
>
> President Woodrow Wilson

C urrency War I began in spectacular fashion in 1921 in the shadow of World War I and wound down to an inconclusive end in 1936. The war was fought in many rounds and on five continents and has great resonance for the twenty-first century. Germany moved first in 1921 with a hyperinflation designed initially to improve competitiveness and then taken to absurd lengths to destroy an economy weighed down by the burden of war reparations. France moved next in 1925 by devaluing the franc before returning to the gold standard, thus gaining an export edge on those like England and the United States who would return to gold at a prewar rate. England broke with gold in 1931, regaining the ground lost to France in 1925. Germany was boosted in 1931 when President Herbert Hoover placed a moratorium on war reparations payments. The moratorium became permanent as a result of the 1932 Lausanne Conference. After 1933 and the rise of Hitler, Germany increasingly went its own way and withdrew from world trade, becoming a more autarkic economy, albeit with links to Austria and Eastern Europe. The United States moved in

1933, also devaluing against gold and regaining some of the competitive edge in export pricing lost to England in 1931. Finally it was the turn of France and England to devalue again. In 1936, France broke with gold and became the last major country to emerge from the worst effects of the Great Depression while England devalued again to regain some of the advantage it had lost against the dollar after FDR's devaluations in 1933.

In round after round of devaluation and default, the major economies of the world raced to the bottom, causing massive trade disruption, lost output and wealth destruction along the way. The volatile and self-defeating nature of the international monetary system during that period makes Currency War I the ultimate cautionary tale for today as the world again confronts the challenge of massive unpayable debt.

Currency War I began in 1921 in Weimar Germany when the Reichsbank, Germany's central bank, set about to destroy the value of the German mark through massive money printing and hyperinflation. Presided over by Reichsbank head Dr. Rudolf von Havenstein, a Prussian lawyer-turned-banker, the inflation proceeded primarily through the Reichsbank's purchases of bills from the German government to supply the government with the money needed to fund budget deficits and government spending. This was one of the most destructive and pervasive monetary debasements ever seen in a major developed economy. A myth has persisted ever since that Germany destroyed its currency to get out from under onerous war reparations demanded by England and France in the Treaty of Versailles. In fact, those reparations were tied to "gold marks," defined as a fixed amount of gold or its equivalent in non-German currency, and subsequent treaty protocols were based on a percentage of German exports regardless of the paper currency value. Those gold- and export-related specifications could not be inflated away. However, the Reichsbank did see an opportunity to increase German exports by debasing its currency both to make German goods more affordable abroad—one typical reason for a debasement—as well as to encourage tourism and foreign investment. These methods could provide foreign exchange needed to pay reparations without diminishing the amount of reparations directly.

As inflation slowly began to take off in late 1921, it was not immediately perceived as a threat. The German people understood that prices were going up, but that did not automatically translate into the equivalent notion that the currency was collapsing. German banks had liabilities nearly equal to their assets and so were largely hedged. Many businesses owned hard assets such as land, plant, equipment and inventories that gained nominal value as the currency collapsed and therefore were also hedged. Some of those companies also owed debts that evaporated as the amounts owed became worthless, and so were enriched by being relieved of their debts. Many large German corporations, predecessors of today's global giants, had operations outside of Germany, which earned hard currency and further insulated their parent companies from the worst effects of the collapse of the mark.

Capital flight is a traditional response to currency collapse. Those who could convert marks into Swiss francs, gold or other stores of value did so and moved their savings abroad. Even the German bourgeoisie was not immediately alarmed as losses in the value of their currency were offset by stock market gains. The fact that these gains were denominated in soon to be worthless marks had not yet occurred to many. Finally, those who held unionized and government jobs were initially hedged as well because the government simply granted wage increases commensurate with inflation.

Of course, not everyone had a government or union job, stock portfolio, hard assets or foreign operations to insulate them. Those most devastated were middle-class pensioners who no longer qualified for raises and savers who kept their funds in banks rather than stocks. These Germans were completely financially ruined. Many were forced to sell their furniture to raise a few marks to pay for food and keep going. Pianos were particularly in demand and became a form of currency on their own. Some elderly couples whose savings had been destroyed would go into the kitchen, hold hands, place their heads in the oven and turn on the gas in a poignant form of suicide. Property crime became rampant and, in the later stages, riots and looting were common.

In 1922, the inflation turned to hyperinflation as the Reichsbank gave up trying to control the situation and printed money frantically to meet the demands of union and government workers. A single U.S. dollar became so valuable thatAmerican visitors could not spend it because merchants could not locate the millions of marks needed to make change. Diners offered to pay for meals in advance because the price would be vastly higher by the time they finished eating. The demand for banknotes was so great that the Reichsbank engaged numerous private printing firms and used special logistics teams in order to obtain enough paper and ink to keep the printing presses rolling. By 1923, the notes were being printed on one side only to conserve ink.

With economic chaos reigning, France and Belgium invaded the German industrial region of the Ruhr Valley in 1923 in order to secure their interests in reparations. The invasion enabled the occupiers to obtain payment in kind through shipments of manufactured goods and coal. The German workers in the Ruhr responded with work slowdowns, strikes and sabotage. The Reichsbank rewarded the workers and encouraged their resistance by printing more money for higher wages and unemployment benefits.

Germany finally attempted to halt the hyperinflation in November 1923 by creating an alternate currency, the rentenmark, which initially circulated side by side with the paper mark. The rentenmark was backed by mortgages and by the ability to tax the underlying properties. Their issuance and circulation were carefully managed by the newly appointed currency commissioner, Hjalmar Schacht, a seasoned private banker who would soon replace von Havenstein as head of the Reichsbank. When the final collapse of the mark came shortly after the rentenmark was introduced, one rentenmark was roughly equal to one trillion marks. The rentenmark was a temporary fix and was soon replaced by a new reichsmark backed directly by gold. By 1924, the old hyperinflated paper marks were literally being swept away into dustbins, drains and sewers.

Economic historians customarily treat the 1921-1924 hyperinflation of the Weimar Republic separately from the worldwide beggar-thy-neighbor competitive devaluations of 1931-1936, but this ignores the continuity of competitive devaluations in the interwar period. The Weimar hyperinflation actually achieved a number of important political goals, a fact that had repercussions throughout the 1920s and 1930s. Hyperinflation unified the German people in opposition to "foreign speculators" and it forced France to show its hand in the Ruhr Valley, thus creating a case for German rearmament. Hyperinflation also evoked some sympathy from England and the United States for alleviation of the harshest demands for reparations emanating from the Versailles Treaty. While the collapse of the mark was not directly linked to the value of reparations payments, Germany could at least argue that its economy had collapsed because of hyperinflation, justifying some form of reparations relief. The currency collapse also strengthened the hand of German industrialists who controlled hard assets in contrast to those relying solely on financial assets. These industrialists emerged from the hyperinflation more powerful than before because of their ability to hoard hard currency abroad and buy up assets of failed enterprises on the cheap at home.

Finally, the hyperinflation showed that countries could, in effect, play with fire when it came to paper currencies, knowing that a simple resort to the gold standard or some other tangible asset such as land could restore order when conditions seemed opportune— exactly what Germany did. This is not to argue that German hyperinflation in 1922 was a carefully thought-out plan, only that hyperinflation can be used as a policy lever. Hyperinflation produces fairly predictable sets of winners and losers and prompts certain behaviors and therefore can be used politically to rearrange social and economic relations among debtors, creditors, labor and capital, while gold is kept available to clean up the wreckage if necessary.

Of course, the costs of hyperinflation were enormous. Trust in German government institutions evaporated and lives were literally destroyed. Yet the episode showed that a major country with natural resources, labor, hard assets and gold available to preserve wealth could emerge from hyperinflation relatively intact. From 1924 to 1929, immediately after the hyperinflation, German industrial production expanded at a faster rate than any other major economy, including the United States. Previously countries had gone off the gold standard in times of war, a notable example being England's suspension of gold convertibility during and immediately after the Napoleonic Wars. Now Germany had broken the link to gold in a time of peace, albeit the hard peace of the Versailles Treaty. The Reichsbank had demonstrated that in a modern economy a paper currency, unlinked to gold, could be debased in pursuit of purely political goals and those goals could be achieved. This lesson was not lost on other major industrial nations.

At exactly the same time the Weimar hyperinflation was spiraling out of control, major industrial nations sent representatives to the Genoa Conference in Italy in the spring of 1922 to consider a return to the gold standard for the first time since before World War I. Prior to 1914, most major economies had a true gold standard in which paper notes existed in a fixed relationship to gold, so both paper and gold coins circulated side by side with one freely convertible into the other. However, these gold standards were mostly swept aside with the coming of World War I as the need to print currency to finance war expenditures became paramount. Now, in 1922, with the Versailles Treaty completed and war reparations established, although on an unsound footing, the world looked again to the anchor of a gold standard.

Yet important changes had taken place since the heyday of the classical gold standard. The United States had created a new central bank in 1913, the Federal Reserve System, with unprecedented powers to regulate interest rates and the supply of money. The interaction of gold stocks and Fed money was still an object of experimentation in the 1920s. Countries had also grown used to the convenience of issuing paper money as needed during the war years of 1914–1918, while citizens had likewise become accustomed to accepting paper money after gold coins had been withdrawn from circulation. The major powers came to the Genoa Conference with a view to reintroducing gold on a more flexible basis, more tightly controlled by the central banks themselves.

From the Genoa Conference there emerged the new gold exchange standard, which differed from the former classical gold standard in significant ways. Participating countries agreed that central bank reserves could be held not only in gold but in the currencies of other nations; the word "exchange" in "gold exchange standard" simply meant that certain foreign exchange balances would be treated like gold for reserve purposes. This outsourced the burden of the gold standard to those countries with large gold holdings such as the United States. The United States would be responsible for upholding the gold value of the dollar at the $20.67 per ounce ratio while other nations could hold dollars as a gold proxy. Under this new standard, international accounts would still be settled in gold, but a country might accumulate large balances of foreign exchange before redeeming those balances for bullion.

In addition, gold coins and bullion no longer circulated as freely as before the war. Countries still offered to exchange paper notes for gold, but typically only in large minimum quantities, such as four-hundred-ounce bars, valued at the time at $8,268 each, equivalent today to over $110,000. This meant that gold bullion would be used only by central banks, commercial banks and the wealthy, while others would use paper notes backed by the promises of governments to maintain their gold equivalent value. Paper money would still be "as good as gold," but the gold itself would disappear into central bank vaults. England codified these arrangements in the Gold Standard Act of 1925, intended to facilitate the new gold exchange standard.

Notwithstanding the return to a modified gold standard, the currency wars continued and gained momentum. In 1923, the French franc collapsed, although not nearly as badly as the mark had a few years earlier. This collapse memorably paved the way for a golden age of U.S. expatriates living in Paris in the mid-1920s, including Scott and Zelda Fitzgerald and Ernest Hemingway, who reported on the day-to-day effects of the collapse of the French franc for the *Toronto Star*. Americans could afford a comfortable lifestyle in Paris by converting dollars from home into newly devalued francs.

Serious flaws in the gold exchange standard began to emerge almost as soon as it was adopted. The most obvious was the instability that resulted from large accumulations of foreign exchange by surplus countries, followed by unexpected demands for gold from the deficit countries. In addition, Germany, potentially the largest economy in Europe, lacked sufficient gold to support a money supply large enough to facilitate the international trade that it needed to return its economy to growth. There was an effort to remedy this deficiency in 1924 in the form of the Dawes Plan, named after the American banker and later U.S. vice president Charles Dawes, who was the plan's principal architect. The Dawes Plan was advocated by an international monetary committee convened to deal with the lingering problems of reparations under the Versailles Treaty. The Dawes Plan partially reduced the German reparations payments and provided new loans to Germany so that it could obtain the gold and hard currency reserves needed to support its economy. The combination of the Genoa Conference of 1922, the new and stable rentenmark of 1923 and the Dawes Plan of 1924 finally stabilized German finance and allowed its industrial and agricultural bases to expand in a noninflationary way.

The system of fixed exchange rates in place from 1925 to 1931 meant that, for the time being, currency wars would play out using the gold account and interest rates rather than exchange rates. The smooth functioning of the gold exchange standard in this period depended on the so-called "rules of the game." These expected nations experiencing large gold inflows to ease monetary conditions, accomplished in part by lowering interest rates, to allow their economies to expand, while those experiencing gold outflows would tighten monetary conditions and raise interest rates, resulting in an economic contraction. Eventually the contracting economy would find that prices and wages were low enough to cause its goods to be cheaper and more competitive internationally, while the expanding economy would experience the opposite. At this point the flows would reverse, with the former gold outflow country attracting inflows as it ran a trade surplus based on cheaper goods, while the expanding economy would begin to run a trade deficit and experience gold outflows.

The gold exchange standard was a self-equilibrating system with one critical weakness. In a pure gold standard, the gold supply was the monetary base and did the work of causing economic expansion and contraction, whereas, under the gold exchange standard, currency reserves also played a role. This meant that central banks were able to make interest rate and other monetary policy decisions involving currency reserves as part of the adjustment process. It was in these policy-driven adjustments, rather than the operation of gold itself, that the system eventually began to break down.

One of the peculiarities of paper money is that it is simultaneously an asset of the party holding it and a liability of the bank issuing it. Gold, on the other hand, is typically only an asset, except in cases—uncommon in the 1920s—where it is loaned from one bank to another. Adjustment transactions in gold are therefore usually a zero-sum game. If gold moves from England to France, the money supply of England decreases and the money supply of France increases by the amount of the gold.

The system could function reasonably well as long as France was willing to accept sterling in trade and redeposit the sterling in English banks to help maintain the sterling money supply. However, if the Banque de France suddenly withdrew these deposits and demanded gold from the Bank of England, the English money supply would contract sharply. Instead of smooth, gradual adjustments as typically occurred under the classical gold standard, the new system was vulnerable to sharp, destabilizing swings that could quickly turn to panic.

A country running deficits under the gold exchange standard could find itself like a tenant whose landlord does not collect rent payments for a year and then suddenly demands immediate payment of twelve months' back rent. Some tenants would have saved for the inevitable rainy day, but many others would not be able to resist the easy credit and would find themselves short of funds and facing eviction. Countries could be similarly embarrassed if they were short of gold when a trading partner came to redeem its foreign exchange. The gold exchange standard was intended to combine the best features of the gold and paper systems, but actually combined some of the worst, especially the built-in instability resulting from unexpected redemptions for gold.

By 1927, with gold and foreign exchange accumulating steadily in

France and flowing heavily from England, it was England's role under the rules of the game to raise interest rates and force a contraction, which, over time, would make its economy more competitive. But Montagu Norman, governor of the Bank of England, refused to raise rates, partly because he anticipated a political backlash and also because he felt the French inflow was due to an unfairly undervalued franc. The French, for their part, refused to revalue, but suggested they might do so in the future, creating further uncertainty and encouraging speculation in both sterling and francs.

Separately, the United States, after cutting interest rates in 1927, began a series of rate increases in 1928 that proved highly contractionary. These rate increases were the opposite of what the United States should have done under the rules of the game, given its dominant position in gold and continuing gold inflows. Yet just as domestic political considerations caused England to refuse to raise rates in 1927, the Fed's decision to raise rates the following year when it should have lowered them was also driven by domestic concerns, specifically the fear of an asset bubble in U.S. stock prices. In short, participants in the gold exchange standard were putting domestic considerations ahead of the rules of the game and thereby disrupting the smooth functioning of the gold exchange standard itself.

There was another flaw in the gold exchange standard that ran deeper than the lack of coordination by the central banks of England, the United States, France and Germany. This flaw involved the price at which gold had been fixed to the dollar in order to anchor the new standard. Throughout World War I, countries had printed enormous amounts of paper currency to finance war debts while the supply of gold expanded very little. Moreover, the gold that did exist did not remain static but flowed increasingly toward the United States, while relatively little remained in Europe. Reconciling the postwar paper-gold ratio with the prewar gold price posed a major dilemma after 1919. One choice was to contract the paper money supply to target the prewar gold price. This would be highly deflationary and would cause a steep decline in overall price levels in order to get back to the prewar price of gold. The other choice was to revalue gold upward so as to support the new price level given the expansion in the paper money supply. Raising the price of gold meant permanently devaluing the currency. The choice was between deflation and devaluation.

It is one thing when prices drift downward over time due to innovation, scalability or other efficiencies. This might be considered "good" deflation and is familiar to any contemporary consumer who has seen prices of computers or wide-screen TVs fall year after year. It is another matter when prices are forced down by unnecessary monetary contraction, credit constraints, deleveraging, business failures, bankruptcies and mass unemployment. This may be considered "bad" deflation. This bad deflation was exactly what was required in order to return the most important currencies to their prewar parity with gold.

The choice was not as stark in the United States because, although the U.S. had expanded its money supply during World War I, it had also run trade surpluses and had greatly increased its gold reserves as a result. The ratio of paper currency to gold was not as badly out of line relative to the prewar parity as it was in England and France.

By 1923, France and Germany had both confronted the wartime inflation issue and devalued their currencies. Of the three major European powers, only England took the necessary steps to contract the paper money supply to restore the gold standard at the prewar level. This was done at the insistence of Winston Churchill, who was chancellor of the exchequer at the time. Churchill considered a return to the prewar gold parity to be both a point of honor and a healthy check on the condition of English finances. But the effect on England's domestic economy was devastating, with a massive decline of over 50 percent in the price level, a high rate of business failures and millions of unemployed. Churchill later wrote that his policy of returning to a prewar gold parity was one of the greatest mistakes of his life. By the time massive deflation and unemployment hit the United States in 1930, England had already been living through those conditions for most of the prior decade.

The 1920s were a time of prosperity in the United States, and both the French and German economies grew strongly through the middle part of the decade. Only England lagged. If England had turned the corner on unemployment and deflation by 1928, the world as a whole might have achieved sustained global economic growth of a kind not seen since before World War I. Instead, global finance soon turned dramatically for the worse.

The start of the Great Depression is conventionally dated by economists from October 28, 1929, Black Monday, when the Dow Jones Industrial Average fell 12.8 percent in a single day. However, Germany had fallen into recession the year before and England had never fully recovered from the depression of 1920–1921. Black Monday represented the popping of a particularly prominent U.S. asset bubble in a world already struggling with the effects of deflation.

The years immediately following the 1929 U.S. stock market crash were disastrous in terms of unemployment, declining production, business failures and human suffering. From the perspective of the global financial system, however, the most dangerous phase occurred during the spring and summer of 1931. The financial panic that year, tantamount to a global run on the bank, began in May with the announcement of losses by the Credit-Anstalt bank of Vienna that effectively wiped out the bank's capital. In the weeks that followed, a banking panic gripped Europe, and bank holidays were declared in Austria, Germany, Poland, Czechoslovakia and Yugoslavia. Germany suspended payments on its foreign debt and imposed capital controls. This was the functional equivalent of going off the new gold exchange standard, since foreign creditors could no longer convert their claims on German banks into gold, yet officially Germany still claimed to maintain the value of the reichsmark in a fixed relationship to gold.

The panic soon spread to England, and by July 1931 massive gold outflows had begun. Leading English banks had made leveraged investments in illiquid assets funded with short-term liabilities, exactly the type of investing that destroyed Lehman Brothers in 2008. As those liabilities came due, foreign creditors converted their sterling claims into gold that soon left England headed for the United States or France or some other gold power not yet feeling the full impact of the crisis. With the outflow of gold becoming acute and the pressures of the bank run threatening to destroy major banks in the City of London, England went off the gold standard on September 21, 1931. Almost immediately sterling fell sharply against the dollar and continued dropping, falling 30 percent in a matter of months. Many other countries, including Japan, the Scandinavian nations and members of the British Commonwealth, also left the gold standard and received the short-run benefits of devaluation. These benefits worked to the disadvantage of the French franc and the currencies of the other gold bloc nations, including Belgium, Luxembourg, the Netherlands and Italy, which remained on the gold exchange standard.

The European bank panic abated after England went off the gold standard; however, the focus turned next to the United States. While the U.S. economy had been contracting since 1929, the devaluation of sterling and other currencies against the U.S. dollar in 1931 put the burden of global deflation and depression more squarely on the United States. Indeed, 1932 was the worst year of the Great Depression in the United States. Unemployment reached 20 percent and investment, production and price levels had all plunged by double-digit amounts measured from the start of the contraction.

In November 1932, Franklin D. Roosevelt was elected president to replace Herbert Hoover, whose entire term had been consumed by a stock bubble, a crash and then the Great Depression itself. However, Roosevelt would not be sworn in as president until March 1933, and in the four months between election and inauguration the situation deteriorated precipitously, with widespread U.S. bank failures and bank runs. Millions of Americans withdrew cash from the banks and stuffed it in drawers or mattresses, while others lost their entire life savings because they did not act in time. By Roosevelt's inauguration, Americans had lost faith in so many institutions that what little hope remained seemed embodied in Roosevelt himself.

On March 6, 1933, two days after his inauguration, Roosevelt used emergency powers to announce a bank holiday that would close all banks in the United States. The initial order ran until March 9 but was later extended for an indefinite period. FDR let it be known that the banks would be examined during the holiday and only sound banks would be allowed to resume business. The holiday ended on March 13, at which time some banks reopened while others remained shut. The entire episode was more about confidence building than sound banking practice, since the government had not in fact examined the books of every bank in the country during the eight days they were closed.

The passage of the Emergency Banking Act on March 9, 1933, was of far greater significance than the bank inspections in terms of rebuilding confidence in the banks. The act allowed the Fed to make loans to banks equal to 100 percent of the par value of any government securities and 90 percent of the face value of any checks or other liquid short-term paper they held. The Fed could also make unsecured loans to any bank that was a member of the Federal Reserve System. In practice, this meant that banks could obtain all the cash they needed to deal with bank runs. It was not quite deposit insurance, which would come later that year, but it was the functional equivalent because now depositors did not have to worry that banks would literally run out of cash.

Interestingly, Roosevelt's initial statutory authority for the bank closure in March was the 1917 Trading with the Enemy Act, which had become law during World War I and granted any president plenary emergency economic powers to protect national security. In case the courts might later express any doubt about the president's authority to declare the bank holiday under this 1917 wartime statute, the Emergency Banking Act of 1933 ratified the original bank holiday after the fact and gave the president explicit rather than merely implicit authority to close the banks.

When the banks did reopen on March 13, 1933, depositors lined up in many instances not to withdraw money but to redeposit it from their coffee cans and mattresses, where it had been hoarded during the panic of the preceding months. Although very little had changed on bank balance sheets, the mere appearance of a housecleaning during the holiday combined with the Fed's new emergency lending powers had restored confidence in the banks. With that behind him, FDR now confronted an even more pernicious problem than a bank run. This was the problem of deflation now being imported into the

United States from around the world through exchange rate channels. CWI had now arrived at the White House doorstep.

When England and others went off the gold standard in 1931, the costs of their exports went down compared to costs in other competing nations. This meant that competing nations had to find ways to lower their costs to also remain competitive in world markets. Sometimes this cost cutting took the form of wage reductions or layoffs, which made the unemployment problem worse. In effect, the nations that had devalued by abandoning gold were now exporting deflation around the world, exacerbating global deflationary trends.

Inflation was the obvious antidote to deflation, but the question was how to achieve inflation when a vicious cycle of declining spending, higher debt burdens, higher unemployment, money hoarding and further spending declines had taken hold. Inflation and currency devaluation are substantially the same thing in terms of their economic effects: both decrease the domestic cost structure and make imports more expensive and exports less expensive to other countries, thus helping to create domestic jobs. England, the Commonwealth and Japan had gone this route in 1931 with some success. The United States could, if it so chose, simply devalue against sterling and other currencies, but this might have prompted further devaluations against the dollar with no net gain. Continuation of paper currency wars on a tit-for-tat basis did not seem to offer a permanent solution. Rather than devalue against other paper currencies, FDR chose to devalue against the ultimate currency—gold.

But gold posed a unique problem in the United States. In addition to official holdings in the Federal Reserve Banks, gold was in private circulation in the form of gold coins used as legal tender and coins or bars held in safe-deposit boxes and other secure locations. This gold could properly be viewed as money, but it was money being hoarded and not spent or put into circulation. The easiest way to devalue the dollar against gold was to increase the dollar price of gold, which Roosevelt could do with his emergency economic powers. FDR could declare that gold would now be convertible at $25 per ounce or $30 per ounce instead of the gold standard price of $20.67 per ounce. The problem was that the benefit of this increase in the gold price would go in large measure to the private gold hoarders and would do nothing to free up the hoards or put them back in circulation. In fact, more people might convert paper dollars to gold bullion in anticipation of further gold price increases, and those hoarding gold might sit tight for the same reason, with their original convictions having already been confirmed. Roosevelt needed to ensure that any gains from the revaluation of gold would go to the government and not the hoarders, while citizens would be left with no forms of money except paper. If gold could be removed from private hands and if citizens could be made to expect further devaluations in their paper money, they might be inclined to start spending it rather than hold on to a depreciating asset.

A prohibition on the hoarding or possession of gold was integral to the plan to devalue the dollar against gold and get people spending again. Against this background, FDR issued Executive Order 6102 on April 5, 1933, one of the most extraordinary executive orders in U.S. history. The blunt language over the signature of Franklin Delano Roosevelt speaks for itself:

> I, Franklin D. Roosevelt . . . declare that [a] national emergency still continues to exist and . . . do hereby prohibit the hoarding of gold coin, gold bullion, and gold certificates within the . . . United States by individuals, partnerships, associations and corporations. . . . All persons are hereby required to deliver, on or before May 1, 1933, to a Federal reserve bank . . . or to any member of the Federal Reserve System all gold coin, gold bullion and gold certificates now owned by them. . . . Whoever willfully violates any provision of this Executive Order . . . may be fined not more than $10,000 or . . . may be imprisoned for not more than ten years.

The people of the United States were being ordered to surrender their gold to the government and were offered paper money at the exchange rate of $20.67 per ounce. Some relatively minor exceptions were made for dentists, jewelers and others who made "legitimate and customary" use of gold in their industry or art. Citizens were allowed to keep $100 worth of gold, about five ounces at 1933 prices, and gold in the form of rare coins. The $10,000 fine proposed in 1933 for those who continued to hoard gold in violation of the president's order is equivalent to over $165,000 in today's money, an extraordinarily large statutory fine.

Roosevelt followed up with a series of additional orders, including Executive Order 6111 on April 20, 1933, which banned the export of gold from the United States except with the approval of the secretary of the Treasury. Executive Order 6261 on August 29, 1933, ordered U.S. gold mines to sell their production to the U.S. Treasury at a price to be set by the Treasury, in effect nationalizing the gold mines.

In a rapid sequence of moves, FDR had deftly confiscated private gold, banned its export abroad and captured the gold mining industry. As a result, Roosevelt greatly increased the U.S. hoard of official gold. Contemporary estimates were that citizens surrendered over five hundred metric tons of gold to the Treasury in 1933. The gold depository at Fort Knox was constructed in 1937 for the specific purpose of holding the gold that had been confiscated from U.S. citizens. There was no longer enough room in the basement of the Treasury.

It is difficult to imagine such a scenario playing out today, although the legal authority of the president to seize gold still exists. The difficulty in imagining this happening lies not in the impossibility of a similar crisis but rather in the political backlash that would ensue in an age of pervasive talk radio, social media, outspoken cable channel anchors and greatly diminished trust by U.S. citizens in their government. Of these factors, the loss of trust is the most powerful. FDR had his talk radio opponents after all, most famously Father Charles Coughlin, with an audience in the 1930s estimated to be larger than Rush Limbaugh's audience today. While it was not quite Twitter or Facebook, there was no shortage of social media, including newspapers and especially word of mouth readily constructed from a dense web of families, churches, social clubs and ethnic bonds. A powerful rebuke to FDR's gold confiscations could easily have emerged, yet it did not. People were desperate and trusted

FDR to do the right things to fix the economy, and if an end to gold hoarding seemed necessary, then people were willing to turn in their coins and bars and gold certificates when ordered to do so.

Today's electronic social media have a powerful amplifying effect on popular sentiment, but it is still the sentiment that counts. The residue of trust in leadership and economic policy in the early twenty-first century has worn thin. It is not difficult to imagine some future dollar collapse necessitating gold seizures by the government. It is difficult to imagine that U.S. citizens would willingly go along as they did in 1933.

Roosevelt's gold confiscation left unanswered the question of what new value the dollar would have relative to gold for purposes of international trade and settlements. Having confiscated Americans' gold at the official price of $20.67 per ounce, FDR proceeded to buy more gold in the open market beginning in October 1933, driving up its price slowly and thereby devaluing the dollar against it. Economist and historian Alan Meltzer describes how FDR would occasionally choose the price of gold while lying in bed in his pajamas, in one instance instructing the Treasury to bid up the price by twenty-one cents because it was three times his lucky number, seven. The story would be humorous if it did not describe an act of theft from the American people; profits from the increased value of gold now accrued to the Treasury and not the citizens who had formerly owned it. Over the next three months, FDR gradually moved the price of gold up to $35 per ounce, at which point he decided to stabilize the price. From start to finish, the dollar was devalued about 70 percent when measured against gold.

As the coup de grace, Congress passed the Gold Reserve Act of 1934, which ratified the new $35 per ounce price of gold and voided so-called gold clauses in contracts. A gold clause was a covenant designed to protect both parties from the uncertainties of inflation or deflation. A typical provision said that in the event of a change in the dollar price of gold, any dollar payments under the contract would be adjusted so that the new dollar obligation equaled the former dollar obligation when measured against a constant weight of gold. FDR's attack on gold clauses was highly controversial and was litigated to the Supreme Court in the 1935 case of *Norman v. Baltimore & Ohio Railroad Co.*, which finally upheld the elimination of gold clauses in a narrow 5–4 decision, with the majority opinion written by Chief Justice Charles Evans Hughes. It was only in 1977 that Congress once again permitted the use of gold clauses in contracts.

Finally the Gold Reserve Act of 1934 also established the Treasury's exchange stabilization fund, to be financed with the profits from gold confiscation, which the Treasury could use on a discretionary basis for currency market exchange intervention and other open market operations. The exchange stabilization fund is sometimes referred to as the Treasury's slush fund, because the money does not have to be appropriated by Congress as part of the budget process. The fund was famously used by Treasury Secretary Robert Rubin in 1994 to stabilize Mexican money markets after the collapse of the peso in December of that year. The exchange stabilization fund had been little used and was mostly unknown even inside Washington policy circles from 1934 to 1994. Members of Congress voting for the Gold Reserve Act in 1934 could hardly have conceived that they might be facilitating a Mexican bailout sixty years later.

The English break with gold in 1931 and the U.S. devaluation against gold in 1933 had the intended effects. Both the English and U.S. economies showed immediate benefits from their devaluations as prices stopped falling, money supplies grew, credit expansion began, industrial production increased and unemployment declined. The Great Depression was far from over, and these signs of progress were from such depressed levels that the burden on businesses and individuals remained enormous. A corner had been turned, however, at least for those countries that had devalued against gold and against other countries.

Now the gold bloc countries, which had benefitted from the first wave of devaluations in the 1920s, began to absorb the deflation that had been deflected by the United States and England. This led finally to the Tripartite Agreement of 1936, another in that seemingly endless string of international monetary conferences and understandings that had begun with Versailles in 1919. The Tripartite

Agreement was an informal agreement reached among England, the United States and France, which acted for itself and on behalf of the gold bloc. The official U.S. version released by Treasury Secretary Henry Morgenthau on September 25, 1936, said that the goal was "to foster those conditions which safeguard peace and will best contribute to the restoration of order in international economic relations." The heart of the agreement was that France was allowed to devalue slightly. The United States said, with reference to the French devaluation, "The United States Government . . . declares its intention to continue to use appropriate available resources so as to avoid . . . any disturbance of the basis of international exchange resulting from the proposed readjustment." This was a "no retaliation" pledge from the United States—another sign that the currency wars were ending for now.

All three parties pledged to maintain currency values at the newly agreed levels against gold, and therefore one another, except as needed to promote domestic growth. The exception made for internal growth was highly significant politically and further evidence that, while currency wars may play out on an international stage, they are driven by domestic political considerations. In this regard, Morgenthau's statement read, "The Government of the United States must, of course, in its policy toward international monetary relations take into full account the requirements of internal prosperity." The UK and French versions of the agreement, issued as a series of three separate communiqués rather than a single treaty document, contained substantially similar language. This "internal prosperity" language was not gratuitous, since all three countries were still struggling with the effects of the Great Depression. They could be expected to abandon the agreement readily if deflation or high unemployment were to return in such a way as to require further inflationary medicine through the exchange rate mechanism or devaluation against gold. Ultimately the Tripartite Agreement was toothless, because growth at home would always trump international considerations, yet it did mark an armistice in the currency wars.

Switzerland, the Netherlands and Belgium also subscribed to the agreement after France had led the way. This completed the cycle of competitive devaluations that had begun with Germany, France and the rest of the gold bloc in the 1920s, continued with the UK in 1931, culminated with the United States in 1933 and now came full circle back to the gold bloc again in 1936. The temporary elixir of currency devaluation had been passed from country to country like a single canteen among thirsty soldiers. The more durable fix of cheapening currencies against gold in order to encourage commodity price inflation and to escape deflation had also now been shared by all.

One positive consequence of the currency devaluations by France and the new pledge of exchange rate stability in the Tripartite Agreement was the resumption of international gold shipments among trading nations. The era of suspension of gold exports and central bank hoarding of gold was beginning to thaw. The U.S. Treasury, in a separate announcement less than three weeks after the Tripartite Agreement, said, "The Secretary of the Treasury states that . . . the United States will also sell gold for immediate export to, or earmark for the account of, the exchange equalization or stabilization funds of those countries whose funds likewise are offering to sell gold to the United States." The United States was willing to lift its ban on gold exports to those countries that would reciprocate. The new price of gold in international transactions was set at $35 per ounce, where it would remain until 1971.

The combination of a final round of devaluations, pledges to maintain new parities and resumption of gold sales might have worked to launch a new era of monetary stability based on gold. But it was a case of too little, too late. The economic destruction wrought by Versailles reparations and Weimar hyperinflation had given rise in Germany to the corporatist, racist Nazi party, which came to power in early 1933. In Japan, a military clique adhering to a twentieth-century version of the feudal code of Bushido had taken control of the Japanese government and launched a series of military invasions and conquests throughout East Asia. By 1942, large parts of the world were at war in an existential struggle between the Allied and Axis powers. Devaluations and struggles over war debts and reparations left over from World War I were forgotten. The next time international monetary issues were revisited, in 1944, the world would be a far different place.

In the end, the flaws of both the 1925 gold exchange standard and U.S. monetary policy from 1928 to 1931 were too much for the global monetary system to bear. Devaluing countries such as France and Germany gained a trade advantage over those who did not devalue. Countries such as England, which had tried to return to the prewar gold standard, suffered massive unemployment and deflation, and countries such as the United States, which had massive gold inflows, failed to live up to their international responsibilities by actually tightening credit conditions during a time when they should have been loosening.

The extent to which these imbalances and misguided policies contributed to the Great Depression have been debated ever since. It is certainly the case that the failure of the gold exchange standard has led many economists today to generally discredit the use of gold in international finance. Yet it seems at least fair to ask whether the problem was gold itself or the price of gold, which stemmed from a nostalgic desire for a prewar peg, combined with undervalued currencies and misguided interest rate policies, that really doomed the system. Perhaps a more pure form of gold standard, rather than the hybrid gold exchange standard, and a more realistic gold price, equivalent to $50 per ounce in 1925, would have proved less deflationary and more enduring. We will never know. What followed after 1936 was not a continuation of a currency war but the bloodiest real war in history.

CHAPTER 5

Currency War II (1967–1987)

"The dollar is our currency, but it's your problem."

U.S. Treasury Secretary John Connally
to foreign finance ministers, 1971

"I don't give a shit about the lira."

President Richard M. Nixon, 1972

As World War II wound down, the major Allied economic powers, led by the United States and England, planned for a new world monetary order intended to avoid the mistakes of Versailles and the interwar period. These plans were given final shape at the Bretton Woods Conference held in New Hampshire in July 1944. The result was a set of rules, norms and institutions that shaped the international monetary system for the next three decades.

The Bretton Woods era, 1944 to 1973, while punctuated by several recessions, was on the whole a period of currency stability, low inflation, low unemployment, high growth and rising real incomes. This period was, in almost every respect, the opposite of the CWI period, 1921–1936. Under Bretton Woods, the international monetary system was anchored to gold through a U.S. dollar freely convertible into gold by trading partners at $35 per ounce and with other currencies indirectly anchored to gold through fixed exchange rates against the U.S. dollar. Short-term lending to particular countries in the event of trade deficits would be provided by the International Monetary Fund. Countries could only devalue their currencies with IMF permission and that would generally be granted only in cases of persistent trade deficits accompanied by high inflation. Although conceived in the form of a grand international agreement, the Bretton Woods structure was dictated almost single-handedly by the United States at a time when U.S. military and economic power, relative to the rest of the world, was at a height not seen again until the fall of the Soviet Union in 1991.

Despite the persistence of Bretton Woods into the 1970s, the seeds of Currency War II were sown in the mid- to late 1960s. One can date the beginning of CWII from 1967, while its antecedents lie in the 1964 landslide election of Lyndon B. Johnson and his "guns and butter" platform. The guns referred to the war in Vietnam and the butter referred to the Great Society social programs, including the war on poverty.

Although the United States had maintained a military presence in Vietnam since 1950, the first large-scale combat troop deployments took place in 1965, escalating the costs of the war effort. The Democratic landslide in the 1964 election resulted in a new Congress that convened in January 1965, and Johnson's State of the Union address that month marked the unofficial launch of the full-scale Great Society agenda.

This convergence of the costs of escalation in Vietnam and the Great Society in early 1965 marked the real turning away from America's successful postwar economic policies. However, it would take several years for those costs to become apparent. America had built up a reservoir of economic strength at home and political goodwill abroad and that reservoir now slowly began to be drained.

At first, it seemed that the United States could afford both guns and butter. The Kennedy tax cuts, signed by President Johnson shortly after President John F. Kennedy's assassination in 1963, had given a boost to the economy. Gross domestic product rose over 5 percent in the first year of the tax cuts and growth averaged over 4.8 percent annually during the Kennedy-Johnson years. But almost from the start, inflation accelerated in the face of the twin budget and trade deficits that Johnson's policies engendered.

Inflation, measured year over year, almost doubled from an acceptable 1.9 percent in 1965 to a more threatening 3.5 percent in 1966. Inflation then ran out of control for twenty years. It was not until 1986 that inflation returned to the level of just over 1 percent. In one incredible five-year stretch from 1977 to 1981, cumulative inflation was over 50 percent; the value of the dollar was cut in half.

U.S. citizens in this period made the same analytic mistake as their counterparts in Weimar Germany had in 1921. Their initial perception was that prices were going up; what was really happening was that the currency was collapsing. Higher prices are the symptom, not the cause, of currency collapse. The arc of Currency War II is really the arc of U.S. dollar inflation and the decline of the dollar.

Despite the centrality of U.S. policies and U.S. inflation to the course of CWII, the opening shots were fired not in the United States but in Britain, where a sterling crisis had been brewing since 1964 and came to a boil in 1967 with the first major currency devaluation since Bretton Woods. While sterling was less significant than the dollar in the Bretton Woods system, it was still an important reserve and trade currency. In 1945, UK pounds sterling comprised a larger percentage of global reserves—the combined holdings of all central banks—than the dollar. This position deteriorated steadily, and by 1965 only 26 percent of global reserves were in sterling. The British balance of payments had been deteriorating since the early 1960s, but grew sharply negative in late 1964.

Instability in sterling arose not only because of short-term trade imbalances but because of the global imbalance between the total sterling reserves held outside Britain and the dollar and gold reserves available inside Britain to redeem those external balances. In the mid-1960s there were about four times as many external sterling claims as internal reserves. This situation was highly unstable and made Britain vulnerable to a run on the bank if sterling holders tried to redeem sterling for dollars or gold en masse. A variety of techniques was orchestrated to support sterling and keep the sterling bears off balance, including international lines of credit, swap lines with the New York Fed, a UK austerity package and surprise currency market interventions. But the problem remained.

Three minor sterling crises arose between 1964 and 1966, but were eventually subdued. A fourth sterling crisis, in mid-1967, however, proved fatal to sterling parity. Numerous factors contributed to the timing, including closure of the Suez Canal during the 1967 Six-Day War between the Arabs and Israel and the expectation that the UK might be required to devalue in order to join the European Economic Community. Inflation was now on the rise in the United Kingdom as it was in the United States. In the UK, inflation was rationalized as necessary to combat rising unemployment, but its impact on the value of the currency was devastating. After an unsuccessful effort to fend off continued selling pressure, sterling formally devalued against the dollar on November 18, 1967, from $2.80 to $2.40 per pound sterling, a 14.3 percent devaluation.

The first significant crack in the Bretton Woods facade had now appeared after twenty years of success in maintaining fixed exchange rates and price stability. If the UK could devalue, so could others. U.S. officials had worked hard to prevent the devaluation of sterling, fearing the dollar would be the next currency to come under pressure. Their fears would soon be realized. The United States was experiencing the same combination of trade deficits and inflation that had unhinged sterling, with one crucial difference. Under Bretton Woods, the value of the dollar was not linked to other currencies but to gold. A devaluation of the dollar therefore meant an upward revaluation in the dollar price of gold. Buying gold was the logical trade if you expected dollar devaluation, so speculators turned their attention to the London gold market.

Since 1961, the United States and other leading economic powers had operated the London Gold Pool, essentially a price-fixing open market operation in which participants combined their gold and dollar reserve resources to maintain the market price of gold at the Bretton Woods parity of $35 per ounce. The Gold Pool included the United States, United Kingdom, Germany, France, Italy, Belgium, the Netherlands and Switzerland, with the United States providing 50 percent of the resources and the remainder divided among the other seven members. The pool was partly a response to an outbreak of panic buying of gold in 1960, which had temporarily driven the market price of gold up to $40 per ounce. The Gold Pool was both a buyer and a seller; it would buy on price dips and sell into rallies in order to maintain the $35 price. But by 1965 the pool was almost exclusively a seller.

■ The End of Bretton Woods

The public attack on the Bretton Woods system of a dominant dollar anchored to gold began even before the 1967 devaluation of sterling. In February 1965, President Charles de Gaulle of France gave an incendiary speech in which he claimed that the dollar was finished as the lead currency in the international monetary system. He called for a return to the classical gold standard, which he described as "an indisputable monetary base, and one that does not bear the mark of any particular country. In truth, one does not see how one could really have any standard criterion other than gold." France backed up the words with action. In January 1965, France converted $150 million of dollar reserves into gold and announced plans to convert another $150 million soon. Spain followed France and converted $60 million of its own dollar reserves into gold. Using the price of gold in June 2011 rather than the $35 per ounce price in 1965, these redemptions were worth approximately $12.8 billion by France and $2.6 billion by Spain and at the time represented significant drains on U.S. gold reserves. De Gaulle helpfully offered to send the French navy to the United States to ferry the gold back to France.

These redemptions of dollars for gold came at a time when United States businesses were buying up European companies and expanding operations in Europe with grossly overvalued dollars, something De Gaulle referred to as "expropriation." De Gaulle felt that if the United States had to operate with gold rather than paper money, this predatory behavior would be forced to a halt. However, there was fierce resistance to a pure gold standard in the late 1960s—as in the 1930s, it would have necessitated a devaluation of dollars and other currencies against gold. The biggest beneficiaries of a rise in the dollar price of gold would have been the major gold-producing nations, including the repugnant apartheid regime in South Africa and the hostile communist regime in the USSR. These geopolitical considerations helped to tamp down the enthusiasm for a new version of the classical gold standard.

Despite the scathing criticisms coming from France, the United States did have one staunch ally in the Gold Pool—Germany. This was crucial, because Germany had persistent trade surpluses and was accumulating gold both from the IMF as part of operations to support sterling and through its participation as an occasional buyer in the Gold Pool itself. If Germany were suddenly to demand gold in exchange for its dollar reserve balances, a dollar crisis much worse than the sterling crisis would result. However, Germany secretly assured the United States it would not dump dollars for gold, as revealed in a letter from Karl Blessing, president of the Deutsche Bundesbank, the German central bank, to William McChesney Martin, the chairman of the Board of Governors of the Federal Reserve. Dated March 30, 1967, the "Blessing Letter" provided:

> *Dear Mr. Martin,*
>
> *There occasionally has been some concern . . . that . . . expenditures resulting from the presence of American troops in Germany [could] lead to United States losses of gold. . . .*
>
> *You are, of course, well aware of the fact that the Bundesbank over the past few years has not converted any . . . dollars . . . into gold. . . .*
>
> *You may be assured that also in the future the Bundesbank intends to continue this policy and to play its full part in contributing to international monetary cooperation.*

It was extremely comforting for the United States to have this secret assurance from Germany. In return, the United States would continue to bear the costs of defending Germany from the Soviet troops and tanks stationed in the woods immediately surrounding Berlin and throughout Eastern Europe.

Germany, however, was not the only party with potential gold claims on the dollar, and in the immediate aftermath of the 1967 sterling devaluation the United States had to sell over eight hundred metric tons of gold at artificially low prices to maintain the dollar-gold parity. In June 1967, just one year after withdrawing from NATO's military command, France withdrew from the Gold Pool as well. The other members continued operations, but it was a lost cause: claims on gold by overseas dollar holders had become an epidemic. By March 1968, the gold outflow from the pool was running at the rate of thirty metric tons per hour.

The London gold market was closed temporarily on March 15, 1968, to halt the outflow, and remained closed for two weeks, an eerie echo of the 1933 U.S. bank holiday. A few days after the closure, the U.S. Congress repealed the requirement for a gold reserve to back the U.S. currency; this freed the U.S. gold supply to be available for sale at the $35 price if needed. This was all to no avail. By the end of March 1968, the London Gold Pool had collapsed. Thereafter, gold was considered to move in a two-tier system, with a market price determined in London and an international payments price under Bretton Woods at the old price of $35 per ounce. The resulting "gold window" referred to the ability of countries to redeem dollars for gold at the $35 price and sell the gold on the open market for $40 or more.

The two-tier system caused speculative pressures to be directed to the open market while the $35 price remained available only to central banks. However, the U.S. allies reached a new, informal agreement not to take advantage of the gold window by acquiring gold at the cheaper official price. The combination of the end of the Gold Pool, the creation of two-tier system and some short-term austerity measures put in place by the United States and United Kingdom helped to stabilize the international monetary system in late 1968 and 1969, yet the dénouement of Bretton Woods was clearly in sight.

On November 29, 1968, not long after the collapse of the London Gold Pool, *Time* reported that among the problems of the monetary system was that "the volume of world trade is rising far more quickly than the global supply of gold." Statements like this illustrate one of the great misunderstandings about the role of gold. It is misguided to say that there is not enough gold to support world trade, because quantity is never the issue; rather, the issue is one of price. If there was inadequate gold at $35 per ounce, the same amount of gold would easily support world trade at $100 per ounce or higher. The problem *Time* was really alluding to was that the price of gold was artificially low at $35 per ounce, a point on which the magazine was correct. If the price of gold was too low, the problem was not a shortage of gold but an excess of paper money in relation to gold. This excess money was reflected in rising inflation in the United States, the United Kingdom and France.

In 1969, the IMF took up the "gold shortage" cause and created a new form of international reserve asset called the special drawing right, or SDR. The SDR was manufactured out of thin air by the IMF without tangible backing and allocated among members in accordance with their IMF quotas. It was promptly dubbed "paper gold" because it represented an asset that could be used to offset balance of payments deficits in the same manner as gold or reserve currencies.

The creation of the SDR was a little-understood novelty at the time. There were several small issuances in 1970–1972 and another issuance in response to the oil price shock and global inflation in 1981. Thereafter, the issuance of SDRs came to a halt for almost thirty years. It was only in 2009, in the depths of a depression that had begun in 2007, that another, much larger amount of SDRs were printed and handed out to members. Still, the original issuance of SDRs in 1970 was a reflection of how badly unbalanced the supply of paper money had become in relation to gold and of the desperation with which the United States and others clung to the gold parity of $35 per ounce long after that price had become infeasible.

The entire period of 1967 to 1971 is best characterized as one of confusion and uncertainty in international monetary affairs. The devaluation of sterling in 1967 had been somewhat of a shock even though the instability in sterling had been diagnosed by central bankers years before. But the following years were marked by a succession of devaluations, revaluations, inflation, SDRs, the collapse of the Gold Pool, currency swaps, IMF loans, a two-tiered gold price and other ad hoc solutions. At the same time, the leading economies of the world were undergoing internal strains in the form of student riots, labor protests, antiwar protests, sexual revolution, the Prague Spring, the Cultural Revolution and the continuing rise of the counterculture. All of this was layered onto rapid technological change summed up in the ubiquity of computers, the fear of thermonuclear war and plain awe at landing a man on the moon. The whole world seemed at once to be on a wobbly foundation in a way not seen perhaps since 1938.

Yet through all of this, one thing seemed safe. The value of the U.S. dollar remained fixed at one thirty-fifth of an ounce of pure gold and the United States seemed prepared to defend this value despite the vast increase in the supply of dollars and the fact that convertibility was limited to a small number of foreign central banks bound to honor a gentleman's agreement not to press too hard for conversion. Then suddenly this last anchor snapped too.

On Sunday, August 15, 1971, President Richard Nixon preempted the most popular show in America, *Bonanza,* to present a live television announcement of what he called his New Economic Policy, consisting of immediate wage and price controls, a 10 percent surtax on imports and the closing of the gold window. Henceforth, the dollar would no longer be convertible into gold by foreign central banks; the conversion privilege for all other holders had been ended years before. Nixon wrapped his actions in the American flag, going so far as to say, "I am determined that the American dollar must never again be a hostage in the hands of international speculators." Of course, it was U.S. deficits and monetary ease, not speculators, that had brought the dollar to this pass, but, as with FDR, Nixon was not deterred by the facts. The last vestige of the 1944 Bretton Woods gold standard and the 1922 Genoa Conference gold exchange standard was now gone.

Nixon's New Economic Policy was immensely popular. Press coverage was overwhelmingly favorable, and on the first trading day after the speech the Dow Jones Industrial Average had its largest one-day point gain in its history up until then. The announcement has been referred to ever since as the Nixon Shock. The policy was conceived in secret and announced unilaterally without consultation with the IMF or other major participants in Bretton Woods. The substance of the policy itself should not have been a shock to U.S. trading partners—de facto devaluation of the dollar against gold, which was what the New Economic Policy amounted to, was a long time coming, and the pressure on the dollar had accelerated in the weeks leading to the speech. Switzerland had redeemed dollar paper for over forty metric tons of gold as late as July 1971. French redemptions of dollars for gold had enabled France to become a gold power, ranking behind only the United States and Germany, and it remains so today.

What most shocked Europeans and the Japanese about the New Economic Policy was not the devaluation of the dollar, but the 10 percent surtax on all goods imported into the United States. Abandoning the gold standard, by itself, did not immediately change the relative values of currencies—sterling, the franc, and the yen all had their established parities with the dollar, and the German mark and Canadian dollar had already been floated by the time of Nixon's speech. But what Nixon really wanted was for the dollar to devalue immediately against all the major currencies and, better yet, to float down thereafter so that the dollar could indulge in continual devaluation in the foreign exchange markets. However, that would take time and negotiations to formalize, and Nixon did not want to wait. His 10 percent surtax had the same immediate economic impact as a 10 percent devaluation. The surtax was like a gun to the head of U.S. trading partners. Nixon would rescind the surtax once he got the devaluations he sought, and the task of negotiating those devaluations was delegated to his flamboyant Treasury secretary, John Connally of Texas.

International response to the 1971 Nixon gambit was not long in arriving. By late August, Japan had announced that it would allow the yen to float freely against the dollar. To no one's surprise, the yen immediately rose 7 percent against the dollar. Combined with the 10 percent surtax, this amounted to a 17 percent increase in the U.S. dollar price of Japanese imports to the United States, which was welcome news to U.S. car and steel producers. Switzerland created "negative interest rates," in the form of fees charged on Swiss franc bank deposits, to discourage capital inflows and help prop up the dollar.

In late September, the council of the General Agreement on Tariffs and Trade (GATT) met to consider whether the U.S. import surtax was a violation of free trade rules. There was no justification for the surtax and U.S. deputy undersecretary of state Nathaniel Samuels made almost no effort to defend it, other than to suggest that the surtax would be lifted when the U.S. balance of payments improved. Under the GATT rules, retaliation would likely have been justified. However, the U.S. trading partners had no stomach for a trade war. Memories of the 1930s were still too fresh and the role of the United States as a superpower balance to the Soviet Union and military protector of Japan and Western Europe was too important to risk a major confrontation over trade. Japan and Western Europe would simply have to suffer a weaker dollar; the question was to what extent and on whose terms.

An international conference in London was organized under the auspices of the so-called Group of Ten, or G10, in late September. These were the wealthiest nations in the world at the time, which importantly included Switzerland, even though it was not then an IMF member. Connally put on a performance worthy of his Texas pedigree. He told the delegates that the United States demanded an immediate $13 billion swing in its trade balance, from a $5 billion deficit to an $8 billion surplus, and that this demand was nonnegotiable. He then refused to engage in discussions about how this might be achieved; he told the delegates it was up to them to formulate a plan, and upon his review he would let them know whether they had been successful. The nine other members of the G10 were left to mutter among themselves about Connally's arrogance and to think about what kind of swing in the U.S. trade balance they might be willing to orchestrate.

Two weeks later, in early October, the key players met again in Washington at the annual meeting of the IMF. Little progress had been made since the London conference, but the implications of Nixon's 10 percent surtax were beginning to sink in. The Canadian trade minister, Jean-Luc Pépin, estimated that the surtax would destroy ninety thousand Canadian jobs in its first year. Some dollar devaluation had already taken place on the foreign exchange markets, where more countries had begun to float their currencies against the dollar and where immediate gains of 3 percent to 9 percent had occurred in various currencies. But Nixon and Connally were seeking total devaluation more in the 12 percent to 15 percent range, along with some assurance that those levels would stick and not be reversed by the markets. The IMF, not surprisingly given its research-dominated staff, began vetting a number of technical solutions. These included wider trading "bands" within which currencies could fluctuate before requesting formal devaluation, and possibly the expanded use of SDRs and the creation of a world central bank. These debates were irrelevant to Connally. He wanted an immediate response to the immediate problem and would use the blunt instrument of the surtax to force the issue for as long as it took. However, he did soften his views slightly at the IMF meeting by indicating that the surtax might be lifted if the U.S. trade balance moved in the right direction even if its ultimate goals had not yet been achieved.

There was one other issue on which the United States seemed willing to show some flexibility and on which the Europeans were quite focused. While the United States had announced it would no longer redeem dollars for gold, it had not officially changed the dollar-gold parity; it still regarded the dollar as worth one thirty-fifth of an ounce of gold, even in its nonconvertible state. An increase in the price of gold would be just as much of a devaluation of the dollar as an upward revaluation of the other currencies. This was symbolically important to the Europeans and would be seen by them as a defeat for the United States in the currency war despite U.S. indifference. The Germans and French would also benefit because they held large gold hoards and an increase in the dollar price of gold would mean an increase in the dollar value of their gold reserves.

Nixon and Connally did not really seem to care; having closed the gold window, the price of gold seemed somewhat irrelevant, and devaluation by whatever method was all just a means to an end. By the end of the IMF meeting, it seemed that some combination of continued upward revaluation of most currencies against the dollar on foreign exchange markets, some flexibility on timing of trade deficit reduction by the United States and a U.S. willingness to explicitly raise the dollar price of gold might form the basis of a lasting currency realignment consistent with Nixon's goals.

By early December, the endgame had begun with another G10 meeting, convened at the ornate Palazzo Corsini in Rome. This time, Connally was ready to deal. He proposed an average revaluation of foreign currencies of 11 percent and a devaluation of the dollar against gold of 10 percent. The combination of the two meant an effective increase of over 20 percent in the dollar price of foreign exports into the United States. In exchange, the United States would drop the 10 percent surtax.

The Europeans and Japanese were in shock: a total swing of perhaps 12 percent to 15 percent might have been acceptable, but 20 percent was too much to bear all at once. Moreover, the members of G10 began to position themselves against one another. A 20 percent swing against the dollar would be one thing if all countries did it at once, but if, for example, the UK revalued only 15 percent while Germany did the full 20 percent, then Germany would be disadvantaged against the UK *and* the United States. France wanted to limit the size of the dollar devaluation against gold so that more of the adjustment would be pushed onto a German revaluation in which France would not fully participate. And so it went.

By now the negotiations were almost nonstop. A few days after the Rome meeting, President Nixon met one-on-one with President Georges Pompidou of France in the Azores, where Pompidou pressed the case for an increase in the dollar price of gold as part of a package deal. Nixon conducted the negotiations in a sleep-deprived state because he had stayed up most of the night to follow a Washington Redskins football game in local time. In the end, Nixon agreed to the French demands and Pompidou returned to France a hero for having humbled the Americans in the delicate matter of the dollar and gold. Still, Nixon did not leave empty-handed, because Pompidou agreed to push for significant reductions in the stiff tariffs on U.S. imports imposed by the European Common Market.

The tentative agreements reached at Palazzo Corsini and in the Azores were ratified two weeks later by the G10 in a meeting held in the historic red castle of the Smithsonian Institution, adjacent to the National Mall in Washington, D.C. The venue gave its name to the resulting Smithsonian Agreement. The dollar was devalued about 9 percent against gold, and the major currencies were revalued upward between 3 percent and 8 percent against the dollar—a total adjustment of between 11 percent and 17 percent, depending on the currency. Important exceptions were England and France, which did not revalue but still went up about 9 percent relative to the dollar because of the devaluation against gold. The Japanese suffered the largest total adjustment, 17 percent—even more than the Germans— but they drew the least sympathy from Connally since their economy was growing at over 5 percent per year. The signatories agreed to maintain these new parities in a trading band of 2.25 percent up or down—a 4.5 percent band in total—and the United States agreed to remove the despised 10 percent import surtax; it had served its purpose. No provision for a return to the convertible gold standard was made, although technically gold had not yet been abandoned. As one writer observed, "Instead of refusing to sell gold for $35 an ounce, the Treasury will simply refuse to sell . . . for $38 an ounce."

The Smithsonian Agreement, like the Nixon Shock four months earlier, was extremely popular in the United States and led to a significant rally in stocks as investors contemplated higher dollar profits in steel, autos, aircraft, movies and other sectors that would benefit from either increased exports or fewer imports, or both. Presidential aide Peter G. Peterson estimated that the dollar devaluation would create at least five hundred thousand new jobs over the next two years.

Unfortunately, these euphoric expectations were soon crushed. Less than two years later, the United States found itself in its worst recession since World War II, with collapsing GDP, skyrocketing unemployment, an oil crisis, a crashing stock market and runaway inflation. The lesson that a nation cannot devalue its way to prosperity eluded Nixon, Connally, Peterson and the stock market in late 1971 as it had their predecessors during the Great Depression. It seemed a hard lesson to learn.

As with the grand international monetary conferences of the 1920s and 1930s, the benefits of the Smithsonian Agreement, such as they were, proved short-lived. Sterling devalued again on June 23, 1972, this time in the form of a float instead of adherence to the Smithsonian parities. The pound immediately fell 6 percent and was down 10 percent by the end of 1972. There was also great concern about the contagion effect of the sterling devaluation on the Italian lira. Nixon's chief of staff briefed him on this new European monetary crisis. Nixon's immortal response, captured on tape, was: "I don't care. Nothing we can do about it. . . . I don't give a shit about the lira."

On June 29, 1972, Germany imposed capital controls in an attempt to halt the panic buying of the mark. By July 3, both the Swiss franc and the Canadian dollar had joined the float. What had started as a sterling devaluation had turned into a rout of the dollar as investors sought the relative safety of German marks and Swiss francs. In June 1972, John Connally resigned as Treasury secretary, so the new secretary, George P. Shultz, was thrown into this developing dollar crisis almost immediately upon taking office. With the help of Paul Volcker, also at Treasury, and Fed chairman Arthur Burns, Shultz was able to activate swap lines, which are basically short-term currency lending facilities, between the Fed and the European central banks, and started intervening in markets to tame the dollar panic. By now, all of the "bands," "dirty floats," "crawling pegs" and other devices invented to maintain some semblance of the Bretton Woods system had failed. There was nothing left for it but to move all of the major currencies to a floating rate system. Finally, in 1973, the IMF declared the Bretton Woods system dead, officially ended the role of gold in international finance and left currency values to fluctuate against one another at whatever level governments or the markets desired. One currency era had ended and another had now begun, but the currency war was far from over.

The age of floating exchange rates, beginning in 1973, combined with the demise of the dollar link to gold put a temporary end to the devaluation dramas that had occupied international monetary affairs since the 1920s. No longer would central bankers and finance ministries anguish over breaking a parity or abandoning gold. Now markets moved currencies up or down on a daily basis as they saw fit. Governments did intervene in markets from time to time to offset what they saw as excesses or disorderly conditions, but this was usually of limited and temporary effect.

■ The Return of King Dollar

In reaction to the gradual demise of Bretton Woods, the major Western European nations embarked on a thirty-year odyssey of currency convergence, culminating with the European Union and the euro, which was finally launched in 1999. As Europe moved fitfully toward currency stability, the former twin anchors of the world monetary system, the dollar and gold, were far from stable. Despite the expectations of growth and higher employment coming from the dollar devaluations, the United States suffered three recessions from 1973 to 1981. In all, there was a 50 percent decline in the purchasing power of the dollar from 1977 to 1981. Oil prices quadrupled during the 1973–1975 recession and doubled again from that new, higher level in 1979. The average annual price of gold went from $40.80 per ounce in 1971 to $612.56 per ounce in 1980, including a short-term superspike to $850 per ounce in January 1980.

In the eyes of many, it was a world gone mad. A new term, "stagflation," was used to describe the unprecedented combination of high inflation and stagnant growth happening in the United States. The economic nightmare of 1973 to 1981 was the exact opposite of the export-led growth that dollar devaluation was meant to achieve. The proponents of devaluation could not have been more wrong.

With faith in the dollar near the breaking point, new leadership and new policies were desperately needed. The United States found both with the appointment of Paul Volcker as chairman of the Federal Reserve Board by President Jimmy Carter in August 1979 and the election of Ronald Reagan as president of the United States in November 1980.

Volcker had been undersecretary of the Treasury from 1969 to 1974 and had been intimately involved in the decisions to break with gold and float the dollar in 1971–1973. He was now living with the consequences of those decisions, but his experience left him extremely well prepared to use the levers of interest rates, open market operations and swap lines to reverse the dollar crisis just as he and Arthur Burns had done during the sterling crisis of 1972.

As for inflation, Volcker applied a tourniquet and twisted it hard. He raised the federal funds rate to a peak of 20 percent in June 1981, and the shock therapy worked. Partly because of Volcker, annual inflation collapsed from 12.5 percent in 1980 to 1.1 percent in 1986. Gold followed suit, falling from an average price of $612.56 in 1980 to $317.26 by 1985. Inflation had been defeated and gold had been subdued. King Dollar was back.

Although Volcker's efforts were heroic, he was not the sole cause of declining inflation and a stronger dollar. Equal credit was due to the low-tax and deregulatory policies of Ronald Reagan. The new president entered office in January 1981 at a time when American economic confidence had been shattered by the recessions, inflation and oil shocks of the Nixon-Carter years. Although the Fed was independent of the White House, Reagan and Volcker together constructed a strong dollar, implemented a low-tax policy that proved to be a tonic for the U.S. economy and launched the United States on one of its strongest periods of growth in history. Volcker's hard-money policies combined with Reagan's tax cuts helped gross domestic product achieve cumulative real growth of 16.6 percent in the three-year span from 1983 to 1985. The U.S. economy has not seen such levels of growth in any three-year period since.

The strong dollar, far from hurting growth, seemed to encourage it when combined with other progrowth policies. However, unemployment remained high for years after the last of the three recessions ended in 1982. The trade deficits with Germany and Japan were growing as the stronger dollar sent Americans shopping for German cars and Japanese electronics, among other goods.

By early 1985, the combination of U.S. industries seeking protection from imports and Americans looking for jobs led to the usual cries from unions and industrial-state politicians for devaluation of the dollar to promote exports and discourage imports. The fact that this policy had failed spectacularly in 1973 did not deter the weak-dollar crowd. The allure of a quick fix for industries in decline and those with structural inadequacies is politically irresistible. So, under the guidance of another Treasury secretary from Texas, James A. Baker, a worthy successor to John Connally, the United States made another demand on the world for a cheap dollar.

This time the method of devaluation was different. There were no longer any fixed exchange rates or gold conversion ratios to break. Currencies traded freely against one another and exchange rates were set by the foreign exchange market, consisting mostly of large international banks and their corporate customers. Part of the dollar's strength in the early 1980s stemmed from the fact that foreign investors wanted dollars to invest in the United States because of its strong economic growth. The strong dollar was a vote of confidence in the United States, not a problem to be solved. However, domestic politics dictated another fate for the dollar, a recurring theme in the currency wars. Because the market was pushing the dollar higher, it would require government intervention in the exchange markets on a massive scale if the dollar was to be devalued. This kind of massive intervention required agreement and coordination by the major governments involved.

Western Europe and Japan had no appetite for dollar devaluation; however, memories of the Nixon Shock were still fresh and no one could be sure that Baker would not resort to import surtaxes just as Connally had in 1971. Moreover, Western Europe and Japan were just as dependent on the United States for their defense and national security against the communist bloc as they had been in the 1970s. On the whole, it seemed better to negotiate with the United States on a dollar devaluation than be taken by surprise again.

The Plaza Accord of September 1985 was the culmination of this multilateral effort to drive the dollar down. Finance ministers from West Germany, Japan, France and the United Kingdom met with the U.S. Treasury secretary at the Plaza Hotel in New York City to work out a plan of dollar devaluation, principally against the yen and the mark. Central banks committed over $10 billion to the exercise, which worked as planned over several years. From 1985 to 1988, the dollar declined over 40 percent against the French franc, 50 percent against the Japanese yen and 20 percent against the German mark.

The Plaza Accord was a success if measured solely as an exercise in devaluation, but the economic results were disappointing. U.S. unemployment remained high, at 7.0 percent in 1986, while growth slowed considerably to only 3.2 percent in 1987. Once again, the quick fix had proved chimerical and, once again, there was a high price to pay in the form of inflation, which took off with a lag after the Plaza Accord, shooting back up to 6.1 percent in 1990. Devaluation and currency wars never produce either the growth or the jobs that are promised, but they reliably produce inflation.

The Plaza Accord was deemed too successful by the parties and occasioned one last adjustment to put the brakes on the dollar's rapid decline from the heights of 1985. The G7, consisting of the Plaza Accord parties plus Canada and Italy, met at the Louvre in Paris in early 1987 to sign the Louvre Accord, meant to stabilize the dollar at the new, lower level. With the Louvre Accord, Currency War II ended, as the G7 finance ministers decided that, after twenty years of turmoil, enough was enough.

By 1987, gold was gone from international finance, the dollar had been devalued, the yen and mark were ascendant, sterling had faltered, the euro was in prospect and China had not yet taken its own place on the stage. For now, there was relative peace in international monetary matters, yet this peace rested on nothing more substantial than faith in the dollar as a store of value based on a growing U.S. economy and stable monetary policy by the Fed. These conditions largely prevailed through the 1990s and into the early twenty-first century, notwithstanding two mild recessions along the way. The currency crises that did arise were nondollar crises, such as the sterling crisis of 1992, the Mexican peso crisis of 1994 and the Asia-

Russia financial crisis of 1997–1998. None of these crises threatened the dollar—in fact, the dollar was typically a safe haven when they arose. It seemed as though it would take either a collapse in growth or the rise of a competing economic power—or both—to threaten the supremacy of the dollar. When these factors finally did converge, in 2010, the result would be the international monetary equivalent of a tsunami.

CHAPTER 6

Currency War III (2010–)

> "The purpose . . . is not to push the dollar down. This should not be regarded as some sort of chapter in a currency war."
>
> Janet Yellen,
> Vice Chair of the Federal Reserve,
> commenting on quantitative easing,
> November 16, 2010

> "Quantitative easing also works through exchange rates. . . . The Fed could engage in much more aggressive quantitative easing . . . to further lower . . . the dollar."
>
> Christina D. Romer,
> former Chair of the Council of Economic Advisers,
> commenting on quantitative easing,
> February 27, 2011

Three supercurrencies—the dollar, the euro and the yuan—issued by the three largest economies in the world—the United States, the European Union and the People's Republic of China—are the superpowers in a new currency war, Currency War III, which began in 2010 as a consequence of the 2007 depression and whose dimensions and consequences are just now coming into focus.

No one denies the importance of other major currencies in the global financial system, including Japanese yen, UK pounds sterling, Swiss francs, and those of the remaining BRICs: Brazilian real, Russian ruble, Indian rupee and South African rand. These currencies derive their importance from the size of the economies that issue them and the volume of trade and financial transactions in which those countries engage. By these measures, the indigenous dollars issued by Australia, New Zealand, Canada, Singapore, Hong Kong and Taiwan, as well as the Norwegian krone, South Korean won and UAE dirham, all have pride of place. But the combined GDP of the United States, European Union and China—almost 60 percent of global GDP—creates a center of gravity to which all other economies and currencies are peripheral in some way.

Every war has its main fronts and its romantic and often bloody sideshows. World War II was the greatest and most expansive military conflict in history. The U.S. perspective on World War II is neatly divided into Europe and the Pacific, while a Japanese perspective would encompass an imperial empire stretching from Burma to an overextended attack at Pearl Harbor. The English, it seems, fought everywhere at once.

So it is with currency wars. The main battle lines being drawn are a dollar-yuan theater across the Pacific, a dollar-euro theater across the Atlantic and a euro-yuan theater in the Eurasian landmass. These battles are real but the geographic designations are metaphorical. The fact is, currency wars are fought globally in all major financial centers at once, twenty-four hours per day, by bankers, traders, politicians and automated systems—and the fate of economies and their affected citizens hang in the balance.

Participation in currency wars today is no longer confined to the national issuers of currency and their central banks. Involvement extends to multilateral and global institutions such as the IMF, World Bank, Bank for International Settlements and United Nations, as well as private entities such as hedge funds, global corporations and private family offices of the superrich. Whether as speculators, hedgers or manipulators these private institutions have as much influence over the fate of currencies as the nations that issue them. To see that the battle lines are global, not neatly confined to nation-states, one need only consider the oft-told story of the hedge fund run by George Soros that "broke the Bank of England" in 1992 on a massive currency bet. Today there are many more hedge funds with many more trillions of dollars in leverage than Soros would have imagined twenty years ago.

Battles in the Pacific, Atlantic and Eurasian theaters of Currency

War III have commenced with important sideshows playing out in Brazil, Russia, the Middle East and throughout Asia. CWIII will not be fought over the fate of the real or the ruble, however; it will be fought over the relative values of the euro, the dollar and the yuan, and this will affect the destinies of the countries that issue them as well as their trading partners.

The world is now entering its third currency war in less than one hundred years. Whether it ends tragically as in CWI or is managed to a soft landing as in CWII remains to be seen. What is clear is that—considering the growth since the 1980s of national economies, money printing and leverage through derivatives—this currency war will be truly global and fought on a more massive scale than ever. Currency War III will include both official and private players. This expansion in size, geography and participation exponentially increases the risk of collapse. Today the risk is not just of devaluation of one currency against another or a rise in the price of gold. Today the risk is the collapse of the monetary system itself—a loss of confidence in paper currencies and a massive flight to hard assets. Given these risks of catastrophic failure, Currency War III may be the last currency war—or, to paraphrase Woodrow Wilson, the war to end all currency wars.

■ The Pacific Theater

The struggle between China and the United States, between the yuan and the dollar, is the centerpiece of global finance today and the main front in Currency War III. The evolution of this struggle begins with the emergence of China from a quarter century of economic isolation, social chaos and the doctrinaire suppression of free markets by the communist regime.

The modern Chinese economic miracle began in January 1975 with the Four Modernizations plan announced by Premier Zhou Enlai, which affected agriculture, industry, defense and technology. Implementation was delayed, however, due to disruptions caused by Zhou's death in January 1976, followed by the death of Communist

Party chairman Mao Zedong in September of that year and the arrest one month later of the radical Gang of Four, including Madame Mao, after a brief reign.

Mao's designated successor, Hua Guofeng, carried forward Zhou's vision and made a definitive break with the Maoist past at a National Party Congress in December 1978. Hua was aided in this by the recently rehabilitated and soon to be dominant Deng Xiaoping. Real change began the next year, followed by a period of experimentation and pilot programs aimed at increasing autonomy in decision making on farms and in factories. In 1979, China took the landmark decision to create four special economic zones offering favorable work rules, reduced regulation and tax benefits designed to attract foreign investment, especially in manufacturing, assembly and textile industries. They were the precursors of a much larger program of economic development zones launched in 1984 involving most of the large coastal cities in eastern China. Although China grew rapidly in percentage terms in the mid-1980s, it was working from a low base and neither its currency nor its bilateral trade relations with major countries such as the United States and Germany gave much cause for concern.

Today's currency war is marked by claims of Chinese undervaluation, yet as late as 1983 the yuan was massively *overvalued* at a rate of 2.8 yuan to one dollar. However, this was at a time when exports were a relatively small part of Chinese GDP and the leadership was more focused on cheap imports to develop infrastructure. As the export sector grew, China engaged in a series of six devaluations over ten years so that, by 1993, the yuan had been cheapened to a level of 5.32 yuan to the dollar. Then, on January 1, 1994, China announced a reformed system of foreign exchange and massively devalued the yuan to 8.7 to the dollar. That shock caused the U.S. Treasury to label China a currency "manipulator" pursuant to the 1988 Trade Act, which requires the Treasury to single out countries that are using exchange rates to gain unfair advantage in international trade. That was the last time Treasury used the manipulator label against China despite veiled threats to do so ever since. A series of mild revaluations followed in response so that, by 1997, the yuan was pegged at 8.28 to the dollar, where it remained practically unchanged until 2004.

In the late 1980s, China suffered a significant bout of inflation, which prompted popular discontent and a conservative backlash led by old-guard communists against the economic reform and opening programs of Deng. Separately, a liberal protest movement, led by students and intellectuals seeking democratic reform, also contributed to political upheaval. These conservative and liberal movements collided violently and tragically in the Tiananmen Square massacre of June 4, 1989, when People's Liberation Army troops, acting on orders from the Communist Party leadership, used live fire and tanks to clear human rights and prodemocracy protestors from the square in the center of Beijing adjacent to the old imperial Forbidden City. Hundreds were killed. There was a slowdown of the Chinese economy after 1989, partly as a result of efforts to curb inflation and partly as a foreign reaction to the Tiananmen Square massacre. This pause proved temporary, however.

In the 1990s, China finally broke the "iron rice bowl," the welfare policy that had previously guaranteed the Chinese people food and some social services at the cost of slow growth and inefficiency. Something resembling a market economy began to appear, which meant that Chinese workers had the opportunity to do better for themselves but had no guaranteed support if they failed. The key to this new social contract was the steady creation of millions of jobs for the new job seekers. With memories of Tiananmen fresh in their minds and the historical memory of over a century of chaos, the leadership knew the survival of the Communist Party and the continuation of political stability depended on job creation; everything else in Chinese policy would be subordinate to that goal. The surest way to rapid, massive job creation was to become an export powerhouse. The currency peg was the means to this end. For the Communist Party of China, the dollar-yuan peg was an economic bulwark against another Tiananmen Square.

By 1992, reactionary elements in China opposed to reform again began to push for a dismantling of Deng's special economic zones and other programs. In response, a visibly ailing and officially retired Deng Xiaoping made his famous New Year's Southern Tour, a personal visit to major industrial cities, including Shanghai, which generated support for continued economic development and which politically disarmed the reactionaries. The 1992 Southern Tour marked a second-stage takeoff in Chinese economic growth, with real GDP more than doubling from 1992 to 2000. However, the effect of this spectacular growth in the 1990s on U.S.-China economic relations was muted by the continuing U.S response to the Tiananmen Square massacre, which included economic sanctions and a general cooling of direct foreign investment by U.S. firms in China. A series of blunders and miscalculations, including the firing of a NATO cruise missile at the Chinese embassy in Belgrade in 1999, served to increase tensions. Economic relations were kept in an adversarial state by the April 2001 collision of a Chinese jet fighter with a U.S. reconnaissance plane, killing the Chinese pilot and causing the emergency landing of the U.S. plane on Chinese territory and temporary imprisonment of the crew.

Ironically, it was the al-Qaeda attacks on September 11, 2001, and China's resulting firm support for the U.S.-led global war on terror that finally broke the ice and helped U.S.-China relations get back on track. Despite almost twenty-five years of significant economic progress by China, beginning in 1976, it was only in 2002 that U.S.-China bilateral trade and investment codependence kicked into high gear.

That year, 2002, also marked the beginning of Fed chairman Alan Greenspan's experiment with sustained ultralow interest rates. Greenspan had started to cut rates in the summer of 2000 following the tech bubble collapse. The resulting decline of over 4.75 percent in the fed funds rate from July 2000 to July 2002 could be viewed as a normal cyclical easing designed to help the economy out of a rut. What happened next was an extraordinary period of over two additional years during which the effective fed funds rate never rose above 1.8 percent and dropped below 1.0 percent in December 2003. As late as October 2004, the effective fed funds rate was 1.76 percent, almost exactly where it had been in July 2002.

This low rate policy was justified initially as a response to the challenges of the 2000 tech bubble collapse, the 2001 recession, the 9/11 attacks and Greenspan's fears of deflation. Yet it was primarily fear of deflation that caused Greenspan to keep rates low for far longer than would ordinarily be justified by a mild recession. China was now exporting its deflation to the world, partly through a steady supply of cheap labor. Greenspan's low rate policy, partly intended to offset the effects of Chinese deflation in the United States, sowed the seeds of the full-scale currency war that emerged later in the decade.

Greenspan's low rates were not only a policy response to potential deflation; they were also a kind of intravenous drug to Wall Street. The Federal Open Market Committee, the body that sets the fed funds target rate, was now acting like a meth lab for hyperactive deal junkies on the Street. Lower rates meant that all types of dubious or risky deals could begin to look attractive, because marginal borrowers would ostensibly be able to afford the financing costs. Low rates also set off a search for yield by institutional investors who needed higher returns than were being offered in risk-free government securities or highly rated bonds. The subprime residential loan market and the commercial real estate market both exploded in terms of loan originations, deal flow, securitizations and underlying asset prices due to Greenspan's low rate policies. The great real estate bubble of 2002 to 2007 was under way.

In September 2002, just as the low rate policy was taking off, Greenspan gained an ally, Ben Bernanke, appointed as a new member of the Fed Board of Governors. Bernanke's deeply rooted fear of deflation was even greater than Greenspan's. Bernanke would quickly establish his deflation-fighting credentials with a speech to the National Economists Club in Washington, D.C., just two months after being sworn in as a Fed governor. The speech, entitled "Deflation: Making Sure 'It' Doesn't Happen Here," was widely noted at the time for its reference to Milton Friedman's idea of dropping freshly printed money from helicopters to prevent deflation if necessary, and earned Bernanke the sobriquet "Helicopter Ben."

Bernanke's 2002 speech was the blueprint for the 2008 bailouts and the 2009 policy of quantitative easing. Bernanke spoke plainly

about how the Fed could print money to monetize government deficits, whether they arose from tax cuts or spending increases, saying:

> A broad-based tax cut . . . accommodated by a program of open
> market purchases . . . would almost certainly be an effective
> stimulant to consumption. . . . A money-financed tax cut is
> essentially equivalent to Milton Friedman's famous "helicopter
> drop" of money. . . .
>
> Of course . . . the government could . . . even acquire existing
> real or financial assets. If . . . the Fed then purchased an equal
> amount of Treasury debt with newly created money, the whole
> operation would be the economic equivalent of direct open market
> operations in private assets.

Bernanke was explaining how the Treasury could issue debt to buy
private stock and the Fed could finance that debt by printing money.
This is essentially what happened when the Treasury took over AIG,
GM and Citibank and bailed out Goldman Sachs, among others. It
had all been spelled out by Bernanke years earlier.

With Bernanke on the board, Greenspan had the perfect soul
mate, and in time the perfect successor, in his antideflationary cru-
sade. The Greenspan-Bernanke fear of deflation is the one constant
of the entire 2002–2011 period. In their view, deflation was the enemy and China, because of low wages and its low production costs—
from ignoring safety and pollution—was an important source.

Despite its economic miracle, China ran trade deficits with the
world as late as 2004. This is not unusual in the early stages of a
developing economy, when efforts at export success must be tem-
pered by the need to import infrastructure components, industrial
equipment, raw materials and technology with which to launch exports. China did run a bilateral trade surplus with the United States;
however, this was not initially cause for concern. In 1997 the U.S.
trade deficit with China was less than $50 billion. Then the deficit
grew steadily, and in the space of three years, from 2003 to 2006, it
exploded from $124 billion to $234 billion. This period, beginning
in 2003, marks the intensification of concern about the U.S.-China

bilateral trade relationship and the role of the dollar-yuan exchange rate in that relationship. In 2006, Senator Charles E. Schumer of New York called the U.S. trade deficit "a slow bleeding at the wrists for the U.S. economy" and pointed to China as a leading contributor.

China's internal deflation is exported to the United States through the currency exchange rate and ends up threatening deflation in the United States. This begins with the Chinese policy decision to peg the exchange rate between the yuan and the dollar. The yuan does not trade freely on international currency markets in the same way that dollars, euros, sterling, yen and other convertible currencies do. The use of the yuan and its availability to settle transactions are tightly controlled by the People's Bank of China, or PBOC, the country's central bank.

When a Chinese exporter ships goods abroad and earns dollars or euros, it must hand over those currencies to the People's Bank of China in exchange for yuan at a rate fixed by the bank. When an exporter needs some dollars or euros to buy foreign materials or other imports, it can get them, but the PBOC makes only enough dollars or euros available to pay for the imports and no more; the rest is kept by the bank.

The process of absorbing all the surplus dollars entering the Chinese economy, especially after 2002, produced a number of unintended consequences. The first problem was that the PBOC did not just take the surplus dollars, but rather purchased them with newly printed yuan. This meant that as the Fed printed dollars and those dollars ended up in China to purchase goods, the PBOC had to print yuan to soak up the surplus. In effect, China had outsourced its monetary policy to the Fed, and as the Fed printed more, the PBOC also printed more in order to maintain the pegged exchange rate.

The second problem was what to do with the newly acquired dollars. The PBOC needed to invest its reserves somewhere, and it needed to earn a reasonable rate of return. Central banks are traditionally ultraconservative in their investment policies, and the PBOC is no exception, preferring highly liquid government securities issued by the United States Treasury. As a result, the Chinese acquired massive quantities of U.S. Treasury obligations as their trade surplus with the United States persisted and grew. By early 2011, Reuters estimated that total Chinese foreign reserves in all currencies were approximately $2.85 trillion, with about $950 billion of that invested in U.S. government obligations of one kind or another. The United States and China were locked in a trillion-dollar financial embrace, essentially a monetary powder keg that could be detonated by either side if the currency wars spiraled out of control.

The United States desperately urged China to increase the value of the yuan in order to reduce the growing U.S. trade deficits with China and slow the massive accumulation of dollar-denominated assets by the PBOC. These pleas met with very limited success. From 2004 through mid-2005 the yuan remained pegged at about 8.28 yuan to one dollar, about where it had been since 1997. Suddenly, over the course of two days in late July 2005, the yuan increased in value from 8.28 to 8.11 to the dollar, an increase of almost 3 percent. From that sudden upward revaluation, the yuan began a long, gradual revaluation over the next three years, eventually reaching the level of about 6.82 to one dollar in mid-July 2008.

Then the PBOC again slammed on the brakes and held the yuan steady around the 6.83 level for the next two years. In June 2010, a second round of revaluation commenced, which by August 2011 brought the yuan slowly but steadily above 6.40 yuan to the dollar. This rise in the dollar value of the yuan was hardly smooth and was never without acrimony. The rhetorical and political battles between China and the United States from 2004 to 2011 on the subject of exchange rates dominated U.S.-Chinese economic relations despite a host of other important bilateral issues, including Iran and North Korea.

It is intriguing to think about how imbalances such as the U.S. bilateral trade deficit with China and China's massive accumulation of U.S. government debt would have evolved under the Bretton Woods system. China's accumulation of U.S. debt would have begun the same way and there would always have been a desire to hold some amount of U.S. Treasury securities for diversification and liquidity-management reasons. But at some point, China would have asked to cash in some of its Treasury securities for U.S. gold held in reserves, as was allowed under Bretton Woods. A relatively small redemption, say, $100 billion of Treasury notes, done in early 2008 when gold was about $1,000 per ounce, would have equaled 100 million ounces of gold, or about 2,840 metric tons. This amounts to 35 percent of the entire official gold supply of the United States. Indeed, a full redemption of all U.S. government securities by China would have wiped out the U.S. gold supply completely and left the United States with no gold and China the proud owner of over 9,000 metric tons. One can imagine Chinese naval vessels arriving in New York Harbor and a heavily armed U.S. Army convoy moving south down the Palisades Interstate Parkway from West Point to meet the vessels and load the gold on board for shipment to newly constructed vaults in Shanghai. No doubt such a scene would have been shocking to the American people, yet that imagined shock proves a larger point. America has, in fact, run trade deficits large enough to wipe out its gold hoard under the old rules of the game. Still, the idea of the gold standard was not to deplete nations of gold, but rather to force them to get their financial house in order long before the gold disappeared. In the absence of a gold standard and the real-time adjustments it causes, the American people seem unaware of how badly U.S. finances have actually deteriorated.

While this example may seem extreme, it is exactly how most of the world monetary system worked until forty years ago. In 1950, the United States had official gold reserves of over 20,000 metric tons. Due to persistent large trade deficits, at the time with Europe and Japan rather than China, U.S. gold reserves had dropped to just over 9,000 metric tons when Nixon closed the gold window in 1971. That drop of 11,000 metric tons in the twenty-one years from 1950 to 1971 went mostly to a small number of export powerhouses. Over the same period, German gold reserves rose from zero to over 3,600 metric tons. Italy's gold hoard went from 227 metric tons to over 2,500 metric tons. France went from 588 metric tons to over 3,100 metric tons. The Netherlands, another rising gold power, went from 280 metric tons to almost 1,700 metric tons. Not all of these expanding gold reserves came from the United States. Another gold power, the United Kingdom, saw its gold reserves drop from over 2,500 metric tons in 1950 to only 690 metric tons by 1971. But in general, U.S. gold was moving from the United States to its trading partners as part of the automatic rebalancing contemplated by the Bretton Woods system.

China's rise to export powerhouse status did not take place in this golden age of the 1950s and 1960s. It took place largely in the early twenty-first century, when claims were settled in paper IOUs or their electronic equivalents. This meant that China did not receive any official gold for its export success. It also meant that there was no effective check on the ability of the United States to print money, borrow and keep spending beyond its means. This borrowing and spending binge was encouraged by the ultralow interest rate policies of Greenspan and Bernanke. Absent a gold standard or some other monetary constraint to apply the brakes, China and the United States hurtled toward CWIII with no compass and no map for navigating paper claims of an unprecedented magnitude.

The principal accusation leveled by the United States against China, discussed repeatedly in the press but never formally alleged by the White House since 1994, is that China manipulates its currency in order to keep Chinese exports cheap for foreign buyers. But China's export machine is not an end in itself—it is a means to an end. The real end of Chinese policy is one familiar to politicians everywhere—jobs. China's coastal factories, assembly plants and transportation hubs are at the receiving end of a river of humanity that flows from China's central and southern rural provinces, carrying tens of millions of mostly younger workers in search of steady work at wages only one-tenth of what a comparable job would pay in the United States.

These newly arrived workers live in crowded dormitories, work seventy-hour weeks, take public transportation, eat noodles and rice and have few if any amenities or leisure pursuits. The little they manage to save is remitted back to the village or farm they came from to support aging parents or other relatives with no social safety net. Yet from the perspective of the rural Chinese, this life is the Chinese Dream, a twenty-first-century counterpart to the more expansive twentieth-century American Dream of a home, car and good schools that came along with a steady job in midcentury America. Of course, those rural immigrants to the cities just need to look around to see the Mercedes, Cadillacs and high-rise luxury apartments of China's new rich to know there is something beyond the dormitory and the city bus.

No one knows better than the Chinese Communist Party leadership what would happen if those jobs were not available. The study of Chinese history is the study of periodic collapse. In particular, the 140-year period from 1839 to 1979 was one of almost constant turmoil. It began with the Opium Wars (1839–1860) and continued through the Taiping Rebellion (1850–1864), the Boxer Rebellion (1899–1901), the fall of the Qing Dynasty in 1912, the warlord and gangster period of the 1920s, civil war between nationalists and communists in the early 1930s, Japanese invasion and World War II (1931–1945), the communist takeover in 1949, the Great Leap Forward (1958–1961), the Cultural Revolution (1966–1976), and finally the death of Mao and the downfall of the Gang of Four in 1976. These events were not just noteworthy points in a chronological history but involved continuing episodes of external war, civil war, widespread famine, mass rape, terror, mass refugee migrations, corruption, assassination, confiscation, political executions and the absence of any effective political center or rule of law. By the late 1970s, Chinese culture and civilization were politically, morally and physically exhausted, and the people, along with the Communist Party, wanted nothing more than stability and economic growth. Liberal democracy and civil rights could wait.

This is why the Tiananmen Square demonstrations in 1989 were as troubling to the Chinese leaders as their violent suppression was shocking to the West. From their perspective, Tiananmen seemed to put China on the edge of chaos again after just ten years of growth and stability. The Chinese Communist Party leadership understood that the nineteenth-century Taiping Rebellion had begun with a single disappointed student and soon embroiled the southern half of the empire in a civil war resulting in twenty million deaths. Chinese history is proof that a social network does not require the Internet but spreads just as powerfully by word of mouth and by what the Chinese call *dazibao,* or big-character posters. The Chinese leaders also understood that the Tiananmen protests were fueled not just by prodemocracy sentiments but by student and worker resentment at higher food prices and slower job growth as China's policy makers hastened to tamp down the economy to fight the inflation that had begun to take off in the late 1980s.

Of course, the United States also cared about job creation. The 2001 recession had been mild in statistical terms with regard to GDP and industrial output, but the number of unemployed in America spiked up sharply, from 5.6 million people at the end of 2000 to over 8.2 million at the end of 2001. Despite a technical recovery in 2002, the number of unemployed continued to grow and reached over 8.6 million people at the end of 2002. From there, it declined very slowly so that there were still over 7.2 million unemployed at the end of 2005. When the recession of 2007 began, America was still working off this high base of unemployed, and the total number skyrocketed to over 15.6 million unemployed by October 2009. Including those employed part-time but seeking longer hours and those not officially unemployed but desiring a job, the total number of unemployed and underemployed Americans at the end of 2009 stood at over 25 million men and women. Every one of those 25 million Americans has a face, a name and a family. In our statistical age, economists prefer to present this phenomenon in percentage terms, such as 6.0 percent unemployment for year-end 2002 and 9.9 percent for 2009, but reciting the actual numbers of affected persons—more than 25 million—helps to bring home the depths of the employment problem. America desperately needed to create jobs.

For a while, this human tragedy was masked by the easy money policies of Greenspan and Bernanke and the resulting euphoria of credit card spending, rising home prices, rising stock prices and large no-down-payment mortgages for all comers. Although there were some complaints about Chinese currency manipulation and lost American jobs in 2004 and 2005, these complaints were muted by the highly visible but ultimately nonsustainable prosperity of those years resulting from the easy money. When the music stopped abruptly in 2007 and the United States careened into the Panic of 2008, there was no longer a place for Chinese policy makers to hide.

Now U.S. politicians, led most noisily by Senator Charles Schumer, publicly attacked the pegging of the yuan-dollar exchange rate and blamed the Chinese for lost jobs in the United States. A bipartisan group of U.S. senators, including Schumer, wrote a letter to the Bush White House in 2008, stating, "The unfair price advantage that the undervalued [Chinese currency] gives Chinese firms has forced many American companies to declare bankruptcy or even go out of business, harming our workers, families and middle class." Senator Schumer and his ilk were undaunted by the fact that there is scant evidence to support this linkage between jobs and exchange rates. It seems unlikely that the typical North Carolina furniture maker would be willing to work for the $118 per month made by his Chinese counterpart. Even if the yuan doubled in value, the Chinese furniture maker would earn only the equivalent of $236 per month—still not high enough to make his U.S. counterpart competitive. None of this mattered to the dollar demagogues. In their view, the Chinese currency was clearly to blame and now the Chinese must respond to their demands for revaluation.

The administration of President George W. Bush was well aware of this chorus of complaints but was also attuned to the importance of close relations with China on a number of other issues. China was the largest purchaser of Iranian oil exports and was therefore in a position to influence Iran in its confrontation with the United States over nuclear weapons development. China was an indispensible economic lifeline to the hermetically sealed regime of North Korea, with which it shared a common border, and so was also in a position to help the United States achieve its strategic goals on the Korean peninsula. Large U.S. corporations eyed the Chinese market enviously and were looking for direct market access through expansion, acquisitions or joint ventures with Chinese partners, all of which required Chinese government approvals. China had suffered a loss of face in 2005 when the China National Offshore Oil Corporation withdrew its takeover bid for U.S.-based Unocal Oil after the U.S. House of Representatives voted 398–15 to call on President Bush to review the bid on national security grounds. Such rejections could easily result in tit-for-tat denial of U.S. acquisitions in China. In short, America had as much to lose as to gain from any confrontation with China, and a continuing high-level expert dialogue seemed like a more fruitful approach.

President Bush addressed the need to keep U.S.-Chinese currency tensions under control by launching the China-U.S. Strategic Economic Dialogue in 2006. These meetings were continued by the Obama administration in expanded form and renamed the Strategic and Economic Dialogue (S&ED) to reflect the inclusion of the U.S. secretary of state and a Chinese state councilor with responsibility for foreign policy. The inclusion of foreign policy officials along with economic officials was a clear recognition of the interconnectedness of the geopolitical and financial aspects of national policy in the twenty-first century.

The Strategic and Economic Dialogue was one of several bilateral and multilateral forums designed in part to deal with the advent of a new currency war. It has helped to avoid an escalation in tensions over the currency manipulation charges, but has done nothing to make the issue go away. A series of bilateral summits between President Hu of China and President Obama of the United States were also convened, but neither the S&ED nor the bilateral summits have produced major progress.

The United States has now chosen the G20 as the main arena to push China in the direction of revaluation, both because of the possibility of attracting allies to join the effort and because the Chinese are more deferential to global opinion than to U.S. opinion alone. Recent significant progress on yuan revaluation has tended to occur not in conjunction with S&ED meetings but rather in advance of G20 meetings. For example, a small but still noteworthy revaluation of the yuan from 6.83 on June 15, 2010, to 6.79 on June 25, 2010, occurred immediately in advance of the G20 leaders' summit in Toronto. Another rally in the yuan from 6.69 on November 1, 2010, to 6.62 on November 11, 2010, coincided with the G20 leaders' summit in Seoul. This demonstrates that the Chinese are attentive to the G20 in ways that they may not be when it comes to other forums.

By the spring of 2011 the U.S.-China Pacific theater in the currency war was quiet. However, the core issues were still unresolved. Employment stress in both China and the United States meant that tensions could erupt at any time. A leadership change in China in 2012 and a presidential election in the United States the same year raised the specter of domestic political forces being a catalyst for further international confrontation.

■ The Atlantic Theater

The Atlantic theater, the relationship between the dollar and the euro, is better understood as one of codependence rather than confrontation. This is because of the much larger scale and degree of interconnectedness between U.S. and European capital markets and banking systems compared to any other pair of financial relationships in the world. This interdependence was never on more vivid display than in the immediate aftermath of the bankruptcy of the Lehman Brothers investment bank in September 2008. Although the bankruptcy was filed in U.S. federal courts after a failed bailout attempt led by the U.S. Treasury, some of the largest financial victims and worst-affected parties were European hedge funds that had done over-the-counter swaps business or maintained clearing accounts at Lehman's London affiliates. This transatlantic fiasco, heavily reported at the time, was amplified in December 2010 when the Fed, in response to disclosures required by the new Dodd-Frank Act, released extensive details of its emergency lending and bailout operations to Europe during the Panic of 2008.

The euro-dollar exchange rate in early 2011 was almost exactly where it was in 2007. The euro was worth $1.30 in early January 2007 and traded right around $1.30 four years later, but this equivalence should not be mistaken for stability. In fact the euro-dollar relationship has been highly volatile, with the euro trading as high as $1.59 in July 2008 and as low as $1.10 in June 2010.

The euro and dollar are best understood as two passengers on the same ship. At any given time, one passenger may be on a higher deck and the other on a lower one. They can change places at will and move higher or lower relative to each other, but at the end of the day they are on the same vessel moving at the same speed heading for the same destination. The day-to-day fluctuations reflect technical factors, short-term supply and demand requirements, fears of default or disintegration of the euro followed quickly by relief at the latest rescue or bailout package. Through it all, the euro-dollar pair travel on, never separated by more than the dimensions of the vessel on which they both sail.

The United States nevertheless has its hands full on the currency war's Atlantic front, not in trying to strengthen the euro excessively but rather in making sure it does not fall apart altogether. The euro itself is a kind of miracle of modern monetary creation, having been invented by the members of the European Union after thirty years of discussion and ten years of intensive technical study and planning. It was the capstone of a European project begun after World War II and intended to preserve the peace.

Beginning at the end of the Renaissance in the mid-sixteenth century, Europe had been racked for over four hundred years by the battles waged during the Reformation, the Counter-Reformation, the Thirty Years' War, the English Revolution, the wars of Louis XIV, the Seven Years' War, the French Revolution, the Napoleonic Wars, the Franco-Prussian War, World War I, World War II, the Holocaust, the dropping of the Iron Curtain and the nuclear terror of the Cold War. By the late twentieth century, Europe was highly cynical about nationalist claims and the potential for military advantage. The old ethnic, national and religious divides were still there. What was needed was a unifying force—something that would tie economies so closely together that war would be unthinkable, if not impossible.

Starting with the six-nation Coal and Steel Community in 1951, Europe progressed through various forms of free trade areas, common markets and monetary systems. The Maastricht Treaty of 1992, named after the city in the Netherlands where it was negotiated and signed, provided for the formation of a political entity, the European Union, and ultimately led to the creation of the euro in

1999. The euro was to be issued by the new European Central Bank. By 2011, the euro was used by seventeen member states.

Yet from the start, analysts warned that a single currency backed by a single central bank was incompatible with the diverse fiscal policies of the member countries adopting the euro. Countries that had historically been profligate and had defaulted on debt or devalued their currencies, such as Greece or Spain, would be awkward partners in a union that included fiscally prudent countries like Germany.

It took ten years for all the flaws in this grand scheme to be fully revealed, although they were there from the start. A toxic combination of venal government ministers, Wall Street hit-and-run derivatives scam artists and willfully blind European Union officials in Brussels allowed countries such as Greece to run deficits and borrow at levels far in excess of Maastricht Treaty limits while burying the true costs in out years and off-balance-sheet contracts. Meanwhile investors happily snapped up billions of euros in sovereign debt from the likes of Greece, Portugal, Spain, Ireland and other eurozone member states at interest rates only slightly higher than solid credits such as Germany. This was done on the basis of high ratings from incompetent ratings agencies, misleading financial statements from government ministries and wishful thinking by investors that a euro sovereign would never default.

The path to the 2010 European sovereign debt crisis was partly the fruit of a new entente among banks, borrowers and bureaucrats. The banks would buy the European sovereign bonds and book the related profits secure in the belief that no sovereign would be allowed to fail. The sovereigns happily issued the bonds in order to finance nonsustainable spending that largely benefitted public unions. The interests of the bureaucrats in Brussels were perhaps most insidious of all. If the European sovereign debt crisis resolved itself, everyone would praise the success of the euro project. If some European sovereign debt failed, the bureaucrats' solution would be more, not less, integration and more, not less, oversight from Brussels. By turning a blind eye to the recklessness, Brussels had constructed a no-lose situation. If the euro succeeded they won praise and if the euro came under stress they won power. The stress came soon enough.

The European banks gorged not only on euro sovereign debt but also on debt issued by Fannie Mae and the full alphabet soup of fraudulent Wall Street structured products such as collateralized debt obligations, or CDOs. These debts were originated by inexperienced local bankers around the United States and repackaged in the billions of dollars by the likes of Lehman Brothers before they went bust. The European banks were the true weak links in the global financial system, weaker even than Citigroup, Goldman Sachs and the other bailed-out icons of American finance.

By 2010, European sovereign finance was a complex web composed of cross-holdings of debt. Of the $236 billion of Greek debt, $15 billion was owed to UK entities, $75 billion was owed to French entities and $45 billion was owed to German entities. Of the $867 billion of Irish debt, $60 billion was owed to French entities, $188 billion was owed to UK entities and $184 billion was owed to German entities. Of the $1.1 trillion of Spanish debt, $114 billion was owed to UK entities, $220 billion was owed to French entities and $238 billion was owed to German entities. The same pattern prevailed in Italy, Portugal and the other heavily indebted members of the euro system. The mother of all inter-European debts was the $511 billion that Italy owed to France.

While this sovereign debt was owed to a variety of institutions, including pension funds and endowments, the vast majority was owed to other countries' banks. This was the reason for the Fed's secret bailout of Europe in 2008 and why the Fed fought so hard to keep the details confidential until some of it was forced into the open by the Dodd-Frank legislation of 2010. This was the reason Fannie Mae and Freddie Mac bondholders never took any losses when those companies were bailed out by the U.S. taxpayers in 2008. This was why the leading states, Germany and France, rallied quickly to prop up sovereign borrowers in the periphery such as Greece, Ireland and Portugal when the euro sovereign crisis reached a critical stage in 2010. The impetus behind all three bailouts was that the European banking system was insolvent. Subsidizing Greek pensioners and

Irish banks was a small price to pay to avoid watching the whole rotten edifice collapse.

However, in the European sovereign debt crisis, Europe was not alone. Both the United States and China supported the European bailouts for different but ultimately self-interested reasons. Europe is a massive export market for the United States. A strong euro keeps up the European appetite for U.S. machines, aircraft, pharmaceuticals, software, agricultural produce, education and the variety of goods and services the United States has to offer. A collapse of the euro would mean a collapse in trade between the two giants of global output. A collapse of a European sovereign could take down the European banks and the euro with it, as investors instantaneously developed a revulsion for all debt denominated in euros and fled from European banks. The consequences of a European sovereign debt default for U.S. exporters to Europe would be too great; here was an entire continent that was too big too fail. The U.S. bailouts, swap lines and support for issuers like Fannie Mae were all part of a multifaceted, multiyear effort to prop up the value of the euro.

China also had an interest in propping up the euro, but its efforts came with a political agenda. Europe is a huge export market for China as well as the United States, and to that extent China's interests are the same as the United States. But China's banks are not nearly as entwined with Europe's as are America's, which gives China more degrees of freedom in terms of deciding how and when to help. The European sovereign debt crisis offered China the chance to diversify its reserves and investment portfolios away from dollars and toward euros, to acquire leading-edge technology systems that had been denied it by the United States and to develop platforms from which it could engage in large-scale technology transfer back to China.

Germany welcomed the U.S. and Chinese support for the euro. As an export powerhouse, Germany might have been expected to favor a weak euro for the same reason that the United States favors a weak dollar and China favors a weak yuan: to gain an edge in the currency wars with a cheap currency that promotes exports. Germany, however, was not only an external exporter; it was an *internal* exporter within the European Union. For those eurozone exports, there was no currency consideration since both the exporter and the importer, for instance Germany and Spain, used the euro. If the euro were to collapse or members broke away from the euro and reverted to their old currencies at devalued levels, those markets might be lost.

Conventional wisdom had it that Germany anguished over support for Greece and Ireland and the other weak links in the euro chain. In fact, Germany had no attractive alternatives. The costs of a euro collapse far outweighed the costs of regional bailouts. Germany actually benefitted from the European sovereign debt crisis. The continued existence of the euro gave Germany a dominant position inside Europe while a somewhat weaker euro internationally enabled it to gain market share in the rest of the world. The sweet spot for Germany was a euro that was weak enough to help exports to the United States and China but not so weak as to collapse. Germany was successful in finding that sweet spot during 2010 despite the sturm und drang surrounding the euro itself.

With the self-interests of the United States, China and Germany all pointing in the same direction, there would be no doubt for now about the survival of the euro. That the banks were flush with rotten assets, that the periphery nations were running nonsustainable fiscal policies and that the people of Greece, Ireland, Portugal and Spain were facing austerity in order to keep the assembly lines moving in Seattle and Shanghai were all matters that could wait for another day. For now, the center held.

■ The Eurasian Theater

If the relationship between the euro and the dollar can be described as codependent, the relationship between the euro and the yuan is simply dependent. China is fast emerging as a potential savior of certain peripheral European economies such as Greece, Portugal and Spain based on Chinese willingness to buy some of their sovereign bonds in the midst of the European sovereign debt crisis. However, Chinese intentions toward Europe and the euro are based on self-interest and cold calculation.

China has a vital interest in a strong euro. The European Union surpasses the United States as China's largest trading partner. If European turmoil were to result in countries such as Greece or Ireland leaving the euro, those countries would return to their former currencies at greatly devalued rates relative to the yuan. This would badly hurt China's exports to parts of Europe. China's interest in supporting the euro is as great or greater than its interest in maintaining the yuan peg against the dollar.

China's motives in Europe include diversifying its reserve position to include more euros, winning respect or friendship among the European countries that it assists directly with bond purchases, and gaining a quid pro quo in connection with such purchases. This quid pro quo can take many forms, including direct foreign investment in sensitive infrastructure such as ports and power generation, access to sensitive European technology and the ability to purchase advanced weapons systems normally reserved for NATO allies and friends such as Israel. China's interests in supporting the euro are not at all adverse to those of Germany, even though Germany and China compete fiercely for export business around the world.

By buying sovereign bonds from peripheral European states, China helps Germany to bear the costs of the European bailouts. By helping to prop up the euro, China helps Germany avoid the losses it would suffer if the euro collapsed, including catastrophic damage to German banks. It is a no-lose situation for China and one that secures its Eurasian flank while it fights the United States head-on. China's main front in the currency wars is the United States, and it has so far avoided a conflagration on the Eurasian front. This is due both to European weakness and Chinese finesse.

The United States likewise supports the euro, and for the same reasons as China: a catastrophic collapse of the euro would weaken its value relative to the dollar and hurt U.S. exports that compete with European exports in markets of the Middle East, Latin America and South Asia. China and the United States not only want the euro to survive; they also want to see it gain strength relative to the dollar and yuan in order to help their own exports. Europe, China and the United States are united in their efforts to avoid a euro collapse despite their mixed motives and adversarial postures in other arenas.

This much unity of purpose probably means that the euro will muddle through the current crisis and remain intact for the foreseeable future, despite potential bond restructurings and austerity plans. Whether this balancing act can be continued and whether China's charm offensive in Europe will be maintained remains to be seen. If the euro actually does collapse, China could suffer massive losses on its bond positions, a revaluation of the yuan and lost exports all at the same time. China may yet come into confrontation with Europe on a number of issues, but for now it is all quiet on China's western front.

■ Global Skirmishes

Apart from the big three theaters in the currency war—the Pacific (dollar-yuan), the Atlantic (euro-dollar) and the Eurasian (euro-yuan)—there are numerous other fronts, sideshows and skirmishes going on around the world. The most prominent of these peripheral actions in the currency war is Brazil.

As late as 1994, Brazil maintained a peg of its currency, the real, to the U.S. dollar. However, the global contagion resulting from the Mexican "Tequila Crisis" of December 1994 put pressure on the real and forced Brazil to defend its currency. The result was the Real Plan, by which Brazil engaged in a series of managed devaluations of the real against the dollar. The real was devalued about 30 percent from 1995 to 1997.

After this success in managing the dollar value of the real to a more sustainable level, Brazil once again became the victim of contagion. This time the crisis did not arise in Latin America but from East Asia. This new financial crisis broke out in 1997 and spread around the world from Thailand to Indonesia, South Korea, and

Russia and finally came to rest in Brazil, where the IMF arranged a monetary firewall with emergency funding as the Fed frantically cut U.S. interest rates to provide needed global liquidity. In the aftermath of that financial storm, and under IMF prompting, Brazil moved to a free-floating currency and a more open capital account, but it still experienced periodic balance-of-payments crises and required IMF assistance again in 2002.

Brazil's fortunes took a decided turn for the better with the 2002 election to the presidency of Luiz Inácio Lula da Silva, known as Lula. Under his leadership from 2003 through 2010, Brazil underwent a vast expansion of its natural resource export capacity along with significant advances in its technology and manufacturing base. Its Embraer aircraft became world-class and catapulted Brazil to the position of the world's third largest aircraft producer. Its huge internal market also became a magnet for global capital flows seeking higher returns, especially after the collapse of yields in U.S. and European markets following the Panic of 2008.

Over the course of 2009 and 2010, the real rallied from fewer than 2.4 reais to the dollar to 1.69 reais to the dollar. This 40 percent upward revaluation of the real against the dollar in just two years was enormously painful to the Brazilian export sector. Brazil's bilateral trade with the United States went from an approximately $15 billion surplus to a $6 billion deficit over the same two-year period. This collapse in the trade surplus with the United States was what prompted Brazilian finance minister Guido Mantega to declare in late September 2010 that a global currency war had begun.

Because of the yuan-dollar peg maintained by China, a 40 percent revaluation of the real against the dollar also meant a 40 percent revaluation against the yuan. Brazil's exports suffered not only at the high end against U.S. technology but also at the low end against Chinese assembly and textiles. Brazil fought back with currency intervention by its central bank, increases in reserve requirements on any local banks taking short positions in dollars, and other forms of capital controls.

In late 2010, Lula's successor as president, Dilma Rousseff, vowed to press the G20 and the IMF for rules that would identify currency manipulators—presumably both China *and* the United States—in order to relieve the upward pressure on the real. Brazil's efforts to restrain the appreciation of the real met with some short-term success in late 2010 but immediately gave rise to another problem—inflation. Brazil was now importing inflation from the United States as it tried to hold the real steady against the dollar in the face of massive money printing by the Fed.

Brazil was now experiencing the same dilemma as China, having to choose between inflation and revaluation. When the United States is printing dollars and another country is trying to peg its currency to the dollar, that country ends up printing local currency to maintain the peg, which causes local inflation. As a consequence, investors chasing high returns around the world, the so-called hot money, poured into Brazil from the United States. The situation had deteriorated to the point that a Nomura Global Economics research report in early 2011 declared Brazil the biggest loser in the currency wars. This was true up to a point, based on the appreciation of the real. By April 2011, Brazil was "waving the white flag in the currency war," in the words of a *Wall Street Journal* analysis. Brazil appeared resigned to a higher value for the real after currency controls, taxes on foreign investments and other measures had failed to stop its appreciation.

Lacking the reserves and surpluses of the Chinese, Brazil was unable to maintain a peg against the dollar by simply buying all the dollars that arrived on its doorstep. Brazil was stuck between the rock of currency appreciation and the hard place of inflation. As was the case with the United States and the Europeans, albeit for different reasons, Brazil increasingly looked to the G20 for help in the currency wars.

Brazil is an important case because of its geographic, demographic and economic scale, but it is by no means the only country caught in the cross fire of a currency war among the dollar, euro and yuan. Other countries implementing or considering capital controls to stem inflows of hot money, especially dollars, include India, Indonesia, South Korea, Malaysia, Singapore, South Africa, Taiwan and Thailand. In every case, the fear is that their currencies will become overvalued and their exports will suffer as the result of the Fed's easy money policies and the resulting flood of dollars sloshing around the world in search of high yields and more rapid growth.

These capital controls took various forms depending on the preferences of the central banks and finance ministries imposing them. In 2010, Indonesia and Taiwan curtailed the issuance of short-term investment paper, which forced hot money investors to invest for longer periods of time. South Korea and Thailand imposed withholding taxes on interest paid on government debt to foreign investors as a way to discourage such investment and to reduce upward pressure on their currencies. The case of Thailand was ironic because Thailand was the country where the 1997–1998 financial panic began. In that panic, investors were trying to get their money out of Thailand and the country was trying to prop up its currency. In 2011 investors were trying to get their money into Thailand and the country was trying to hold down its currency. There could be no clearer example of the shift in financial power between emerging markets such as Thailand and developed markets such as the United States over the past ten years.

None of these peripheral, mostly Asian, countries trying to hold down the value of their currencies is the issuer of a widely accepted reserve currency, and none has the sheer economic scale of the United States, China or the eurozone when it comes to the ability to fight a currency war by direct market intervention. These countries too would need a multilateral forum within which to resolve the stresses caused by Currency War III. While the IMF has traditionally provided such a forum, increasingly all of the large trading economies, whether G20 members or not, are looking to the G20 for guidance or new rules of the game to keep the currency wars from escalating and causing irreparable harm to themselves and the world.

CHAPTER 7

The G20 Solution

"Let me put it simply . . . there may be a contradiction between the interests of the financial world and the interests of the political world. . . . We cannot keep constantly explaining to our voters and our citizens why the taxpayer should bear the cost of certain risks and not those people who have earned a lot of money from taking those risks."

Angela Merkel,
Chancellor of Germany, at the G20 Summit,
November 2010

The Group of Twenty, known as G20, is an unaccountable and very powerful organization that arose from the need to resolve global issues in the absence of true world government. The name G20 refers to its twenty member entities. They are a mixture of what were once the world's seven largest economies, grouped as the G7, consisting of the United States, Canada, France, Germany, the United Kingdom, Italy and Japan, and some fast-growing, newly emerging economies such as Brazil, China, South Korea, Mexico, India and Indonesia. Others were included more for their natural resources or for reasons of geopolitics rather than the dynamism of their economies; examples are Russia and Saudi Arabia. Still others were added for geographic balance, including Australia, South Africa, Turkey and Argentina. The European Union was invited for good measure, even though it is not a country, because its central bank issues one of the world's reserve currencies. Some economic heavyweights such as Spain, the Netherlands and Norway were officially left out, but they are sometimes invited to attend the G20 meetings anyway because of their economic importance. G20 and Friends might be a more apt appellation.

The G20 operates at multiple levels. Several times each year the finance ministers and central bank heads meet to discuss technical issues and try to reach consensus on specific goals and their implementation. The most important meetings, however, are the leaders' summits, attended by presidents, prime ministers and kings, which meet periodically to discuss global financial issues, with emphasis on the structure of the international monetary system and the need to contain currency wars. It is at these leaders' summits, both in the formal sessions and informally in the suites, that the actual deals shaping the global financial system are made. Interspersed among the presidents and prime ministers at these meetings is that unique breed of international bureaucrat known as the sherpa. The sherpas are technical experts in international finance who assist the leaders with agendas, research and drafting of the opaque communiqués that follow each confab. All roads toward the resolution of the looming currency wars point in the direction of G20 as the principal forum.

The G20 is well suited to be inclusive of Chinese participation. China often resists compromise in bilateral meetings, viewing requests for concessions as bullying and their assent as a loss of face. This is less of a problem in G20, where multiple agendas are implemented at once. Smaller participants enjoy the chance to have their voices heard in G20 because they lack the leverage to move markets on their own. The United States benefits from having its allies in the room and avoids charges of acting unilaterally. So the advantages of G20 to all parties are apparent.

President George W. Bush and President Nicolas Sarkozy of France were instrumental in changing the G20 from merely a finance ministers' meeting, which it had been since its beginning in 1999, to a leaders' meeting, which it has been since 2008. In the immediate aftermath of the Lehman Brothers and AIG collapses in September 2008, attention turned to a previously scheduled G20 meeting of finance ministers in November. The Panic of 2008 was one of the greatest financial catastrophes in history and the role of

China as one of the largest investors in the world and a potential source of rescue capital was undeniable. At the time, the G7 was the leading forum for economic coordination, but China was not in the G7. In effect, Sarkozy and Bush reenacted the scene in *Jaws* where Roy Scheider, after seeing the shark for the first time, says to Robert Shaw, "We're gonna' need a bigger boat." Politically and financially, G20 is a much bigger boat than G7.

In November 2008, President Bush convened the G20 Leaders' Summit on Financial Markets and the World Economy, at which every president, prime minister, chancellor or king of a member country was present. Instantly the G20 morphed from a finance ministers' technical session to a gathering of the most powerful leaders in the world. Unlike various regional summits, every corner of the globe had its representatives and, unlike the UN General Assembly, everyone was in the room at the same time.

Based on the urgency of the financial crisis and the ambitious agenda laid down by the G20 in November 2008, the leaders' summits continued through four more meetings over the course of 2009 and 2010. For 2011, the G20 leaders decided to hold a single meeting in Cannes, France, in November. This sequence of summits was the closest thing the world had ever seen to a global board of directors, and it seemed here to stay.

The G20 is perfectly suited to U.S. Treasury secretary Timothy Geithner's modus operandi, which he calls "convening power." Author David Rothkopf brought this concept to light in a highly revealing interview he conducted with Geithner for his book *Superclass*, about the mores of the global power elite. When he was president of the New York Fed in 2006, Geithner told Rothkopf:

> We have a convening power here that is separate from the formal authority of our institution. . . . I think the premise going forward is that you have to have a borderless, collaborative process. It does not mean it has to be universal. . . . It just needs a critical mass of the right players. It is a much more concentrated world. If you focus on the limited number of the ten to twenty large institutions that have some global reach, then you can do a lot.

Geithner's notion of convening power states that, in a crisis, an ad hoc assembly of the right players could come together on short notice to address the problem. They set an agenda, assign tasks, utilize staff and reassemble after a suitable interval, which could be a day or month, depending on the urgency of the situation. Progress is reported and new goals are set, all without the normal accoutrements of established bureaucracies or rigid governance.

This process was something Geithner learned in the depths of the Asian financial crisis in 1997. He saw it again when it was deployed successfully in the bailout of Long-Term Capital Management in 1998. In that crisis, the heads of the "fourteen families," the major banks at the time, came together with no template, except possibly the Panic of 1907, and in seventy-two hours put together a $3.6 billion all-cash bailout to save capital markets from collapse. In 2008, Geithner, then president of the New York Fed, revived the use of convening power as the U.S. government employed ad hoc remedies to resolve the failures of Bear Stearns, Fannie Mae and Freddie Mac from March to July of that year. When the Panic of 2008 hit with full force in September, the principal players were well practiced in the use of convening power. The first G20 leaders' meeting, in November 2008, can be understood as Geithner's convening power on steroids.

It was in the G20 that the United States chose to advance its vision for a kind of global grand bargain, which Geithner has promoted under the name "rebalancing." To understand rebalancing and why this has been critical to growth in the U.S. economy, one need only recall the components of gross domestic product. For the United States, GDP grew to roughly $14.9 trillion in early 2011. The components broke down as follows: consumption, 71 percent; investment, 12 percent; government spending, 20 percent; and net exports, minus 3 percent. This was barely above the level the U.S. economy had reached before the recession of 2007. The economy was not growing nearly fast enough to reduce unemployment significantly from the very high levels reached in early 2009.

The traditional cure for a weak economy in the United States has always been the consumer. Government spending and business investment might play a role, but the American consumer, at 70 percent or more of GDP, has always been the key to recovery. Some combination of low interest rates, easier mortgage terms, wealth effects from a rising stock market and credit card debt has always been enough to get the consumer out of her funk and get the economy moving again.

Now the standard economic playbook was not working. The consumer was overleveraged and overextended. Home equity had evaporated; indeed many Americans owed more on their mortgages than their houses were worth. The consumer was stretched, with unemployment high, retirement looming and kids' college bills coming due. And it seemed the consumer would stay stretched for years.

In theory, business investment could expand on its own, but it made no sense to invest in plant and equipment beyond a certain point if the consumer was not there to buy the resulting goods and services. Besides, high U.S. corporate tax rates led many corporations to keep their earnings offshore so that much of their new investment took place outside the United States and did not contribute to U.S. GDP. Investment remained in the doldrums and would stay there as long as the consumer was in hibernation.

With the consumer out of action and investment weak, the Keynesians in the Bush and Obama administrations next turned to government spending to stimulate the economy. However, after four stimulus plans from 2008 to 2010 failed to create net new jobs, a revulsion to more spending emerged. This revulsion was fanned by a Tea Party movement, threats from ratings agencies to downgrade U.S. creditworthiness and a Republican tidal wave of victories in the 2010 midterm elections. It became clear that the American people wanted someone to put the lid back on Uncle Sam's cookie jar. It remained to be seen how much in the way of spending cuts could be enacted, but it was apparent that greatly increased government spending was off the table.

So a process of elimination led the Obama administration to see that if consumption, investment and government spending were out of play, the only way to get the economy moving was through net exports—there was nothing else left. In the State of the Union address on January 27, 2010, President Obama announced the National Export Initiative, intended to double U.S. exports in five years. Achieving this could have profound effects. A doubling of exports could add 1.3 percent to U.S. GDP, moving growth from an anemic 2.6 percent to a much more robust 3.9 percent or higher, which might be enough to accelerate the downward trajectory of unemployment. Doubling exports was a desirable goal if it could be achieved. But could it? If so, at what cost to our trading partners and the delicate balance of growth around the world?

At this point U.S. economic policy crashed headlong into the currency wars. The traditional and fastest way to increase exports had always been to cheapen the currency, exactly what Montagu Norman did in England in 1931 and what Richard Nixon did in the United States in 1971. America and the world had been there before and the global results had been catastrophic. Once again a cheap dollar was the preferred policy and once again the world saw a catastrophe in the making.

China's GDP composition was in some ways the mirror image of the United States. Instead of the towering 70 percent level of the United States, consumption was only 38 percent of the Chinese economy. Conversely, net exports, which produced a negative 3 percent drag on the U.S. economy, actually added 3.6 percent to the Chinese total. China's growth was heavily driven by investment, which totaled 48 percent of GDP versus only 12 percent for the United States. Given these mirror image economies, a simple rebalancing seemed in order. If China could increase consumption, in part by buying goods and services from the United States, including software, video games and Hollywood films, then both countries could grow. All that needed to change was the consumption and export mix. China would dial up consumption and dial down net exports, while the United States did the opposite. Those new export sales to China would create jobs in the United States for good measure. This could not be done through exchange rates alone; however, Geithner said repeatedly that upward revaluation of the yuan was an important part of the overall policy approach.

One reason the Chinese did not consume more was that their

social safety net was weak, so individuals saved excessively to pay for their own retirement and health care. Another factor working against Chinese consumption was a millennia-old Confucian culture that discouraged ostentatious displays of wealth. Yet U.S. policy makers were not looking for a prospending cultural revolution; something more modest would suffice. Just a few percentage points of increase in consumption by China in favor of U.S. exports could allow the United States to ignite a self-sustaining recovery.

This was to be a strange kind of rebalancing: the increased Chinese consumption and increased U.S. net exports would come entirely at China's expense. China would have to make all of the adjustments, with regard to their currency, their social safety net and twenty-five hundred years of Confucian culture, while the United States would do nothing and reap the benefits of increased net exports to a fast-growing internal Chinese market. This was a particularly soft option for the United States. It required no tangible effort by the United States to improve its business climate by reducing corporate taxes and regulation, providing for sound money or promoting savings and investment. Some of what the United States wanted may have been in China's best interests, but China could not be blamed for believing it was being bullied on behalf of a U.S. plan that above all suited the United States. In the parlance of the G20, "rebalancing" became code for doing what the United States wanted.

The international financial cognoscenti did not have to wait for the January 2010 State of the Union to see where the United States was going with its rebalancing plan. The idea for increased U.S. exports and the associated revaluation of the yuan had already been vetted in September 2009 at the Pittsburgh G20 summit. The first two G20 summits, in Washington and London, had been devoted to an immediate response to the Panic of 2008 and the need to create new liquidity sources through the IMF. These early G20 summits had also been preoccupied with plans to rein in the banks and their greed-based compensation structures, which provided grotesque rewards for short-term gains but caused the long-term destruction of trillions of dollars of global wealth. By the Pittsburgh summit in late

2009, the leaders felt that while vulnerabilities remained, enough stability had returned that they could look past the immediate crisis and begin to think about ways to get the global economy moving again. Pittsburgh would be the last G20 summit before the 2010 State of the Union. If the United States was going to get buy-in for its export-driven rebalancing plan, this was the time.

The Pittsburgh G20 leaders' summit produced a breakthrough plan for the kind of rebalancing of growth that Geithner wanted. The plan was contained in the official leaders' statement as "A Framework for Strong, Sustainable, and Balanced Growth." It was not immediately clear how this rebalancing was to be achieved. Like all such technical statements from large multilateral bodies, it is written in a kind of global elite-speak in which plain language is the first casualty. Buried in Section 20 of the framework, however, is this passage:

> Our collective response to the crisis has highlighted . . . the need for a more legitimate and effective IMF. The Fund must play a critical role in promoting global financial stability and rebalancing growth.

There was no doubt on the part of the participants that rebalancing meant increased consumption by China and increased exports by the United States. Now the IMF was being deputized by the G20 to act as a kind of cop on the beat to see to it that G20 members lived up to any obligations they might undertake in that regard. So the international foundation was laid in Pittsburgh for President Obama's National Export Initiative announced two months later.

The G20's use of the IMF as an outsourced secretariat, research department, statistical agency and policy referee suited both organizations extremely well. It gave the G20 access to enormous expertise without its having to create and build an expert staff on its own. For the IMF, it was more like a reprieve. As late as 2006 many international monetary experts seriously questioned the purpose and continued existence of the IMF. In the 1950s and 1960s, it had provided bridge loans to countries suffering temporary balance of payments difficulties to allow them to maintain their currency peg to the dollar. In the 1980s and 1990s it had assisted developing economies suffering foreign exchange crises by providing finance conditioned upon austerity measures designed to protect foreign bankers and bondholders. Yet with the elimination of gold, the rise of floating exchange rates and the piling up of huge surpluses by developing countries, the IMF entered the twenty-first century with no discernable mission. Suddenly the G20 breathed new life into the IMF by positioning it as a kind of Bank of the G20 or proto–world central bank. Its ambitious leader at the time, Dominique Strauss-Kahn, could not have been more pleased, and he eagerly set about as the global referee for whatever guidelines the G20 might set.

Despite this heady start toward global rebalancing and President Obama's personal buy-in, two G20 summits came and went in 2010 with no significant progress in the commitments of member nations to the Pittsburgh summit goals. The IMF did conduct extensive reviews of the practices of each country under the heading "mutual assessment" and continued allegiance to the framework was paid in the G20 communiqués, but the ambitious goals of rebalancing were essentially ignored, especially by China.

Geithner was blunt in criticizing the Chinese for not allowing greater yuan revaluation. When asked by the *Wall Street Journal* in September 2010 if the Chinese had done enough, he said, "Of course not . . . they've done very, very little." U.S. exports did improve in 2010, but this was mostly because of relatively high growth in emerging markets and a demand for U.S. high-tech products rather than exchange rate changes. The Chinese did allow the yuan to appreciate slightly, mostly to forestall China being branded a currency manipulator by the U.S. Treasury, which could lead to trade sanctions by the U.S. Congress. But neither of these developments came close to meeting Geithner's demands. Even a bilateral summit in January 2011 between President Hu and President Obama, the so-called G2, produced little more than mutually cordial remarks and smiling photo ops. It seemed that if the United States wanted a cheaper dollar it would have to act on its own to get it. Reliance by the world on the G20 had so far proved a dead end.

By June 2011, however, the United States was emerging as a winner in the currency war. Like winners in many wars throughout history, the United States had a secret weapon. That financial weapon was what went by the ungainly name "quantitative easing," or QE, which essentially consists of increasing the money supply to inflate asset prices. As in 1971, the United States was acting unilaterally to weaken the dollar through inflation. QE was a policy bomb dropped on the global economy in 2009, and its successor, promptly dubbed QE2, was dropped in late 2010. The impact on the world monetary system was swift and effective. By using quantitative easing to generate inflation abroad, the United States was increasing the cost structure of almost every major exporting nation and fast-growing emerging economy in the world all at once.

Quantitative easing in its simplest form is just printing money. To create money from thin air, the Federal Reserve buys Treasury debt securities from a select group of banks called primary dealers. The primary dealers have a global base of customers, ranging from sovereign wealth funds, other central banks, pension funds and institutional investors to high-net-worth individuals. The dealers act as intermediaries between the Fed and the marketplace by underwriting Treasury auctions of new debt and making a market in existing debt.

When the Fed wants to reduce the money supply, they sell securities to the primary dealers. The securities go to the dealers and the money paid to the Fed simply disappears. Conversely, when the Fed wants to increase the money supply, they buy securities from the dealers. The Fed takes delivery of the securities and pays the dealers with freshly printed money. The money goes into the dealers' bank accounts, where it can then support even more money creation by the banking system. This buying and selling of securities between the Fed and the primary dealers is the main form of open market operations. The usual purpose of open market operations is to control short-term interest rates, which the Fed typically does by buying or selling the shortest-maturity Treasury securities—instruments such as Treasury bills maturing in thirty days. But what happens when interest rates in the shortest maturities are already zero and the Fed wants to provide additional monetary "ease"? Instead of buying very short maturities, the Fed can buy Treasury notes with intermediate maturities of five, seven or ten years. The ten-year note in particular is the benchmark used to price mortgages and corporate debt. By buying intermediate-term debt, the Fed could provide lower interest rates for home buyers and corporate borrowers to hopefully stimulate more economic activity. At least, this was the conventional theory.

In a globalized world, however, exchange rates act like a water-slide to move the effect of interest rates around quickly. Quantitative easing could be used by the Fed not just to ease financial conditions in the United States but *also in China*. It was the perfect currency war weapon and the Fed knew it. Quantitative easing worked because of the yuan-dollar peg maintained by the People's Bank of China. As the Fed printed more money in its QE programs, much of that money found its way to China in the form of trade surpluses or hot money inflows looking for higher profits than were available in the United States. Once the dollars got to China, they were soaked up by the central bank in exchange for newly printed yuan. The more money the Fed printed, the more money China had to print to maintain the peg. China's policy of pegging the yuan to the dollar was based on the mistaken belief and misplaced hope that the Fed would not abuse its money printing privileges. Now the Fed was printing with a vengeance.

There was one important difference between the United States and China. The United States was a slack economy with little chance of inflation in the short run. China was a booming economy and had bounced back nicely from the Panic of 2008. There was less excess capacity in China to absorb the new money without causing inflation. The money printing in China quickly led to higher prices there. China was now importing inflation from the United States through the exchange rate peg after previously having exported its deflation to the United States the same way.

While yuan revaluation was going slowly in late 2010 and early 2011, inflation in China took off and quickly passed 5 percent on an annualized basis. By refusing to revalue, China was getting inflation instead. The United States was happy either way, because revaluation and inflation both increased the costs of Chinese exports and made the United States more competitive. From June 2010 through January 2011, yuan revaluation had moved at about a 4 percent annualized rate and Chinese inflation was moving at a 5 percent annualized rate so the total increase in the Chinese cost structure by adding revaluation and inflation was 9 percent. Projected over several years, this meant that the dollar would decline over 20 percent relative to the yuan in terms of export prices. This was exactly what Senator Chuck Schumer and other critics in the United States had been calling for. China now had no good options. If it maintained the currency peg, the Fed would keep printing and inflation in China would get out of control. If China revalued, it might keep a lid on inflation, but its cost structure would go up when measured in other currencies. The Fed and the United States would win either way.

While revaluation and inflation might be economic equivalents when it came to increasing costs, there was one important difference. Revaluation could be controlled to some extent since the Chinese could direct the timing of each change in the pegged rate even if the Fed was forcing the overall direction. Inflation, on the other hand, was essentially uncontrolled. It could emerge in one sector such as food or fuel and quickly spread through supply chains in unpredictable ways. Inflation could have huge behavioral impacts and start to feed on itself in a self-fulfilling cycle as merchants and wholesalers raised prices in anticipation of price increases by others.

Inflation was one of the catalysts of the June 1989 Tiananmen Square protests, which ended in massacre. Conservative Chinese counted on a steady relationship between their currency and the dollar and a steady value for their massive holdings of U.S. Treasury debt, exactly as Europe had enjoyed in the early days of Bretton Woods. Now they were betrayed—the Fed was forcing their hand. Given the choice between uncontrolled inflation with unforeseen consequences and a controlled revaluation of the yuan, the Chinese moved steadily in the direction of revaluation beginning in June 2010, increasing dramatically by mid-2011.

The United States had won round one of the currency wars. Like a heavyweight boxing match between the United States and China, it was round one of what promised to be a fifteen-round fight. Both boxers were still standing; the United States had won the round on points, not with a knockout. The Fed was planted in the U.S. corner like a cut man ready to fix any damage. China had help in its corner too—from QE victims around the world. Soon the bell would toll to start round two.

When the principal combatants use their weapons in any war, noncombatants soon suffer collateral damage, and a currency war is no different. The inflation the United States had desperately sought not only found its way to China but also to emerging markets generally. Through a combination of trade surpluses and hot money flows seeking higher investment returns, inflation caused by U.S. money printing soon emerged in South Korea, Brazil, Indonesia, Thailand, Vietnam and elsewhere. Fed chairman Bernanke blithely adopted a "blame the victim" approach, saying that those countries had no one to blame but themselves because they'd refused to appreciate their currencies against the dollar in order to reduce their surpluses and slow down the hot money. In the anodyne language of central bankers, Bernanke said:

> Policy makers in the emerging markets have a range of powerful . . . tools that they can use to manage their economies and prevent overheating, including exchange rate adjustment. . . . Resurgent demand in the emerging markets has contributed significantly to the sharp recent run-up in global commodity prices. More generally, the maintenance of undervalued currencies by some countries has contributed to a pattern of global spending that is unbalanced and unsustainable.

This ignored the fact that many of the commodities that residents of those countries were purchasing, such as wheat, corn, oil, soybeans, lumber, coffee and sugar, are priced on world, not local, markets. As consumers in specific markets bid up prices in response to Fed money printing, prices rose not only in those local markets but also worldwide.

Soon the effects of Fed money printing were felt not only in the relatively successful emerging markets of East Asia and Latin America, but also in the much poorer parts of Africa and the Middle East. When a factory worker lives on $12,000 per year, rising food prices are an inconvenience. When a peasant lives on $3,000 per year, rising food prices are the difference between eating and starving, between life and death. The civil unrest, riots and insurrection that erupted in Tunisia in early 2011 and quickly spread to Egypt, Jordan, Yemen, Morocco, Libya and beyond were as much a reaction to rising food and energy prices and lower standards of living as they were to dictatorships and lack of democracy. Countries in the Middle East strained their budgets to subsidize staples such as bread to mitigate the worst effects of this inflation. This converted the inflation problem into a fiscal problem, especially in Egypt, where tax collection became chaotic and revenues from tourism dried up in the aftermath of the Arab Spring revolutions. The situation become so dire that the G8, meeting in Deauville, France, in May 2011, hastily arranged a $20 billion pledge of new financial support to Egypt and Tunisia. Bernanke was already out of touch with the travails of average Americans; now he was increasingly out of touch with the world.

It remained to be seen whether the G20 could divert the United States from its runaway fiscal and monetary policies, which were flooding the world with dollars and causing global inflation in food and energy prices. For its part, the United States sought allies inside the G20 such as France and Brazil to apply pressure on the Chinese to revalue. The U.S. view was that everyone—Europe, North America and Latin America—would gain exports and growth if China revalued the yuan and increased domestic consumption. This may have been true in theory, but the U.S. strategy of flooding the world with dollars seemed to be causing great harm in the meantime. China and the United States were engaged in a global game of chicken, with China sticking to its export model and the United States trying to inflate away China's export cost advantage. But inflation was not confined to China, and the whole world grew alarmed at the damage. The G20 was supposed to provide a forum to coordinate global economic policies, but it was starting to look more like a playground with two bullies daring everyone else to chose sides.

In the run-up to the G20 leaders' summit in Seoul in November 2010, Geithner tried to paint China into a corner by articulating a percentage test for when trade surpluses became excessive and unsustainable from a global perspective. In general, any annual trade surplus in excess of 4 percent of GDP would be treated as a sign that the currency of the surplus country needed to be revalued in order to tilt the terms of trade away from the surplus country and toward deficit countries like the United States. This was something that used to happen automatically under the classical gold standard but now required central bank currency manipulation.

Geithner's idea went nowhere. He had wanted to target China, yet, unfortunately for his thesis, Germany also became a target, because the German trade surplus was about as large as China's when expressed as a percentage of GDP. By Geithner's own metrics, the Germany currency, the euro, would also have to be revalued upward. This was the last thing Germany and the rest of Europe wanted, given the precarious nature of their economic recoveries, the structural weakness of their banking system and the importance of German exports to Europe's job situation. Finding support in neither Europe nor Asia, Geithner quietly dropped the idea.

Instead of setting firm targets, the Seoul G20 leaders' summit suggested the idea of "indicative guidelines" for determining when trade surpluses might be at unsustainable levels. The exact nature of these guidelines was left to a subsequent meeting of the finance ministers and central bank governors to work out. In February 2011, the ministers and governors met in Paris and agreed in principle on what factors might be included as "indicators," but they did not yet agree on exactly what level of each indicator might be tolerated, or not, within the indicative guidelines. That quantification process was left for a subsequent meeting in April and the entire process was left up to the final approval of the G20 leaders themselves at the annual meeting, in Cannes in November 2011.

Meanwhile, the empowerment of the IMF as the watchdog of the G20 continued apace. In a March 2011 conference in Nanjing,

China, attended by experts and economists, G20 president Nicolas Sarkozy said, with regard to balance of payments, "Greater supervision by the IMF appears indispensible."

Saying that the G20 process moves forward at a glacial pace seems kind. Yet with twenty sovereign leaders and as many different agendas, it was not clear what the alternative would be if a global solution was to be achieved. This is the downside of Geithner's theory of convening power. The absence of governance can be efficient if the people in the room are like-minded or if one party in the room has the ability to coerce the others, as had been true when the Fed confronted the fourteen families at the time of the LTCM bailout. When the assembled parties have widely divergent goals and different views on how to achieve those goals, the absence of leadership means that minute incremental change is the best that can be hoped for. By 2011 it appeared that the changes were so minute and so slow as to be no change at all.

The G20 was far from perfect as an institution, but it was all the world had. The G7 model seemed dead and the United Nations offered nothing comparable. The IMF was capable of good technical analysis; it was useful as a referee of whatever policies the G20 could agree on. But IMF governance was heavily weighted to the old trilateral model of North America, Japan and Western Europe, and its influence was resented in the emerging markets powerhouses such as China, India, Brazil and Indonesia. The IMF was useful; however, change would also be needed there to conform to new global realities.

In late 2008 and early 2009, the G20 was able to coordinate policy effectively because the members were united by fear. The collapse of capital markets, world trade, industrial output and employment had been so catastrophic as to force a consensus on bailouts, stimulus and new forms of regulation on banks.

By 2011, it appeared the storm had passed and the G20 members were back to their individual agendas—continued large surpluses for China and Germany and continued efforts by the United States to undermine the dollar to reverse those surpluses and help U.S. exports. Yet there was no Richard Nixon around to take preemptive action and no John Connally to knock heads. America had lost its clout. It would take another crisis to prompt unified action by the G20. Given the policy of U.S. money printing and its inflationary side effects around the world, it seemed the next crisis would not be long in coming.

That crisis arrived with a jolt near the city of Sendai, Japan, on the afternoon of March 11, 2011. A 9.0 earthquake followed quickly by a ten-meter-high tsunami devastated the northeast coastline of Japan, killing thousands, inundating entire towns and villages, and destroying infrastructure of every kind—ports, fishing fleets, farms, bridges, roads and communications. Within days the worst nuclear disaster since Chernobyl had commenced at a nuclear power plant near Sendai, with the meltdown of radioactive fuel rods in several reactors and the release of radiation in plumes affecting the general public. As the world wrestled with the aftermath, a new front arose in the currency wars. The Japanese yen suddenly surged to a record high against the dollar, bolstered by expectations of massive yen repatriation by Japanese investors to fund reconstruction. Japan held over $2 trillion in assets outside of the country, mostly in the United States, and over $850 billion of dollar-denominated reserves. Some portion of these would have to be sold in dollars, converted to yen and moved back to Japan to pay for rebuilding. This massive sell-dollars/buy-yen dynamic was behind the surge in the yen.

From the U.S. perspective, the rise in the yen relative to the dollar seemed to fit nicely into the U.S. goals, yet Japan wanted the opposite. The Japanese economy was facing a catastrophe, and a cheap yen would help promote Japanese exports and get the Japanese economy back on its feet. The magnitude of the catastrophe in Japan was just too great—for now the U.S. policy of a cheap dollar would have to take a backseat to the need for a cheap yen.

There was no denying the urgency of Japan's need to cash out its dollar assets to fund its reconstruction; this was the force driving the yen higher. Only the force of coordinated central bank intervention would be powerful enough to push back against the flood of yen pouring back into Japan. The yen-dollar relationship was too specialized for G20 action, and there was no G20 meeting imminent anyway. The big three of the United States, Japan and the European Central Bank would address the problem themselves.

Under the banner of the G7, French finance minister Christine Lagarde placed a phone call to U.S. Treasury secretary Geithner on March 17, 2011, to initiate a coordinated assault on the yen. After consultations among the central bank heads responsible for the actual intervention and a briefing to President Obama, the attack on the yen was launched at the open of business in Japan on the morning of March 18, 2011. This attack consisted of massive dumping of yen by central banks and corresponding purchases of dollars, euros, Swiss francs and other currencies. The attack continued around the world and across time zones as European and New York markets opened. This central bank intervention was successful, and by late in the day on March 18 the yen had been pushed off its highs and was moving back into a more normal trading range against the dollar. Lagarde's deft handling of the yen intervention enhanced her already strong reputation for crisis management earned during the Panic of 2008 and the first phase of the euro sovereign debt crisis in 2010. She was the near universal choice to replace the disgraced Dominique Strauss-Kahn as head of the IMF in June 2011.

If the G20 was like a massive army, the G7 had shown it could still play the role of special forces, acting quickly and stealthily to achieve a narrowly defined goal. The G7 had turned the tide at least temporarily. However, the natural force of yen repatriation to Japan had not gone away, nor had the speculators who anticipate and profit from such moves. For a while, it was back to the bad old days of the 1970s and 1980s as a small group of central banks fended off attacks from speculators and the fundamental forces of revaluation. In the larger scheme of things, Japan's need for a weak yen was a setback to the U.S. plan for a weak dollar. The classic beggar-thy-neighbor problem of competitive devaluations had taken on a new face. Now, in addition to China, the United States and Europe all wanting to weaken their currencies, Japan, which had traditionally been willing to play along with U.S. wishes for a stronger yen, found itself in the cheap-currency camp too. Not everyone could cheapen at once; the circle still could not be squared. Ultimately the dollar-yen struggle would be added to the dollar-yuan fight already on the G20 agenda as the world sought a global solution to its currency woes.

PART THREE

THE NEXT GLOBAL CRISIS

CHAPTER 8

Globalization and State Capital

> "It is a doctrine of war not to assume the enemy will not come, but rather to rely on one's readiness to meet him; not to presume that he will not attack, but rather to make one's self invincible."
>
> Sun Tzu, *The Art of War,*
> Late fifth century BC

Historically a currency war involves competitive devaluations by countries seeking to lower their cost structures, increase exports, create jobs and give their economies a boost at the expense of trading partners. This is not the only possible course for a currency war. There is a far more insidious scenario in which currencies are used as weapons, not in a metaphorical sense but in a real sense, to cause economic harm to rivals. The mere threat of harm can be enough to force concessions by rivals in the geopolitical battle space.

These attacks involve not only states but also terrorists, criminal gangs and other bad actors, using sovereign wealth funds, special forces, intelligence assets, cyberattacks, sabotage and covert action. These financial maneuvers are not the kind that are the subject of polite discussion at G20 meetings.

The value of a nation's currency is its Achilles' heel. If the currency collapses, everything else goes with it. While markets today are linked through complex trading strategies, most still remain discrete to some extent. The stock market can crash, yet the bond market might rally at the same time. The bond market may crash due to rising interest rates, yet other markets in commodities, including gold and oil, might hit new highs as a result. There is always a way to make money in one market while another market is falling out of bed. However, stocks, bonds, commodities, derivatives and other investments are all priced in a nation's currency. If you destroy the currency, you destroy all markets and the nation. This is why the currency itself is the ultimate target in any financial war.

Unfortunately, these threats are not given sufficient attention inside the U.S. national security community. Bill Gertz, reporting in the *Washington Times*, noted, "U.S. officials and outside analysts said the Pentagon, the Treasury, and U.S. intelligence agencies are not aggressively studying the threats to the United States posed by economic warfare and financial terrorism. 'Nobody wants to go there,' one official said."

An overview of the forces of globalization and state capitalism, a new version of seventeenth-century mercantilism in which corporations are extensions of state power, is a step toward understanding the grave dangers facing the world economy today. Financial warfare threats can be grasped only in the context of today's financial world. This world is conditioned by the triumph of globalization, the rise of state capitalism and the persistence of terror. Financial warfare is one form of unrestricted warfare, the preferred method of those with inferior weapons but greater cunning.

■ Globalization

Globalization has been emerging since the 1960s but did not gain its name and widespread recognition until the 1990s, shortly after the fall of the Berlin Wall. Multinational corporations had existed for decades, but the new global corporation was different. A multinational corporation had its roots and principal operations in one country but operated extensively abroad through branches and affiliates. It might have a presence in many countries, but it tended to keep the distinct national identity of its home country wherever it operated.

The new global corporation was just that—global. It submerged its national identity as much as possible and forged a new identity as a global brand stripped of national distinction. Decisions about the location of factories and distribution centers and the issuance of shares or bonds in various currencies were based on considerations of cost, logistics and profits without regard to affection for a nominal home country.

Globalization emerged not through the initiation of any new policies but through the elimination of many old ones. From the end of World War II to the end of the Cold War, the world had been divided not only by the Iron Curtain separating the communist and capitalist spheres but also by restrictions imposed by capitalist countries themselves. These restrictions included capital controls that made it difficult to invest freely across borders and taxes that were imposed on cross-border payments made on investments. Stock markets limited membership to local firms and most banks were off-limits to foreign ownership. Courts and politicians tilted the playing field in favor of local favorites, and enforcement of intellectual property rights was spotty at best. The world was highly fragmented, discriminatory and costly for firms with international ambitions.

By the late 1990s, these costs and barriers had mostly been removed. Taxes were reduced or eliminated by treaties. Capital controls were relaxed, and it became easy to move funds into or out of particular markets. Labor mobility improved and enforcement of legal rights became more predictable. Stock exchanges deregulated and merged across borders to create global giants. The expansion of the European Union politically and economically created the world's richest tariff-free market, and the launch of the euro eliminated countless currency conversions and their costs. Russia and China rose as protocapitalist societies eager to adopt many of the new global norms they saw emerging in Western countries. Economic and political walls were coming down while, at the same time, technology facilitated ease of communication and improved productivity. From the point of view of finance, the world was now borderless and moving quickly toward what legendary banker Walter Wriston had presciently called the twilight of sovereignty.

Infinite risk in a borderless world was the new condition of finance. Globalization increased the scale and interconnectedness of finance beyond what had ever existed. While issuance of bonds was traditionally limited by the use to which the borrower put the proceeds, derivatives had no such natural limit. They could be created in infinite amounts by mere reference to the underlying security on which they were based. The ability to sell Nevada subprime mortgage loans to German regional banks after the loans had been bundled, sliced, repackaged and wrapped with worthless triple-A ratings was a wonder of the age.

In a globalized world, what was old was new again. A first age of globalization had occurred from 1880 to 1914, roughly contemporaneous with the classical gold standard, while the period from 1989 to 2007 was really the second age of globalization. In the first, the wonders were not the Internet or jets but radio, telephones and steamships. The British Empire operated an internal market and single-currency zone as vast as the European Union. In 1900, China was open to trade and investment, albeit on coercive terms, Russia had finally begun to throw off its late feudal model and modernize its industry and agriculture, and a unified Germany was becoming an industrial colossus.

The effect of such developments on finance was much the same at the turn of the twentieth century as at the turn of the twenty-first. Bonds could be issued by Argentina, underwritten in London and purchased in New York. Oil could be refined in California and shipped to Japan on credit provided by banks in Shanghai. The newly invented stock ticker brought near real-time information from the New York Stock Exchange to "wire house" brokerage offices in Kansas City and Denver. Financial panics with global repercussions did occur with some frequency, notably the Panic of 1890, involving South American defaults, and the rescue of the leading London bank, Baring Brothers. This first age of globalization was a time of prosperity, innovation, expanding trade and financial integration.

In August 1914, it all collapsed. A London banker, surveying the

scene from the window of his City club early that summer and contemplating the pace of progress in his time, could not have imagined
the run of tragedy that would ensue over the next seventy-five years.
Two world wars, two currency wars, the fall of empires, the Great
Depression, the Holocaust and the Cold War would pass before a
new age of globalization began. In 2011, globalized finance is om-
nipresent; whether it is here to stay remains to be seen. History
shows that civilization and the globalization it presents are no more
than a thin veneer on the jagged edge of chaos.

■ State Capital

Globalization was not the only geopolitical phenomenon developing
in the late twentieth century; state capitalism was another. State
capitalism is the in-vogue name for a new version of mercantilism,
the dominant economic model of the seventeenth through nineteenth
centuries. Mercantilism is the antithesis of globalization. Its adher-
ents rely on closed markets and closed capital accounts to achieve
their goal of accumulating wealth at the expense of others.

Classical mercantilism rests on a set of principles that seem
strange to modern ears. The main forms of wealth are tangible and
found in land, commodities and gold. The acquisition of wealth is a
zero-sum game in which wealth acquired by one nation comes at the
expense of others. International economic conduct involves granting
advantages to internal industries and imposing tariffs on foreign
goods. Trading is done with friendly partners to the exclusion of
rivals. Subsidies and discrimination are legitimate tools to achieve
economic goals. In its most succinct form, the mercantilist takes the
view that trade is war. Success in mercantilism was measured by the
accumulation of gold.

Although mercantilism had its roots in the Hundred Years' War
of the fourteenth and fifteenth centuries, it reached new heights with
the formation of the East India Company in England in 1600 and
the Dutch East India Company in the Netherlands in 1602. While
these companies operated as private stock companies, they were

given wide-ranging monopolies supported by the power to raise armies, negotiate treaties, coin money, establish colonies and act in the place of the government in dealings in Asia, Africa and the Americas. Scholars have focused on the private features of these firms, such as stock ownership, dividends and boards of directors. However, given their quasi-sovereign powers, they are more properly understood as extensions of the sovereign with private owners and managers. This arrangement bears comparison to regional Federal Reserve Banks in the United States, which are privately owned but act as a financial arm of the government.

It was only in the late eighteenth century, with the industrial revolution and the publication of *The Wealth of Nations* by Adam Smith, that a more modern form of laissez-faire capitalism with private ownership and banking arose. Yet through the twentieth century, despite the success of private enterprise, state-controlled businesses still prevailed in societies dominated by communists, fascists, oligarchs and many other antidemocratic forces.

What we today take for granted as the dominant financial paradigm of private capitalist free enterprise and entrepreneurship is, in fact, exceptional in most times and most places. Private enterprise may have the greatest claim to efficiency and wealth creation, but these are not universally held values. Capitalism's claim to dominance in the future of global trade, finance and technology would seem to have no stronger historical basis than the claims of monarchy, imperialism, communism and other systems in their day.

Companies that appear private but have nearly unlimited state resources behind them, such as China Petroleum and Chemical Corporation (known as Sinopec), are able to bid on natural resources, buy competitors and invest in equipment without regard to short-run financial impacts. They are able to gain market share by selling below cost. They do not have to worry about losing access to capital markets in times of economic distress. Such entities need not fear investigation by their own government if they bribe dictators and their troops to protect their interests. This neomercantilism is the power of the state dressed up as a modern corporation: old wine in new bottles.

Exemplars of this new breed of enterprise are sovereign wealth funds, national oil companies and other state-owned enterprises. These entities are plentiful in Russia, China, Brazil, Mexico and other emerging markets. Western Europe also has its state-owned megacorporations. EADS, the European aircraft, defense and space giant, has publicly traded shares but is majority owned by a consortium that includes French and Spanish government holding companies, a Russian state-controlled bank and Dubai Holding. The Italian oil company Eni, owned 30 percent by the state, is another example—just one among many. Americans are tempted to throw stones at these state-owned entities and call them unfair competition, only to be reminded that in 2008 the U.S. government bailed out Citibank, GE and Goldman Sachs. The United States has its own state-sponsored enterprises; it is really not that different.

To understand globalization and state capitalism, a different, non-U.S. perspective is needed. Intelligence analysts are trained to avoid "mirror imaging," which is the tendency to assume that others see the world as we do. In trying to discern the intentions of adversaries, mirror imaging can be a fatal flaw. Threat analysis requires the analyst to put herself in the shoes of Russians, Chinese, Arabs and others to understand not just the differences in language, culture and history but also the differences in motivation and intent. When Russian leaders think of natural gas, they see not only export revenue but also a stranglehold on the industrial economy of Europe. When Chinese strategists consider their holdings of U.S. government bonds, they understand they have a weapon that can either destroy the U.S. economy or blow up in their faces. When Arab rulers move down the path to modernity, they are acutely aware that they are placing themselves in a reactionary and religious vise that can crush them. A twenty-first-century Grand Tour through Dubai, Moscow and Beijing will help us to see ourselves the way billions of Arabs, Asians and Russians see us—and to understand that the dollar's destiny is not entirely in American hands.

■ Dubai

If *Casablanca* were filmed today, it would be called *Dubai*. The classic film centers around Rick's Café Américain, where the owner, played by Humphrey Bogart, offers drinks, music and gambling, with intrigue on the side. The exotic setting was Morocco during World War II. What defined *Casablanca* was its neutral mélange where enemies could mingle at ease. Nazis, refugees and gunrunners sat at adjacent tables to drink champagne and sing "As Time Goes By."

So it is in Dubai, an island of relative calm surrounded by wars in Afghanistan and Libya, instability in Iraq and Lebanon, transition in Tunisia and Egypt, and bitter enmity between Israel and Iran. It is the ultimate bad neighborhood. In place of Rick's, there is Atlantis, an over-the-top resort on the artificial Palm Island, itself dredged from the seafloor and laid out in a palm shape so vast it can be seen from space. Inside Atlantis are the best restaurants in town, where Israeli agents, Iranian provocateurs, Russian hit men, Saudi arms dealers and local smugglers sit side by side, escorted by tall, leggy blondes who look distinctly out of place in the desert.

What they find in Dubai is what Rick's customers found in Casablanca—neutral turf where they can meet, recruit and betray one another without immediate fear of arrest. Dubai is conducive to international intrigue. The weather is excellent from October through March. Dubai is in the midst of a danger zone, surrounded by Mumbai, Lahore, Tehran, Istanbul, Cairo, Khartoum and the pirate dens of Somalia. It has excellent air and telecommunications links with the world. It is famously overbuilt—it boasts the world's tallest building and plenty of postmodern glitz to dazzle visitors from more traditional and repressive societies.

All this glamour and intrigue are also accompanied by some Hollywood-style violence. In March 2009, a Russian warlord was shot dead in the upscale Marina section of Dubai, near some of its best beaches and hotels. Two suspects, one Tajik and one Iranian, were arrested and gave confessions implicating a member of the Russian Duma acting on orders from the strongman of Chechnya, Ramzan Kadyrov. In a touch straight out of Ian Fleming's *The Man with the Golden Gun,* the victim was shot with a gold-plated pistol smuggled in by a Russian diplomat.

An even more spectacular murder took place in January 2010, when Israeli surveillance agents and hit men—working in teams, traveling on fake passports, wearing disguises and using heavily encrypted cell phones—assassinated Mahmoud al-Mabhouh, a senior Hamas operative, in his Dubai hotel room as he waited to complete an arms deal with his Iranian suppliers. Dubai has a low crime rate, but when it comes to terrorists with enemies, even the desert is not safe.

Historically Dubai thrived on two activities, pearl diving and smuggling. Today pearl diving is a small business carried on in part as an attraction for tourists. Smuggling is bigger than ever. The long wharf on the Creek, the old part of Dubai, is piled high with electronics, appliances, spare parts and other goods headed for Iran. The amount of gold and currency inside boxes marked with Sony or HP logos is anybody's guess. Across Baniyas Road, which runs alongside the wharf, are Iranian banks where letters of credit can be arranged on the spot to finance the shipment of goods—without regard to U.S. trade sanctions. On the Creek itself are the dhows— beamy, high-prowed wooden sailing vessels with large lateen rigs ready to embark on the voyage across the Persian Gulf to Bandar Abbas and other ports on the Iranian coast. In Dubai, smuggling is not even vaguely disreputable; it is a way of life.

Dubai is an international financial center and tax haven, its boulevards and backstreets choked with international banks. Dubai is the principal offshore banking center for Iran. Major Dubai banks act as correspondents to Iranian banks for the facilitation of payments and foreign exchange transactions with the rest of the world, including Iran's conversion of its reserves into euros and gold and slow dumping of the dollar. Dubai also acts as the banking center for the Somali pirate trade. While pirates, hostage crews and patrolling navies engage in standoffs in the Arabian Sea, pirate agents make the rounds in Dubai to negotiate ransom and provide wire instructions for final payment.

For tangible wealth, there is the gold souk, one of the largest marketplaces in the world, where gold in every form—jewelry, coins, bars and ingots—is for sale and then reexport in attaché cases to private hoards around the world, no questions asked. Dubai has a commodities center with separate glass skyscrapers named after the Arabic words for gold, silver and diamond. Beneath these towers is one of the largest, most secure vaults in the world, managed by Brink's. With Swiss banking secrecy under attack and oligarchs being harassed in Russia, converting wealth into untraceable gold and securing it in the desert is an attractive strategy.

The gold that changes hands in the souk is the tip of the iceberg of wholesale wealth that transits Dubai. Paper currencies move continuously from engravers to central banks to customers, much of it circulating outside its home country. Dubai is the world's largest transshipment point for paper currencies. At secure sites near the Dubai airport, massive amounts of banknotes are stored, awaiting return to their issuing banks.

Espionage, assassination, gold, currency and an international mix of actors at the crossroads of the world give Dubai its standing as the new Casablanca. Dubai, like Casablanca, is just a mirror of its time and place. Were it not for the corruption and dysfunction of the wider world, Dubai would have no clientele. Every war needs its neutral venue, and in the currency wars Dubai fills the bill. There is no currency anywhere that is not money-good in Dubai—at a price.

■ Moscow

A visitor to Moscow quickly becomes familiar with the sight of the so-called Seven Sisters: a group of gray Soviet-era skyscrapers, each about 150 meters, or 450 feet, high, commissioned by Stalin and built in the late 1940s in a kind of neo-Gothic totalitarian style, with the symmetry, massiveness and reach-for-the-sky spires beloved by bureaucrats everywhere. They are spread around Moscow in a huge ring so that one of them dominates the skyline in any direction. While different in details, they are sufficiently similar in form to create a sense of déjà vu. A visitor can leave one of the sisters, the Moscow State University, say, and travel across the city only to encounter a look-alike, such as the former Leningradskaya Hotel.

There is an eighth sister, newly arrived and set back on a large open site on Nametkina Street, outside the innermost ring roads surrounding central Moscow. It is suitably massive and about the same height as the original seven, with a pyramidlike roof reminiscent of the pointed spires of the sisters. But the resemblance ends there. The new sister, finished in 1995, has a gleaming postmodern exterior of blue glass, steel and concrete. In keeping with this up-to-date look, it has an up-to-date function: it is the headquarters of Gazprom, the largest company in Russia, the world's largest natural gas company and the mainstay of the Russian natural resources–based economy. Gazprom and the Russian state are as one in the exploitation of natural gas—what they call the "blue fuel," in reference to the clean burning properties revealed in its blue flame.

Even in an age of government bailouts of entire industries, it is difficult for Westerners to grasp the scope of Gazprom's operations and its links to the Russian government. It is as if ExxonMobil, J. P. Morgan and Time Warner were a single company, with Bill Clinton as its CEO. Gazprom's revenues are about 10 percent of Russia's gross domestic product. Gazprom produces over 85 percent of Russia's natural gas and over 20 percent of the world's supply. It controls almost 20 percent of global gas reserves and 60 percent of Russian gas reserves. It is fully vertically integrated, including exploration, production, transmission, processing, marketing and distribution. In addition to energy, it has major interests in media, banking and insurance, and operates an internal investment company.

Dmitry Medvedev, elected president of Russia in 2008, twice served as chairman of the board of Gazprom. The current chairman, Viktor Zubkov, is the deputy prime minister of Russia—that is, Prime Minister Vladimir Putin's right-hand man. The CEO, Alexey Miller, is a Putin crony from their St. Petersburg days in the 1990s. While the company's stock is traded on several exchanges, it is nevertheless controlled by the Russian state.

Gazprom's long-range plans seem more like a study in military tactics than corporate strategy. It speaks of the Chinese vector, exploitation of the Yamal Peninsula and establishing bases in the Arctic. The military comparison is more than a metaphor. In 2007, the Russian Duma authorized Gazprom to create its own security force, with powers far beyond normal security companies—in effect, a corporate army like the ones the trading firms of the mercantilist age deployed. Gazprom also has a strategic enemy that it is determined to destroy. The enemy's name is Nabucco.

Nabucco is a new natural-gas pipeline consortium backed by members of the European Union and the United States that will allow Europe to obtain natural gas without depending on Russia. It is a direct threat to Gazprom's near monopoly on natural gas supplies to Europe through pipelines transiting Ukraine and Belarus. Nabucco is an attempt to circumvent these pipelines in a way that neither uses Russian natural gas nor passes through Russian territory. Nabucco would source its gas initially in Azerbaijan and later Kazakhstan and Iraq. It will traverse Turkey on its way to Europe.

One of the critical links in the larger Nabucco scheme is the South Caucasus Pipeline that runs through Georgia. With the invasion of Georgia in August 2008, Russian armored columns were used to threaten Nabucco and support Gazprom's dominant position. This invasion came at the height of the U.S. bailout of Fannie Mae, and Russia was one of the largest holders of Fannie Mae bonds at the time. By bailing out Fannie Mae, the Bush administration protected Russia's financial interests with U.S. taxpayer money even as Russia threatened U.S. interests on the energy front. Such is the geopolitical nexus in which the currency wars are fought.

Not only is Russia intent on disrupting Nabucco, it is also sponsoring two alternative pipelines that will deliver gas from Central Asia to Europe but are controlled by Gazprom and transit Russia. Gazprom's goal is to keep Central Asian supplies bottled up inside Russian pipelines before flowing to Europe. Europe's energy supplies are largely held hostage by Russia, and Russia has no intention of letting go.

Russia's use of natural gas as a geopolitical weapon goes beyond threats; it has been put into action several times. On New Year's Day 2006, Gazprom cut off supplies of natural gas to Ukraine. The effects were not limited to Ukraine but were felt throughout Europe. The stated cause was a billing dispute. While Ukraine had agreed to pay Russia for gas it consumed, Russia had agreed to pay Ukraine for the right to transit its territory to deliver gas to the rest of Europe. Russia could pay its transit fees in kind, meaning that it simply charged Ukraine nothing for some of the gas used by Ukraine. None of these payments were at market rates but were privately negotiated and involved middlemen believed to be diverting the payments to offshore accounts of Russian and Ukrainian officials. This mix of private negotiations, middlemen, payments in kind and off-market transactions ensured that the parties were constantly at odds over who owed what to whom.

Ukraine exploited this confusion to cover up its chronic hard currency shortages and late payments. In time, Russia learned that it could use the same ambiguity for its own purposes—using its disputes with Ukraine to halt shipments to Europe while blaming Ukraine for the stoppages. Russia could take the high ground by posing as an aggrieved creditor while showing Europe the implications of energy dependence.

New Year's Day 2009 saw another Russian shutdown of deliveries to Ukraine. This time the consequences were more severe, with widespread factory closings in Eastern Europe and unheated homes in the dead of winter. By January 7 the gas war had escalated and direct Ukrainian supplies were reduced to zero. But then Ukraine diverted the transit supplies to its own use, and the shortages spread throughout Eastern Europe, seriously affecting Hungary, Poland and other states. Russia was holding Ukraine hostage, but Ukraine held the rest of Europe hostage to protect itself—a result that might have been foreseen by Russia. Finally, on January 18, an all-night summit conference between Putin and then Ukrainian prime minister Yulia Tymoshenko produced a new pricing plan, and Russia resumed supplies.

It seems unlikely the world has seen the end of the natural gas wars. Putin has recently suggested that the rest of Europe should help Ukraine with its cash shortages to protect itself from the consequences of future supply disruptions. This regionalizes the problem and shows how aggressively Russia is willing to use the gas weapon and the currency weapon in combination.

Russia recently released its official "National Security Strategy of the Russian Federation up to 2020," an overview of the global strategic opportunities and challenges confronting Russia. In addition to the usual analysis of weapons systems and alliances, the strategy draws the link between energy and national security and considers the global financial crisis, currency wars, supply chain disruptions and struggles for other natural resources, including water. The strategy does not rule out the use of military force to resolve any of these finance- or resource-related struggles.

The perfection of Russia's use of the blue fuel weapon arises in the midst of the global financial crisis. This provides Russia with its own force multiplier—something that amplifies offensive power beyond its normal value. Russia's cutoffs of natural gas are devastating at the best of times. Coming amid a European sovereign debt crisis and housing market collapse, the next gas cutoff could have a catastrophic impact.

Of course, victims of blue fuel warfare have a remedy. They can turn their backs on NATO, the euro, the dollar and the West, and rejoin the Russian sphere of influence in exchange for secure, dependable and reasonably priced energy. Russia does not require its new vassals to adopt the totalitarian political systems of the Soviet past. It only requires that they be dependable allies in geopolitical matters and join a regional ruble currency bloc while maintaining a facade of democracy, as does Russia itself.

Russia also speaks openly of the dethroning of the dollar as the dominant reserve currency. While the Russian ruble is in no position to replace the dollar in international reserves, it could become a regional reserve and trade currency for Russian and Central Asian gas suppliers and Eastern European gas customers, dislodging the dollar to that extent at least. For now, it is enough to say that Russia has warned the world of the coming blue fuel wars in both words and deeds. Energy is a wedge used to forge a regional economic bloc with a regional reserve currency, the ruble. The dollar will be left out in the cold.

■ Beijing

What is most striking about Chinese history is how often and how suddenly it has swerved from order to chaos through the millennia. Despite the appearance of economic dynamism in China today, sudden collapse is entirely possible and could be caused by things such as inflation, rising unemployment, ethnic tensions or a burst housing bubble. Prolonged and widespread unemployment is potentially more destabilizing in China than in the more developed economies, especially when combined with lost upward mobility for tens of millions more citizens.

In addition to normal population stresses, China is sitting on a demographic powder keg in the form of twenty-four million "excess males"—the result of the murder of newborn girls through infanticide and sex-selective abortion under China's one-child policy. Many are now in their early twenties. It is a sad fact that single, unemployed men in their early twenties are often associated with forms of antisocial behavior, including gangs, murder, drugs and alcohol.

Internal social instability caused by the excess population of single men along with food price inflation and mass unemployment is a greater threat in the eyes of Chinese rulers than the U.S. military. This instability can be smoothed over in part through infrastructure investments that create jobs, which China depends on its currency reserves to finance. What happens when the United States devalues those reserves through inflation? While inflation may make sense to U.S. policy makers, the resulting wealth transfer from China to the United States is viewed as an existential threat by the Chinese. Maintaining the real value of its reserves is one of China's keys to maintaining internal social control. The Chinese are warning the United States that they will not tolerate dollar inflation and will take countermeasures to prevent a loss of wealth. The U.S.-Chinese currency war is just getting started, and the Fed's quantitative easing makes it entirely plausible to say the United States fired the first shot.

The clearest exposition of Chinese thinking on financial warfare is an essay called "The War God's Face Has Become Indistinct," included in a book on unrestricted warfare written in 1999 by Colonels Qiao Liang and Wang Xiangsui of the People's Liberation Army. One passage in particular is worth quoting at length:

> Financial warfare has now officially come to war's center stage—a stage that for thousands of years has been occupied only by soldiers and weapons. . . . We believe that before long, "financial warfare" will undoubtedly be an entry in the . . . dictionaries of official military jargon. Moreover, when people revise the history books on twentieth-century warfare . . . the section on financial warfare will command the reader's utmost attention. . . . Today, when nuclear weapons have already become frightening mantelpiece decorations that are losing their real operational value . . . financial war has become a "hyperstrategic" weapon that is attracting the attention of the world. This is because financial war is easily manipulated and allows for concealed actions, and is also highly destructive.

Consideration of such military doctrine suggests that the future of geopolitics might not be the benign multilateral ethos of Davos Man but a rather more dark and dystopian world of resource scarcity, infrastructure collapse, mercantilism and default. China's call to replace the U.S. dollar as the global reserve currency, routinely dismissed by *bien-pensant* global elites, might be taken more seriously if they were as familiar with Chinese financial warfare strategy as with Keynesian theory.

China's main link with the global financial system is the U.S. government bond market. China may be history's oldest civilization and a rising superpower, but on Wall Street it is more likely to be viewed as the best customer in the world. When China needs to buy or sell U.S. Treasury bonds for its reserves, it does so through the network of primary dealers. Large customers like China prefer to trade with primary dealers because their privileged relationship with the Fed gives them the best information about market conditions. Relationships are the key to knowing what is really going on in markets, and China taps into those relationships.

When China calls a bank dealer, the call never goes to voice mail. Direct lines are installed from China's central bank and sovereign wealth funds to arena-sized trading floors at UBS, J. P. Morgan, Goldman Sachs and other major banks. A salesperson knows China is on the line before she picks up the phone. Code names are used so the salesperson and trader can engage in market-making conversations safe from eavesdropping. When China wants to trade U.S. bonds, it typically calls several dealers at once and makes dealers compete for the business. China expects—and gets—the best bids on its bond sales in exchange for the massive volume of business it provides.

Figures on China's purchases of U.S. Treasury bonds are difficult to ascertain because China is nontransparent about its holdings. Not every dollar-denominated bond is issued by the U.S. government and not every government security is issued by the Treasury. Many U.S. government securities are issued by Fannie Mae, Freddie Mac and other agencies, and China holds some dollar-denominated bonds issued by banks and others not part of the U.S. government. There is no doubt, however, that the vast majority of China's dollar holdings are in U.S. Treasury bonds, notes and bills. Official U.S. figures put Chinese holdings of Treasury securities in excess of one trillion dollars, but when government agency securities from Fannie Mae and Freddie Mac are taken into account, the dollar-denominated government securities total is much higher.

China's great fear is that the United States will devalue its currency through inflation and destroy the value of these Chinese holdings of U.S. debt. There has been much speculation that China, in retaliation for U.S. inflation, could dump its one trillion dollars of U.S. Treasury securities in a highly visible fire sale that would cause U.S. interest rates to skyrocket and the dollar to collapse on foreign exchange markets. This would result in higher mortgage costs and lower home prices in the United States, as well as other major financial dislocations. The fear is also that China could use this financial leverage to sway U.S. policy in areas from Taiwan to North Korea to quantitative easing.

These fears are dismissed by most observers. They say that China would never dump its Treasury securities because it has far too many of them. The Treasury market is deep, but not that deep, and the price of Treasuries would collapse long before more than a small fraction of China's bonds could be sold. Many of the resulting losses would fall on the Chinese themselves. In effect, dumping Treasuries would mean economic suicide for the Chinese.

This easy logic ignores other things the Chinese can do that are just as damaging to the United States and far less costly to the Chinese. Treasury securities are sold in many maturities, ranging from thirty days to thirty years. The Chinese could shift the mix of their Treasury holdings from longer to shorter maturities without selling a single bond and without reducing their total holdings. As each long-term note matures, China could reinvest in three-month instruments without reducing its total investment in Treasuries. These shorter maturities are less volatile, meaning the Chinese would be less vulnerable to market shocks. This shift would also make the Chinese portfolio more liquid, vastly facilitating a full Chinese exit from Treasury securities. The Chinese would not have to dump anything but merely wait the six months or so it takes the new notes to mature. The effect is like shortening the time on a detonator.

In addition, the Chinese are aggressively diversifying their cash reserve positions away from dollar-denominated instruments of any kind. Again, this does not involve dumping and reinvesting by China, but simply deploying its new reserves in new directions. The Chinese earn several hundred billion dollars each year from their trade surplus. This is a massive amount of new money that needs to be invested alongside the reserves they already have. While existing reserves may remain mostly in U.S. Treasury debt, new reserves can be used in any way that makes sense to the Chinese.

Investment options in other currencies are limited. The Chinese can buy bonds in yen, euros and sterling issued by governments and banks outside the United States, but the choices are few—there simply aren't enough of them. None of those other markets has the depth and quality of the U.S. Treasury market. But China's choices are not limited to bonds. The other leading investment—and the one the Chinese now favor—is commodities.

Commodities include not only obvious things like gold, oil and copper, but also the stocks of mining companies that own commodities—an indirect way of owning the commodity itself—and agricultural land that can be used to grow commodities such as wheat, corn, sugar and coffee. Also included is the most valuable commodity of all—water. Special funds are being organized to buy exclusive rights to freshwater from deep lakes and glaciers in Patagonia. The Chinese can invest in those funds or buy freshwater sources outright.

These commodity investment programs are well under way. Most prominently, between 2004 and 2009 China secretly doubled its official holdings of gold. China used one of its sovereign wealth funds, the State Administration of Foreign Exchange (SAFE), to purchase gold covertly from dealers around the world. Since SAFE is not the same as the Chinese central bank, these purchases were off the books from the central bank's perspective. In a single transaction in 2009, SAFE transferred its entire position of five hundred metric tons of gold to the central bank in a bookkeeping entry, after which it was announced to the world. China argues that the secrecy was needed to avoid running up the price of gold due to the adverse market impact that arises when there is a single large buyer in the market. This is a common problem. Nations usually deal with it by announcing long-term buying programs and giving themselves flexibility as to timing, so the market cannot take undue advantage of one buyer. In this case, China went beyond flexible timing and conducted a clandestine operation.

What other financial operations are being pursued in secret today? While the Chinese proceed on numerous fronts, the United States continues to take its dollar hegemony for granted. China's posture toward the U.S. dollar is likely to become more aggressive as its reserve diversification becomes more advanced. China's hard asset endgame is one more ticking time bomb for the dollar.

■ Collapse

After this Cook's Tour of financial hot spots, it is daunting to consider what may be the greatest risk of all—correlation. As applied to global financial warfare scenarios, correlation refers to two or more threats originating abroad that might produce adverse shocks at the same time, either because of coordination or because one acts as a catalyst for the others. If Russia wanted to launch a natural resources attack on the West through a cutoff of natural gas supplies, it might make good sense for the Chinese to accelerate their efforts to diversify away from paper assets into hard assets because of the expected price spikes produced by Russia's move. Conversely, if China were ready to announce an alternative reserve currency backed by commodities, it might make good sense for Russia to announce that it would no longer accept dollars in payment for oil and natural gas exports, except at a greatly devalued exchange rate to the new currency.

At a more malign level, China and Russia might find it beneficial to secretly coordinate the timing of their commodity and currency assaults so as to be self-reinforcing. They could accumulate large positions in advance of their actions using leverage and derivatives. This not only would be a financial attack but would involve advance insider trading to profit from their own misdeeds. Iranians with access to Dubai banks observing these developments might decide to trigger a war with Saudi Arabia or a terrorist attack, not because they were necessarily communicating with the Russians or Chinese, but because the financial force multiplier from an attack would be that much greater.

Throwing a Russian resources assault, a Chinese currency assault and an Iranian military assault at United States interests in a near simultaneous affront would produce predictable effects in the hairtrigger world of capital markets. Markets would experience the financial equivalent of a stroke. They would not just collapse; they might cease to function entirely.

The foregoing threats are fast arriving. They are not extreme worst-case scenarios, but the culmination of events happening to-day. Consider the following:

- October 28, 2008: Interfax reports that Vladimir Putin, prime minister of Russia, advised Wen Jiabao, premier of China, to abandon the U.S. dollar as a transaction and reserve currency.
- November 15, 2008: The Associated Press reports that Iran has converted its financial reserves into gold.
- November 19, 2008: Dow Jones reports that China is considering a target of four thousand metric tons for its official gold reserves to diversify against the risks of holding U.S. dollars.
- February 9, 2009: The *Financial Times* reports that transactions in gold bullion have reached an all-time record.
- March 18, 2009: Reuters reports that the United Nations supports calls for the abandonment of the U.S. dollar as the global reserve currency.
- March 30, 2009: Agence France Presse reports that Russia and China are cooperating on the creation of a new global currency.
- March 31, 2009: The *Financial Times* reports that China and Argentina have entered into a currency swap, which would allow Argentina to use Chinese yuan in lieu of dollars.
- April 26, 2009: Agence France Presse reports that China is calling for the reform of the world monetary system and replacement of the U.S. dollar as the leading reserve currency.
- May 18, 2009: The *Financial Times* reports Brazil and China have agreed to explore conducting bilateral trade without using dollars.
- June 16, 2009: Reuters reports that Brazil, Russia, India and China, at a BRIC summit, call for a more "diversified, stable and predictable currency system."
- November 3, 2009: Bloomberg reports that India has purchased $6.7 billion worth of IMF gold to diversify assets away from the weaker dollar.

- November 7, 2010: World Bank president Robert Zoellick states that the G20 should "consider employing gold as an international reference point of market expectations about inflation, deflation and future currency values."
- December 13, 2010: French president Nicolas Sarkozy calls for the consideration of a wider role for SDRs in the international monetary system.
- December 15, 2010: *BusinessWeek* reports that China and Russia have jointly called for the dollar's role in world trade to be diminished and are launching a yuan-ruble trade currency settlement mechanism.

This is just a sample of the many reports indicating that China, Russia, Brazil and others are seeking an alternative to the dollar as a global reserve currency. A role for commodities as the basis for a new currency is another frequent refrain.

These are daunting trends and pose difficult choices. Upholding U.S. national security interests cannot be done without knowing the dynamics of global capital markets. U.S. dependence on traditional rivals to finance its debt constrains not only fiscal policy but U.S. national security and military options. Geopolitical dominoes are already falling in places such as Pakistan, Somalia, Thailand, Iceland, Egypt, Libya, Tunisia and Jordan. Much larger dominoes are waiting to fall in Eastern Europe, Spain, Mexico, Iran and Saudi Arabia. Challenges to U.S. power grow stronger as the U.S. dollar grows weaker.

Then there are the geopolitical big three—the United States, Russia and China. Of those, the United States is the most secure against foreign financial attack yet seems intent on undermining itself by debasing its dollar. Russia is visibly weak, yet its weakness can be its strength—it has a history of turning its back on the world and surviving in autarky. China appears resilient but, as shown throughout history, is the most fragile, having repeatedly fluctuated between centralized empires and fragmented warring states for five thousand years. It is hard to appreciate how much the Chinese leadership lives in dread of the least sign of unrest from the unemployed, the countryside, the Falun Gong, the Tibetans, the Uighurs, North Korean refugees or the many other centrifugal forces at play. A global economic crisis possessed by a complex dynamic could be a catalyst that undoes sixty years of Chinese Communist Party rule. Waiting in the wings is Iran, which sees U.S. economic weakness as the ultimate force multiplier, something that gives Iran more bang for the buck when it decides to strike its neighbors in the Middle East. We have begun a descent into the maelstrom. The nexus of unrestrained global capital and unstable geopolitics is a beast that has begun to show its claws.

CHAPTER 9

The Misuse of Economics

"Human decisions affecting the future . . . cannot depend on strict mathematical expectation, since the basis for making such calculations does not exist; . . . it is our innate urge to activity which makes the wheels go round, our rational selves choosing . . . but often falling back for our motive on whim or sentiment or chance."

John Maynard Keynes, 1935

I n the late 1940s, economics divorced itself from its former allies in political science, philosophy and law and sought a new alliance with the hard sciences of applied mathematics and physics. It is ironic that economics aligned with the classic physics of causality at exactly the time physicists themselves were embracing uncertainty and complexity. The creation of the Nobel Memorial Prize in Economic Sciences in 1969, seventy-four years after the original Nobel Prize in physics, confirmed this academic metamorphosis. Economists were the new high priests of a large part of human activity—wealth creation, jobs, savings and investment—and came well equipped with the equations, models and computers needed to perform their priestly functions.

There has never been a time since the rise of laissez-faire capitalism when economic systems were entirely free of turmoil. Bubbles, panics, crashes and depressions have come and gone with the regularity of floods and hurricanes. This is not surprising, because the underlying dynamics of economics, rooted in human nature, are always at work. Yet the new scientific economics promised better.

Economists promised that through fine tuning fiscal and monetary policy, rebalancing terms of trade and spreading risk through derivatives, market fluctuations would be smoothed and the arc of growth extended beyond what had been possible in the past. Economists also promised that by casting off the gold standard they could provide money as needed to sustain growth, and that derivatives would put risk in the hands of those best able to bear it.

However, the Panic of 2008 revealed that the economic emperors wore no clothes. Only massive government interventions involving bank capital, interbank lending, money market guarantees, mortgage guarantees, deposit insurance and many other expedients prevented the wholesale collapse of capital markets and the economy. With few exceptions, the leading macroeconomists, policy makers and risk managers failed to foresee the collapse and were powerless to stop it except with the blunt object of unlimited free money.

To explain why, it is illuminating to take 1947, the year of publication of Paul Samuelson's *Foundations of Economic Analysis,* as an arbitrary dividing line between the age of economics as social science and the new age of economics as natural science. That dividing line reveals similarities in market behavior before and after. The collapse of Long-Term Capital Management in 1998 bears comparison to the collapse of the Knickerbocker Trust and the Panic of 1907 in its contagion dynamics and private resolution by bank counterparts with the most to lose. The stock market crash of October 19, 1987, when the Dow Jones Industrial Average dropped 22.61 percent in a single day, is reminiscent of the two-day drop of 23.05 percent on October 28–29, 1929. Unemployment in 2011 is comparable to the levels of the Great Depression, when consistent methodologies for the treatment of discouraged workers are used for both periods. In short, there is nothing about the post-1947 period of so-called hard economic science to suggest that it has had any success in mitigating the classic problems of boom and bust. In fact, there is much evidence to suggest that the modern practice of economics has left society worse off when one considers government deficit spending, the debt overhang, rising income inequality and the armies of long-term unemployed.

Recent failures have stripped economists of their immunity from rigorous scrutiny by average citizens. What works and what does not in economics is no longer just a matter of academic debate when forty-four million Americans are on food stamps. Claims by economic theorists about multipliers, rationality, efficiency, correlation and normally distributed risk are not mere abstractions. Such claims have become threats to the well-being of the nation. Signal failures of economics have arisen in Federal Reserve policy, Keynesianism, monetarism and financial economics. Understanding these failures will allow us to comprehend why growth has stalled and currency wars loom.

■ The Federal Reserve

The U.S. Federal Reserve System is the most powerful central bank in history and the dominant force in the U.S. economy today. The Fed is often described as possessing a dual mandate to provide price stability and to reduce unemployment. The Fed is also expected to act as a lender of last resort in a financial panic and is required to regulate banks, especially those deemed "too big to fail." In addition, the Fed represents the United States at multilateral central-bank meeting venues such as the G20 and the Bank for International Settlements, and conducts transactions using the Treasury's gold hoard. The Fed has been given new mandates under the Dodd-Frank reform legislation of 2010 as well. The "dual" mandate is more like a hydra-headed monster.

From its creation in 1913, the most important Fed mandate has been to maintain the purchasing power of the dollar; however, since 1913 the dollar has lost over 95 percent of its value. Put differently, it takes twenty dollars today to buy what one dollar would buy in 1913. Imagine an investment manager losing 95 percent of a client's money to get a sense of how effectively the Fed has performed its primary task.

The Fed's track record on dollar price stability should be compared to that of the Roman Republic, whose silver denarius maintained 100 percent of its original purchasing power for over two hundred years, until it began to be debased by the Emperor Augustus in the late first century BC. The gold solidus of the Byzantine Empire had an even more impressive track record, maintaining its purchasing power essentially unchanged for over five hundred years, from the monetary reform of AD 498 until another debasement began in 1030.

Fed defenders point out that while the dollar may have lost 95 percent of its purchasing power, wages have increased by a factor of over twenty, so that increased wages offset the decreased purchasing power. The idea that prices and wages move together without harm is known as money neutrality. This theory, however, ignores the fact that while wages and prices have gone up together, the impact has not been uniform across all sectors. The process produces undeserving winners and losers. Losers are typically those Americans who are prudent savers and those living on pensions whose fixed returns are devalued by inflation. Winners are typically those using leverage as well as those with a better understanding of inflation and the resources to hedge against it with hard assets such as gold, land and fine art. The effect of creating undeserving winners and losers is to distort investment decision making, cause misallocation of capital, create asset bubbles and increase income inequality. Inefficiency and unfairness are the real costs of failing to maintain price stability.

Another mandate of the Fed is to function as a lender of last resort. In the classic formulation of nineteenth-century economic writer Walter Bagehot, this means that in a financial panic, when all bank depositors want their money at once, a central bank should lend money freely to solvent banks against good collateral at a high rate of interest to allow banks to meet their obligations to depositors. This type of lending is typically not construed as a bailout, but rather as a way to convert good assets to cash when there is no other ready market for the assets. Once the panic subsides and confidence is restored, the loans can be repaid to the central bank and the collateral returned to the private banks.

In the depths of the Great Depression, when this lender of last resort function was most needed, the Fed failed utterly. More than ten thousand banks in the United States were either closed or taken over and assets in the banking system dropped almost 30 percent. Money was in such short supply that many Americans resorted to barter, in some cases trading eggs for sugar or coffee. This was the age of the wooden nickel, a homemade token currency that could be used by a local merchant to make change for a customer and then accepted later by other merchants in the vicinity in exchange for goods and services.

The next time the lender of last resort function became as critical as it had been in the Great Depression was the Panic of 2008. The Fed acted in 2008 as if a liquidity crisis had begun, when it was actually a solvency and credit crisis. Short-term lending can help ease a liquidity crisis by acting as a bridge loan, but it cannot cure a solvency crisis, when the collateral is permanently impaired. The solution for a solvency crisis is to shut down or nationalize the insolvent banks using existing emergency powers, move bad assets to government control and reprivatize the new solvent bank in a public stock offering to new shareholders. The new bank is then in a position to make new loans. The benefit of putting the bad assets under government control is that they can be funded at low cost with no capital and no mark-to-market accounting for losses. The stockholders and bondholders of the insolvent bank and the FDIC insurance fund would bear the losses on the bad assets, and the taxpayers would be responsible only for any excess losses.

Once again, the Fed misread the situation. Instead of shutting down insolvent banks, the Fed and the Treasury bailed them out with TARP funds and other gimmicks so that bondholders and bank management could continue to collect interest, profits and bonuses at taxpayer expense. This was consistent with the Fed's actual mandate dating back to Jekyll Island—to save bankers from themselves. The Fed almost completely ignored Bagehot's core principles. It did lend freely, as Bagehot recommended, but it took weak collateral, much of which is still lodged on the Fed's books. The Fed charged almost no interest instead of the high rates typically demanded from borrowers in distress. The Fed also lent to insolvent banks rather than just the solvent ones worth saving. The result for the economy even now is that the bad assets are still in the system, bank lending is highly constrained due to a need to rebuild capital and the economy continues to have great difficulty returning to self-sustaining growth.

When most urgently called upon to perform its lender of last resort functions, the Fed has bungled both times. First in 1929–1933, when it should have provided liquidity and did not. Then again in 2007–2009, when it should have closed insolvent banks but instead provided liquidity. The upshot of these two episodes, curiously, is that the Fed has revealed it knows relatively little about the classic arts of banking.

In 1978, the Humphrey-Hawkins Full Employment Act, signed by President Jimmy Carter, added management of unemployment to the Fed's mandate. The act was an explicit embrace of Keynesian economics and mandated the Fed and the executive branch to work together in order to achieve full employment, growth, price stability and a balanced budget. The act set a specific numeric goal of 3 percent unemployment by 1983, which was to be maintained thereafter. In fact, unemployment subsequently reached cyclical peaks of 10.4 percent in 1983, 7.8 percent in 1992, 6.3 percent in 2003 and 10.1 percent in 2009. It was unrealistic to expect the Fed to achieve the combined goals of Humphrey-Hawkins all at once, although Fed officials still pay lip service to the idea in congressional testimony. In fact, the Fed has not delivered on its mandate to achieve full employment. As of 2011, full employment as it is conventionally defined is still five years away, according to the Fed's own estimates.

To these failures of price stability, lender of last resort and unemployment must be added the greatest failure of all: bank regulation. The Financial Crisis Inquiry Commission created by Congress in 2009 to examine the causes of the current financial and economic crisis in the United States heard from more than seven hundred witnesses, examined millions of pages of documents and held extensive hearings in order to reach conclusions about responsibility for the financial crisis that began in 2007. The commission concluded that regulatory failure was a primary cause of the crisis and it laid that failure squarely at the feet of the Fed. The official report reads:

We conclude this crisis was avoidable. The crisis was the result of human action and inaction. . . . The prime example is the Federal Reserve's pivotal failure to stem the flow of toxic mortgages, which it could have done by setting prudent mortgage-lending standards. The Federal Reserve was the one entity empowered to do so and it did not. . . . We conclude widespread failures in financial regulation and supervision proved devastating to the stability of the nation's financial markets. The sentries were not at their posts. . . . Yet we do not accept the view that regulators lacked the power to protect the financial system. They had ample power in many arenas and they chose not to use it. . . . The Federal Reserve Bank of New York and other regulators could have clamped down on Citigroup's excesses in the run-up to the crisis. They did not. . . . In case after case after case, regulators continued to rate the institutions they oversaw as safe and sound even in the face of mounting troubles.

The report goes on for more than five hundred pages to detail the Fed's regulatory failures in minute detail. As noted in the excerpt above, all of the Fed's failures were avoidable.

One last test of Fed competence involves the Fed's handling of its own balance sheet. The Fed may be a central bank, but it is still a bank with a balance sheet and net worth. A balance sheet has two sides: assets, which are the things owned, and liabilities, which are the things owed to others. Net worth, also called capital, equals the assets minus the liabilities. The Fed's assets are mostly government securities it buys, and its liabilities are mostly the money it prints to buy them.

As of April 2011, the Fed had a net worth of approximately $60 billion and assets approaching $3 trillion. If the Fed's assets declined in value by 2 percent, a fairly small event in volatile markets, the 2 percent decline applied to $3 trillion in assets produces a $60 billion loss—enough to wipe out the Fed's capital. The Fed would then be insolvent. Could this happen? It has happened already, but the Fed does not report it because it is not required to revalue its assets to market value. This situation will come to a head when it comes time to unwind the Fed's quantitative easing program by selling bonds. The Fed may ignore mark-to-market losses in the short run, but when it sells the bonds, those losses will have to be shown on the books.

The Federal Reserve is well aware of this problem. In 2008, the Fed sent officials to meet with Congress to discuss the possibility of the Fed propping up its balance sheet by issuing its own bonds as the Treasury does now. In 2009, Janet Yellen, then president of the Federal Reserve Bank of San Francisco, went public with this request in a New York speech. Regarding the power to issue the new Fed Bonds, Yellen said, "I would feel happier having it now" and "It would certainly be a nice thing to have." Yellen seemed eager to get the program under way, and with good reason. The Fed's lurch toward insolvency was becoming more apparent by the day as it piled more leverage on its capital base. By getting permission from Congress to issue new Fed bonds, the Federal Reserve could unwind quantitative easing without having to sell the existing bonds on its books. Sales of the new Fed bonds would be substitutes for sales of the old Treasury bonds to reduce the money supply. By this substitution, the losses on the old Treasury bonds would stay hidden.

This bond scam was shot down on Capitol Hill, and once it failed, the Fed needed another solution quickly. It was running out of time before QE would need to be reversed. The solution was a deal arrived at between the Treasury and the Fed that did not require approval from Congress.

The Fed earns huge profits every year on the interest received on Treasury bonds the Fed owns. The Fed customarily pays these profits back to the Treasury. In 2010, the Fed and Treasury agreed that the Fed could suspend the repayments indefinitely. The Fed keeps the cash and the amount the Fed would normally pay to the Treasury is set up as a liability account—basically an IOU. This is unprecedented and is a sign of just how desperate the situation has become.

Now as losses on future bond sales arise, the Fed does not reduce capital, as would normally occur. Instead the Fed increases the amount of the IOU to the Treasury. In effect, the Fed is issuing private IOUs to the Treasury and using the cash to avoid appearing insolvent. As long as the Fed can keep issuing these IOUs, its capital will not be wiped out by losses on its bond positions. On paper the Fed's capital problem is solved, but in reality the Fed is increasing its leverage and parking its losses at the Treasury. Corporate executives who played these kinds of accounting games would be sent to jail. It should not escape notice that the Treasury is a public institution while the Fed is a private institution owned by banks, so this accounting sham is another example of depriving the taxpayers of funds for the benefit of the banks.

The United States now has a system in which the Treasury runs nonsustainable deficits and sells bonds to keep from going broke. The Fed prints money to buy those bonds and incurs losses by owning them. Then the Treasury takes IOUs back from the Fed to keep the Fed from going broke. It is quite the high-wire act, and amazing to behold. The Treasury and the Fed resemble two drunks leaning on each other so neither one falls down. Today, with its 50-to-1 leverage and investment in volatile intermediate-term securities, the Fed looks more like a poorly run hedge fund than a central bank.

Ed Koch, the popular mayor of New York in the 1980s, was famous for walking around the city and asking passersby, in his distinctive New York accent, "How'm I doin'?" as a way to get feedback on his administration. If the Fed were to ask, "How'm I doin'?" the answer would be that since its formation in 1913 it has failed to maintain price stability, failed as a lender of last resort, failed to maintain full employment, failed as a bank regulator and failed to preserve the integrity of its balance sheet. The Fed's one notable success has been that, under its custody, the Treasury's gold hoard has increased in value from about $11 billion at the time of the Nixon Shock in 1971 to over $400 billion today. Of course, this increase in the value of gold is just the flip side of the Fed's demolition of the dollar. On the whole, it is difficult to think of another government agency that has failed more consistently on more of its key missions than the Fed.

■ Monetarism

Monetarism is an economic theory most closely associated with Milton Friedman, winner of the Nobel Prize in economics in 1976. Its basic tenet is that changes in the money supply are the most important cause of changes in GDP. These GDP changes, when measured in dollars, can be broken into two components: a "real" component, which produces actual gains, and an "inflationary" component, which is illusory. The real plus the inflationary equals the nominal increase, measured in total dollars.

Friedman's contribution was to show that increasing the money supply in order to increase output would work only up to a certain point; beyond that, any nominal gains would be inflationary and not real. In effect, the Fed could print money to get nominal growth, but there would be a limit to how much real growth could result. Friedman also surmised that the inflationary effects of increasing the money supply might occur with a lag, so that in the short run printing money might increase real GDP but inflation would show up later to offset the initial gains.

Friedman's idea was encapsulated in an equation known as the quantity theory of money. The variables are M = money supply, V = velocity of money, P = price level and y = real GDP, expressed as:

$$MV = Py$$

This is stated as: money supply (M) times velocity (V) equals nominal GDP, which can be broken into its components of price changes (P) and real growth (y).

Money supply (M) is controlled by the Fed. The Fed increases money supply by purchasing government bonds with printed money and decreases money supply by selling the bonds for money that then disappears. Velocity (V) is just the measure of how quickly money turns over. If someone spends a dollar and the recipient also spends it, that dollar has a velocity of two because it was spent twice. If instead the dollar is put in the bank, that dollar has a velocity of zero because it was not spent at all. On the other side of the equation, nominal GDP growth has its real component (y) and its inflation component (P).

For decades one of the most important questions to flow from this equation was, is there a natural limit to the amount that the real economy can expand before inflation takes over? Real growth in the economy is limited by the amount of labor and the productivity of that labor. Population grows in the United States at about 1.5 percent per year. Productivity increases vary, but 2 percent to 2.5 percent per year is a reasonable estimate. The combination of people and productivity means that the U.S. economy can grow about 3.5 percent to 4.0 percent per year in real terms. That is the upper limit on the long-term growth of real output, or y in the equation.

A monetarist attempting to fine-tune Fed monetary policy would say that if y can grow at only 4 percent, then an ideal policy would be one in which money supply grows at 4 percent, velocity is constant and the price level is constant. This would be a world of near maximum real growth and near zero inflation.

If increasing the money supply in modest increments were all there was to it, Fed monetary policy would be the easiest job in the world. In fact, Milton Friedman once suggested that a properly programmed computer could adjust the money supply with no need for a Federal Reserve. Start with a good estimate of the natural real growth rate for the economy, dial up the money supply by the same target rate and watch the economy grow without inflation. It might need a little tweaking for timing lags and changes in the growth estimate due to productivity, but it is all fairly simple as long as the velocity of money is constant.

But what if velocity is not constant?

It turns out that money velocity is the great joker in the deck, the factor that no one can control, the variable that cannot be fine-tuned. Velocity is psychological: it all depends on how an individual feels about her economic prospects or about how all consumers in the aggregate feel. Velocity cannot be controlled by the Fed's printing press or advancements in productivity. It is a behavioral phenomenon, and a powerful one.

Think of the economy as a ten-speed bicycle with money supply as the gears, velocity as the brakes and the bicycle rider as the consumer. By shifting gears up or down, the Fed can help the rider accelerate or climb hills. Yet if the rider puts on the brakes hard enough, the bike slows down no matter what gear the bike is in. If the bike is going too fast and the rider puts on the brakes hard, the bike can skid or crash.

In a nutshell, this is the exact dynamic that has characterized the U.S. economy for over ten years. After peaking at 2.12 in 1997, velocity has been declining precipitously ever since. The drop in velocity accelerated as a result of the Panic of 2008, falling from 1.80 in 2008 to 1.67 in 2009—a 7 percent drop in one year. This is an example of the consumer slamming on the brakes. More recently, in 2010 velocity has leveled off at 1.71. When consumers pay down debt and increase savings instead of spending, velocity drops as does GDP, unless the Fed increases the money supply. So the Fed has been furiously printing money just to maintain nominal GDP in the face of declining velocity.

The Fed has another problem in addition to the behavioral and not easily controlled nature of velocity. The money supply that the Fed controls by printing, called the monetary base, is only a small part of the total money supply, about 20 percent, according to recent data. The other 80 percent is created by banks when they make loans or support other forms of asset creation such as money market funds and commercial paper. While the monetary base increased 242 percent from January 2008 to January 2011, the broader money supply increased only 34 percent. This is because banks are reluctant to make new loans and are struggling with the toxic loans still on their books. Furthermore, consumers and businesses are afraid to borrow from the banks either because they are overleveraged to begin with or because of uncertainties about the economy and doubts about their ability to repay. The transmission mechanism from base money to total money supply has broken down.

The $MV = Py$ equation is critical to an understanding of the dynamic forces at play in the economy. If the money (M) expansion mechanism is broken because banks will not lend and velocity (V) is flat or declining because of consumer fears, then it is difficult to see how the economy (Py) can expand.

This brings us to the crux. The factors that the Fed can control, such as base money, are not working fast enough to revive the economy and decrease unemployment. The factors that the Fed needs to accelerate are bank lending and velocity, which result in more spending and investment. Spending, however, is driven by the psychology of lenders, borrowers and consumers, essentially a behavioral phenomenon. Therefore, to revive the economy, the Fed needs to change mass behavior, which inevitably involves the arts of deception, manipulation and propaganda.

To increase velocity, the Fed must instill in the public either euphoria from the wealth effect or fear of inflation. The idea of the wealth effect is that consumers will spend more freely if they feel more prosperous. The favored route to a wealth effect is an increase in asset values. For this purpose, the Fed's preferred asset classes are stock prices and home prices, because they are widely known and closely watched. After falling sharply from a peak in mid-2006, home prices stabilized during late 2009 and rose slightly in early 2010 due to the policy intervention of the first-time home buyer's tax credit. By late 2010, that program was discontinued and home prices began to decline again. By early 2011, home prices nationwide had returned to the levels of mid-2003 and seemed headed for further declines. It appeared there would be no wealth effect from housing this time around.

The Fed did have greater success in propping up the stock market. The Dow Jones Industrial Average increased almost 90 percent from March 2009 through April 2011. The Fed's zero interest rate policy left investors with few places to go if they wanted returns above zero. Yet the stock rally also failed to produce the desired wealth effects. Some investors made money, but many more stayed away from stocks because they had lost confidence in the market after 2008.

Faced with its inability to generate a wealth effect, the Fed turned to its only other behavioral tool—instilling fear of inflation in consumers. To do this in a way that increased borrowing and velocity, the Fed had to manipulate three things at once: nominal rates, real rates and inflation expectations. The idea was to keep nominal rates low and inflation expectations high. The object was to create negative real rates—the difference between nominal rates minus the expected rate of inflation. For example, if inflation expectations are 4 percent and nominal interest rates are 2 percent, then real interest rates are negative 2 percent. When real rates are negative, borrowing becomes attractive and both spending and investment grow. According to the monetarists' formula, this potent combination of more borrowing, which expands the money supply, and more spending, which increases velocity, would grow the economy. This policy of negative real rates and fear of inflation was the Fed's last, best hope to generate a self-sustaining recovery.

Negative interest rates create a situation in which dollars can be borrowed and paid back in cheaper dollars due to inflation. It is like renting a car with a full tank of gas and returning the car with the tank half empty at no charge to the user. Consumers and businesses find this difficult to pass up.

The Fed's plan was to encourage borrowing through negative interest rates and encourage spending through fear of inflation. The resulting combination of leverage and inflation expectations might increase money supply *and* velocity and therefore increase GDP. This could work—but what would it take to increase expectations?

Extensive theoretical work on this had been done by Ben Bernanke and Paul Krugman in the late 1990s as a result of studying a similar episode in Japan during its "lost decade." A definitive summary of this research was written by economist Lars Svensson in 2003. Svensson was a colleague of Bernanke's and Krugman's at Princeton and later became a central banker himself in Sweden. Svensson's paper is the Rosetta stone of the currency wars because it reveals the linkage between currency depreciation and negative real interest rates as a way to stimulate an economy at the expense of other countries.

Svensson discusses the benefits of currency war:

> Even if the . . . interest rate is zero, a depreciation of the currency provides a powerful way to stimulate the economy. . . . A currency depreciation will stimulate an economy directly by giving a boost to export . . . sectors. More importantly . . . a currency depreciation and a peg of the currency rate at a depreciated rate serves as a conspicuous commitment to a higher price level in the future.

Svensson also describes the difficulties of manipulating the public in the course of pursuing these policies:

> If the central bank could manipulate private-sector beliefs, it would make the private sector believe in future inflation, the real interest rate would fall, and the economy would soon emerge from recession. . . . The problem is that private-sector beliefs are not easy to affect.

Here was Bernanke's entire playbook—keep interest rates at zero, devalue the dollar by quantitative easing and manipulate opinion to create fear of inflation. Bernanke's policies of zero interest rates and quantitative easing provided the fuel for inflation. Ironically, Bernanke's fiercest critics were helping his plan by incessantly sounding the inflation alarm; they were stoking inflation fears with language no Fed chairman could ever use himself.

This was central banking with the mask off. It was not the cool, rational, scientific pursuit of disinterested economists sitting in the Fed's marble temple in Washington. Instead it was an exercise in deception and hoping for the best. When prices of oil, silver, gold and other commodities began to rise steeply in 2011, Bernanke was publicly unperturbed and made it clear that actual interest rates would remain low. In fact, increasing inflation anxiety reported from around the world combined with continued low rates was exactly what the theories of Bernanke, Krugman and Svensson advocated. America had become a nation of guinea pigs in a grand monetary experiment, cooked up in the petri dish of the Princeton economics department.

The Bernanke-Krugman-Svensson theory makes it clear that the Fed's public efforts to separate monetary policy from currency wars are disingenuous. Easy money and dollar devaluation are two sides of the same coin, and currency wars are part of the plan. Easy money and dollar devaluation are designed to work together to cause actual inflation and to raise inflation expectations while holding interest rates low to get the lending and spending machine back in gear. This is clear to the Chinese, the Arabs and other emerging markets in Asia and Latin America that have complained vociferously about the Fed's stewardship of the dollar. The question is whether the collapse of the dollar is obvious to the American people.

Fundamentally, monetarism is insufficient as a policy tool not because it gets the variables wrong but because the variables are too hard to control. Velocity is a mirror of the consumer's confidence or fear and can be highly volatile. The money supply transmission mechanism from base money to bank loans can break down because of the lack of certainty and confidence on the part of lenders and borrowers. The danger is that the Fed does not accept these behavioral limitations and tries to control them anyway through communication tinged with deception and propaganda. Worse yet, when the public realizes that it is being deceived, a feedback loop is created in which trust is broken and even the truth, if it can be found, is no longer believed. The United States is dangerously close to that point.

■ Keynesianism

John Maynard Keynes died in 1946 and so never lived to see the errors committed in his name. His death came just one year before the publication of Samuelson's *Foundations of Economic Analysis,* which laid the intellectual base for what became known as neo-Keynesian economics. Keynes himself used few equations in his writings, but did provide extensive analysis in clear prose. It was only in the late 1940s and 1950s that many of the models and graphs associated today with Keynesian economics came into existence. This is where the conceptual errors espoused under the name

"Keynesian" are embedded; what Keynes would have thought of those errors had he lived is open to speculation.

Near the end of his life, Keynes supported a new currency, which he called the bancor, with a value anchored to a commodity basket including gold. He was, of course, a fierce critic of the gold exchange standard of the 1920s, but he was practical enough to realize that currencies must be anchored to something and, for this reason, preferred a global commodity standard to the dollar-and-gold standard that emerged from Bretton Woods in 1944.

Our purpose here is not to review the field of Keynesian economics at large, but rather to zero in on the flaw most relevant to the currency wars. In the case of monetarism, the flaw was the volatility of velocity as expressed in consumer choice. In Keynesianism, the flaw is the famous "multiplier."

The Keynesian multiplier theory rests on the assumption that a dollar of government deficit spending can produce more than a dollar of total economic output after all secondary effects are taken into account. The multiplier is the Bigfoot of economics—something that many assume exists but is rarely, if ever, seen. The foundation of Keynesian public policy is called aggregate demand, or the total of all spending and investment in the domestic economy, excluding inventories. For example, if a worker is fired, he not only loses his income, but he also then stops spending in ways that cause others to lose income as well. The lost income and lost spending cause a drop in aggregate demand, which can feed on itself, leading more businesses to fire more employees, who then spend less, and so on in a vicious circle. Keynesian theory says that government can step in and spend money that individuals cannot or will not spend, thereby increasing aggregate demand. The government spending can reverse the slide and contribute to renewed economic growth.

The problem with this theory of government spending to boost aggregate demand is that governments have no money of their own in the first instance. Governments have to print the money, take the money in the form of taxes or borrow the money from their citizens or from abroad. Printing money can cause nominal growth, but it can also cause inflation, so that real growth is unchanged over time.

Taxing and borrowing may enable the government to spend more, but it means there is less for the private sector to spend or invest, so it is not clear how aggregate demand increases. This is where the multiplier claims to play a role. The idea of the multiplier is that one dollar of government spending will stimulate more spending by others and result in more than one dollar of increased output, and this is the justification for taking the dollar from the private sector.

How much more output is yielded by one dollar of government spending? Put differently, what is the size of the multiplier? In a famous study written just before the start of President Obama's administration, two of Obama's advisers, Christina Romer and Jared Bernstein, looked at the multiplier in connection with the proposed 2009 stimulus program. Romer and Bernstein estimated the multiplier at about 1.54 once the new spending was up and running. This means that for every $100 billion in the Obama spending program, Romer and Bernstein expected output to increase by $154 billion. Since the entire Obama program ended up at $787 billion, the "extra" output just from doing the stimulus program would amount to $425 billion—the largest free lunch in history. The purpose of this stimulus was to offset the effects of the depression that had begun in late 2007 and to save jobs.

The Obama administration ran U.S. fiscal year deficits of over $1.4 trillion in 2009 and $1.2 trillion in 2010. The administration projected further deficits of $1.6 trillion in 2011 and $1.1 trillion in 2012—an astounding total of over $5.4 trillion in just four years. In order to justify the $787 billion program of extra stimulus in 2009 with deficits of this magnitude, it was critical to show that America would be worse off without the spending. The evidence for the Keynesian multiplier had to be rock solid.

It did not take long for the evidence to arrive. One month after the Romer and Bernstein study, another far more rigorous study of the same spending program was produced by John B. Taylor and John F. Cogan of Stanford University and their colleagues. Central to the results shown by Taylor and Cogan is that *all of the multipliers are less than one,* meaning that for every dollar of "stimulus" spending, the amount of goods and services produced by the private sector *declines*. Taylor and Cogan employed a more up-to-date multiplier model that has attracted wider support among economists and uses more realistic assumptions about the projected path of interest rates and expectations of consumers in the face of higher tax burdens in the future. The Taylor and Cogan study put the multiplier effect of the Obama stimulus program at 0.96 in the early stages but showed it falling rapidly to 0.67 by the end of 2009 and to 0.48 by the end of 2010. Their study showed that, by 2011, for each stimulus dollar spent, private sector output would *fall* by almost sixty cents. The Obama stimulus program was hurting the private sector and therefore handicapping the private sector's ability to create jobs.

The Taylor and Cogan study was not the only study to reach the conclusion that Keynesian multipliers are less than one and that stimulus programs destroy private sector output. John Taylor had reached similar conclusions in a separate 1993 study. Empirical support for Keynesian multipliers of less than one, in certain conditions, was reported in separate studies by Michael Woodford of Columbia University, Robert Barro of Harvard and Michael Kumhof of Stanford, among others. A review of the economic literature shows that the methods used by Romer and Bernstein to support the Obama stimulus program were outside the mainstream of economic thought and difficult to support except for ideological reasons.

Keynes's theory that government spending could stimulate aggregate demand turns out to be one that works in limited conditions only, making it more of a special theory than the general theory he had claimed. Stimulus programs work better in the short run than the long run. Stimulus works better in a liquidity crisis than a solvency crisis, and better in a mild recession than a severe one. Stimulus also works better for economies that have entered recessions with relatively low debt levels at the outset. The seminal yet still underappreciated econometric work of Professor Carl F. Christ from the 1960s theorized that both Keynesian *and* monetarist tools work most powerfully for economies that have *started with a balanced budget*. Christ was the first to identify what he called the "government budget restraint," a concept that seems to have been forgotten in the meantime. Christ wrote, "Results suggest forcefully that both the extreme fiscal advocates and the extreme monetary advocates are wrong: Fiscal variables strongly influence the effect of a given change in the . . . money stock, and open market operations strongly influence the effects of given changes in government expenditures and taxation." Christ was saying that the impact of Keynesian stimulus could not be gauged independently of the deficit starting line.

None of the favorable conditions for Keynesian stimulus was present in the United States in early 2009. The country was heavily burdened with debt, was running huge deficits and was suffering from a severe solvency crisis that promised to continue for many years—exactly the wrong environment for Keynesian stimulus. The stimulus spending would increase the deficit and waste valuable resources, but not do much else.

Two years after the Romer and Bernstein study, the economic results were in, and they were devastating to their thesis. Romer and Bernstein had estimated total employment at over 137 million by the end of 2010. The actual number was only about 130 million. They had estimated GDP would increase 3.7 percent by late 2010; however, it had barely increased at all. They had also estimated that recession unemployment would peak at 8 percent; unfortunately, it peaked at 10.1 percent in October 2009. By every measure the economy performed markedly worse than Romer and Bernstein had anticipated using their version of the Keynesian multiplier. From the start, the Obama stimulus was little more than an ideological wish list of favored programs and constituencies dressed up in the academic robes of John Maynard Keynes.

The Romer-Bernstein plan almost certainly saved some jobs in the unionized government sector. However, few had argued that the stimulus would produce no jobs, merely that the hidden costs were too high. The combination of deficit spending, monetary ease and bank bailouts had boosted the economy in the short run. The problem was that the recovery was artificial and not self-sustaining, because it had been induced by government spending and easy money rather than by private sector consumption and investment. This led to a political backlash against further deficit spending and quantitative easing.

The increased debt from the failed Keynesian stimulus became a cause célèbre in the currency wars. These wars were primarily about devaluing a country's currency, which is a form of default. A country defaults to its foreign creditors when its claims suddenly become worth less through devaluation. A country defaults to its own people through inflation and higher prices for imported goods. With debt in the hands of foreign investors reaching unprecedented levels, the international impact of devaluation was that much greater, so the currency wars would be fought that much harder.

Because debt and deficits are now so large, the United States has run out of dry powder. If the United States were struck by another financial crisis or a natural disaster of the magnitude of Hurricane Katrina or greater, its ability to resort to deficit spending would be impaired. If the United States were confronted with a major war in the Middle East or East Asia, it would not have the financial wherewithal to support a war effort as it had done in World War II. Vulnerability to foreign creditors is now complete. In the face of any one of these crises—financial, natural or military—the United States would be forced to resort to emergency measures, as had FDR in 1933 and Nixon in 1971. Bank closings, gold seizures, import tariffs and capital controls would be on the table. America's infatuation with the Keynesian illusion has now resulted in U.S. power being an illusion. America can only hope that nothing bad happens. Yet given the course of events in the world, that seems a slim reed on which to lean.

■ Financial Economics

At about the same time that Paul Samuelson and others were developing their Keynesian theories, another group of economists were developing a theory of capital markets. From the faculties of Yale, MIT and the University of Chicago came a torrent of carefully reasoned academic papers by future Nobel Prize winners such as Harry

Markowitz, Merton Miller, William Sharpe and James Tobin. Their papers, published in the 1950s and 1960s, argued that investors cannot beat the market on a consistent basis and that a diversified portfolio that broadly tracks the market will produce the best results over time. A decade later, a younger generation of academics, including Myron Scholes, Robert C. Merton (son of famed sociologist Robert K. Merton) and Fischer Black, came forward with new theories on the pricing of options, opening the door to the explosive growth of financial futures and other derivatives contracts ever since. The work of these and other scholars, accumulated over fifty years and continuing today, constitutes the branch of economic science known as financial economics.

University biologists working with infectious viruses have airtight facilities to ensure that the objects of their study do not escape from the laboratory and damage the population at large. Unfortunately, no such safeguards are imposed on economics departments. For every brilliant insight there are some dangerous misconceptions that have infected the world's financial bloodstream and caused incalculable harm. None of these ideas has done more harm than the twin toxins of financial economics known as "efficient markets" and the "normal distribution of risk."

The idea behind the efficient market is that investors are solely interested in maximizing their wealth and will respond in a rational manner to price signals and new information. The theory assumes that when material new information arrives it is factored into prices immediately, so that prices move smoothly from one level to another based on the news. Since the markets efficiently price in all of this new information immediately, no investor can beat the market except by pure luck, because any information that an investor might want to use to make an investment decision is already reflected in the market price. Since the next piece of new information is unknowable in advance, future price movements are unpredictable and random.

The idea of normally distributed risk is that since future price movements are random, the severity and frequency of price swings will also be random, like a coin toss or roll of the dice. Mild events happen frequently and extreme events happen infrequently. When the frequent mild events and infrequent severe events are put on a graph, it takes the shape of the famous bell curve. The large majority of outcomes are bunched in the area of low severity, with far fewer events in the high severity region. Because the curve tails off steeply, highly extreme events are so rare as to be almost impossible.

In Figure 1 below, the height of the curve shows how often events happen and the width of the curve shows how severe they are, either positive or negative. The area centered on 0 traces those mild events that happen frequently. Consider the area of the curve beyond –3 and +3 This area represents events of much greater severity, events like stock market crashes or the bursting of housing bubbles. Yet, according to this bell curve, they almost never happen. This is shown by the fact that the curve practically touches the horizontal baseline, which signifies things that never happen at all.

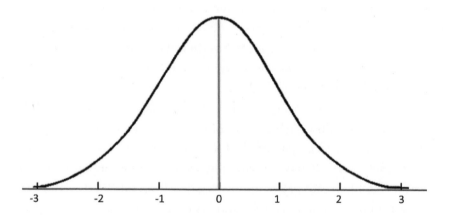

FIGURE 1: A bell curve showing a normal distribution of risk

The problem with the Nobel Prize–winning theories based on the bell curve is that empirical evidence shows they do not correspond to the real world of markets and human behavior. Based on an enormous body of statistical and social science research, it is clear that markets are *not* efficient, that price movements are *not* random and risk is *not* normally distributed.

The academic counterattack on these tenets of financial economics have come from two directions. From the fields of psychology,
sociology and biology came a flood of studies showing that investors
are irrational after all, at least from the perspective of wealth maxi-
mization. From iconoclastic mathematical genius Benoît Mandelbrot
came insights that showed future prices are not independent of the
past—that the market had a kind of "memory" that could cause it
to react or overreact in disruptive ways, giving rise to alternating
periods of boom and bust.

Daniel Kahneman and his colleague Amos Tversky demonstrated
in a series of simple but brilliantly constructed experiments that individuals were full of irrational biases. The subjects of their experiments were more concerned about avoiding a loss than achieving a
gain, even though an economist would say the two outcomes had
exactly the same value. This trait, called risk aversion, helps to explain why investors will dump stocks in a panic but be slow to reen-
ter the market once it turns around.

When economists began searching capital markets data for the
kinds of irrationality that Kahneman and Tversky had demonstrated, they had no trouble finding it. Among the anomalies discovered were that trends, once set in motion, were more likely to
continue than to reverse—the basis of "momentum" investing. It
also appeared that small-cap stocks outperform large-cap stocks.
Others identified the so-called January effect, which showed that
stocks performed better in January than other months. None of
these findings are consistent with efficient markets or random price
movements.

The debate between the efficient markets theorists and the social
scientists would be just another arcane academic struggle but for one
critical fact. The theory of efficient markets and its corollaries of
random price movements and a bell curve distribution of risk had
escaped from the lab and infected the entire trading apparatus of
Wall Street and the modern banking system. The application of
these flawed theories to actual capital markets activity contributed
to the 1987 stock market crash, the 1998 implosion of Long-Term
Capital Management and the greatest catastrophe of all—the Panic

of 2008. One contagious virus that spread the financial economics disease was known as value at risk, or VaR.

Value at risk is the method Wall Street used to manage risk in the decade leading up to the Panic of 2008 and it is still in widespread use today. It is a way to measure risk in an overall portfolio—certain risky positions are offset against other positions to reduce risk, and VaR claims to measure that offset. For example, a long position in ten-year Treasury notes might be offset by a short position in five-year Treasury notes so that the net risk, according to VaR, is much less than either of the separate risks of the notes. There is no limit to the number of complicated offsetting baskets that can be constructed. The mathematics quickly become daunting, because clear relationships such as longs and shorts in the same bond give way to the multiple relationships of many items in the hedging basket.

Value at risk is the mathematical culmination of fifty years of financial economics. Importantly, it assumes that future relationships between prices will resemble the past. VaR assumes that price fluctuations are random and that risk is embedded in net positions—long minus short—instead of gross positions. VaR carries the intellectual baggage of efficient markets and normal distributions into the world of risk management.

The role of VaR in causing the Panic of 2008 is immense but has never been thoroughly explored. The Financial Crisis Inquiry Commission barely considered trading risk models. The highly conflicted and fraudulent roles of mortgage brokers, investment bankers and ratings agencies have been extensively examined. Yet the role of VaR has remained hidden. In many ways, VaR was the invisible thread that ran through all the excesses that led to the collapse. What was it that allowed the banks, ratings agencies and investors to assume that their positions were safe? What was it that gave the Federal Reserve and the SEC comfort that the banks and brokers had adequate capital? Why did bank risk managers continually assure their CEOs and boards of directors that everything was under control? The answers revolve around value at risk and its related models. The VaR models gave the all clear to higher leverage and massive off-balance sheet exposures.

Since the regulators did not know as much about VaR as the banks, they were in no position to question the risk assessments. Regulators allowed the banks to self-regulate when it came to risk and leverage. It was as if the U.S. Nuclear Regulatory Commission allowed the builders of nuclear power plants to set their own safety specifications with no independent review.

Many scholars and practitioners had been aware of the flaws and limitations in VaR. The truth is that the flaws were well known and widely discussed for over a decade both in academia and on Wall Street. The banks continued to use VaR not because it worked but because it permitted a pretense of safety that allowed them to use excessive leverage and make larger profits while being backstopped by the taxpayers when things went wrong. Using VaR to manage risk is like driving a car at a hundred miles per hour while the speedometer has been rigged to stay at fifty miles per hour. Regulators in the backseat of the car glance at the speedometer and see 50, then go back to sleep. Meanwhile the car careens wildly, like something from a scene in *Mad Max*.

The destructive legacy of financial economics, with its false assumptions about randomness, efficiency and normal risk distributions, is hard to quantify, but $60 trillion in destroyed wealth in the months following the Panic of 2008 is a good estimate. Derivatives contracts did not shift risk to strong hands; instead derivatives concentrated risk in the hands of those too big to fail. VaR did not measure risk; it buried it behind a wall of equations that intimidated regulators who should have known better. Human nature and all its quirks were studiously ignored by the banks and regulators. When the financial economy was wrecked and its ability to aid commerce was well and truly destroyed, the growth engine went into low gear and has remained there ever since.

■ Washington and Wall Street—the Twin Towers of Deception

By the start of the new currency war in 2010, central banking was based not on principles of sound money but on the ability of central bankers to use communication to mislead citizens about their true intentions. Monetarism was based on unstable relationships between velocity and money that made it ineffective as a policy tool. Keynesianism was applied recklessly based on a mythical multiplier that was presumed to create income but actually destroyed it. Financial economics was a skyscraper erected on the quicksand of efficient markets and normal risk distributions that bore no relation to real behavior in capital markets. The entire system of fiscal policy, monetary policy, banking and risk management was intellectually corrupt and dishonest, and the flaws persist to this day.

Recently new and better economic paradigms have emerged. However, Washington and Wall Street both have a vested interest in the flawed models from the past. For Washington, Keynesianism is an excuse to expand spending and monetarism is an excuse to concentrate power at the Fed. For Wall Street, the theories of financial economics provide cover for high leverage and deceptive sales practices for off–balance sheet derivatives. On Wall Street, profits come first and good science second. If some theory, however flawed or out of date, can be trotted out with the right academic pedigree to provide a rationale for risk taking, then that is fine. If politicians and regulators are even further behind the learning curve than Wall Street, then that is fine too. As long as the profits continue on Wall Street, the hard questions will not be asked, let alone answered.

CHAPTER 10

Currencies, Capital and Complexity

"The difficulty lies, not in the new ideas, but in escaping
from the old ones."

John Maynard Keynes, 1935

Despite the theoretical and real-world shortcomings of both the Keynesian multiplier and the monetarist quantity approach to money, these are still the dominant paradigms used in public policy when economic growth falters. One need look only at the Obama stimulus and the Bernanke quantitative easing programs to see the hands of John Maynard Keynes and Milton Friedman hard at work. This persistence of the old school is also one driver of the new currency war, because of the expansion of public debt. This debt can be repaid only with help from inflation and devaluation. When growth falters, taking growth from other countries through currency devaluation is irresistible. Far better solutions are needed.

Fortunately, economic science has not stood entirely still. A new paradigm has emerged in the past twenty years from several schools of thought, including behavioral economics and complexity theory, among others. This new thinking comes with a healthy dose of humility—practitioners in many cases acknowledge the limitations of what is possible with the tools at hand. The new schools avoid the triumphalism of Keynes's claim to a "general theory" and Friedman's dictum that inflation is "always and everywhere" monetary.

The most promising new school is complexity theory. Despite the name, complexity theory rests on straightforward foundations. The first is that complex systems are not designed from the top down. Complex systems design themselves through evolution or the interaction of myriad autonomous parts. The second principle is that complex systems have emergent properties, which is a technical way of saying the whole is greater than the sum of its parts—the entire system will behave in ways that cannot be inferred from looking at the pieces. The third principle is that complex systems run on exponentially greater amounts of energy. This energy can take many forms, but the point is that when you increase the system scale by a factor of ten, you increase the energy requirements by a factor of a thousand, and so on. The fourth principle is that complex systems are prone to catastrophic collapse. The third and fourth principles are related. When the system reaches a certain scale, the energy inputs dry up because the exponential relationship between scale and inputs exhausts the available resources. In a nutshell, complex systems arise spontaneously, behave unpredictably, exhaust resources and collapse catastrophically. When you apply this paradigm to finance, you begin to see where the currency wars are headed.

Complexity theory has a strong empirical foundation and has had wide application in a variety of natural and man-made settings, including climate, seismology and the Internet. Significant progress has been made in applying complexity to capital and currency markets. However, a considerable challenge arises when one considers the interaction of human behavior and market dynamics. The complexity of human nature sits like a turbocharger on top of the complexity of markets. Human nature, markets and civilization more broadly are all complex systems nested inside one another like so many Russian *matryoshka* dolls. An introduction to behavioral economics will provide a bridge to a broader consideration of complexity theory and how underlying dynamics may determine the fate of the dollar and the endgame in the currency wars.

■ Behavioral Economics and Complexity

Contemporary behavioral economics has its roots in mid-twentieth-century social science. Pioneering sociologists such as Stanley Milgram and Robert K. Merton conducted wide-ranging experiments and analyzed data to develop new insights into human behavior.

Robert K. Merton's most famous contribution was the formalization of the idea of the self-fulfilling prophecy. The idea is that a statement given as true, even if initially false, can become true if the statement itself changes behavior in such a way as to validate the false premise. Intriguingly, to make his point Merton used the example of a run on the bank in the days before deposit insurance. A bank can begin the day on a sound basis with ample capital. A rumor that the bank is unsound, although false, can start a stampede of depositors trying to get their money out all at once. Even the best banks do not maintain 100 percent cash on hand, so a true bank run can force the bank to close its doors in the face of depositor demands. The bank fails by the end of the day, thus validating the rumor even though the rumor started out as false. The interaction of the rumor, the resulting behavior and the ultimate bank failure is an illustration of a positive feedback loop between information and behavior.

Merton and other leading sociologists of their time were not economists. Yet in a sense they were, because economics is ultimately the study of human decision making with regard to goods in conditions of scarcity. The sociologists cast a bright light on these decision-making processes. Former Bear Stearns CEO Alan Schwartz can attest to the power of Merton's self-fulfilling prophecy. On March 12, 2008, Schwartz told CNBC, "We don't see any pressure on our liquidity, let alone a liquidity crisis." Forty-eight hours later Bear Stearns was headed to bankruptcy after frightened Wall Street banks withdrew billions of dollars of credit lines. For Bear Stearns, this was a real-life version of Merton's thought experiment.

A breakthrough in the impact of social psychology on economics came with the work of Daniel Kahneman, Amos Tversky, Paul Slovic and others in a series of experiments conducted in the 1950s and 1960s. In the most famous set of experiments, Kahneman and Tversky showed that subjects, given the choice between two monetary outcomes, would select the one with the greater certainty of being received even though it did not have the highest expected return. A typical version of this is to offer a subject the prospect of winning money structured as a choice between: A) $4,000 with an 80 percent probability of winning, or B) $3,000 with a 100 percent probability of winning. For supporters of efficient market theory, this is a trivial problem. Winning $4,000 with a probability of 80 percent has an expected value of $3,200 (or $4,000 × .80). Since $3,200 is greater than the alternative choice of $3,000, a rational wealth-maximizing actor would chose A. Yet in one version of this, 80 percent of the participants chose B. Clearly the participants had a preference for the "sure thing" even if its theoretical value was lower. In some ways, this is just a formal statistical version of the old saying "A bird in the hand is worth two in the bush." Yet the results were revolutionary—a direct assault on the cornerstone of financial economics.

Through a series of other elegantly designed and deceptively simple experiments, Kahneman and his colleagues showed that subjects had a clear preference for certain choices based on how they were presented, even though an alternative choice would produce exactly the same result. These experiments introduced an entirely new vocabulary to economics, including certainty (the desire to avoid losses, also called risk aversion), anchoring (the undue influence of early results in a series), isolation (undue weight on unique characteristics versus shared characteristics), framing (undue weight on how things are presented versus the actual substance) and heuristics (rules of thumb). The entire body of work was offered under the title "prospect theory," which marked a powerful critique of the utility theory used by financial economists.

Unfortunately, behavioral economics has been embraced by policy makers to manipulate rather than illuminate behavior based on dubious premises about their superior wisdom. Bernanke's campaign to raise inflationary "expectations" by printing money and devaluing the dollar while holding rates low is the boldest contemporary version of such manipulation, yet there are others. Orchestrated propaganda campaigns have involved off-the-record meetings of corporate CEOs with business reporters requesting that they apply a more favorable spin to business news. These attempted manipulations have their absurd side, as with the phrase "green shoots" repeated ad nauseam by cable TV cheerleaders in the spring of 2009 at a time when America was losing millions of jobs. Tim Geithner's self-proclaimed "Recovery Summer" in 2010 is another example—that summer came and went with no recovery at all for the forty-four million on food stamps. These are all examples of what Kahneman called "framing" an issue to tilt the odds in favor of a certain result.

What Bernanke, Geithner and like-minded behavioralists in policy positions fail to see is something Merton might have easily grasped—the positive feedback effect that arises from framing without substance. If the economy is actually doing well, the message requires no framing and the facts will speak for themselves, albeit with a lag. Conversely, when reality consists of collapsing currencies, failed banks and insolvent sovereigns, talk about green shoots has at best a limited and temporary effect. The longer-term effect is a complete loss of trust by the public. Once the framing card has been played enough times without results, citizens will reflexively disbelieve everything officials say on the subject of economic growth even to the point of remaining cautious if things actually do improve. This does not represent a failure of behavioral economics so much as its misuse by policy makers.

Behavioral economics possesses powerful tools and can offer superb insights despite occasional misuse. It is at its best when used to answer questions rather than force results. Exploration of the paradox of Keynesianism is one possibly fruitful area of behavioral economic research with potential to mitigate the currency wars. Keynesianism was proposed in part to overcome the paradox of thrift. Keynes pointed out that in times of economic distress an individual may respond by reducing spending and increasing savings. However, if everyone does the same thing, distress becomes even worse because aggregate demand is destroyed, which can cause businesses to close and unemployment to rise. Keynesian-style government spending was thought to replace this shortage of private spending. Today government spending has grown so large and sovereign debt burdens so great that citizens rightly expect that some combination of inflation, higher taxation and default will be required to reconcile the debt burden with the means available to pay it. Government spending, far from stimulating more spending, actually makes the debt burden worse and may increase this private propensity to save. Here is a conundrum that behavioral economists seem well suited to explore. The result may be the discovery that short-term government austerity brightens long-run economic prospects by increasing confidence and the propensity to spend.

■ Complexity Theory

Our definition of complex systems included spontaneous organization, unpredictability, the need for exponentially greater energy inputs and the potential for catastrophic collapse. Another way to understand complexity is to contrast it with that which is merely complicated. A Swiss watch may be complicated, but it is not complex. The number and size of various gears, springs, jewels, stems and casings make it complicated. Yet the parts do not communicate with one another. They touch but do not interact. One gear does not enlarge itself because the other gears think it is a good idea. The springs do not spontaneously self-organize into a liquid metallic soup. The watch is complicated; however, complexity is much more than complication.

Complex systems begin with individual components called autonomous agents, which make decisions and produce results in the system. These agents can be marine species in the oceanic food chain or individual investors in currency markets; the dynamics are the same. To be complex, a system first requires diversity in the types of agents. If the agents are alike, nothing very interesting will happen.

If they are diverse, they will respond differently to various inputs, producing more varied results.

The second element is connectedness. The idea is that the agents are connected to one another through some channel. This can consist of electrical lines in the case of a power grid or Twitter feeds in the case of a social network, but somehow the agents must have a way to contact one another.

The third element is interdependence, which means that the agents influence one another. If someone is not sure how cold it is outside and she looks out the window to see everyone wearing down coats, she might choose to wear one too. The decision is not automatic—she might choose to wear only a sweater—but in this case a decision to wear a warm coat is partly dependent on others' decisions.

The last element is adaptation. In complex systems, adaptation means more than change; rather it refers specifically to learning. Investors who repeatedly lose money on Wall Street themes such as "buy and hold" may learn over time that they need to consider alternative strategies. This learning can be collective in the sense that lessons are shared quickly with others without each agent having to experience them directly. Agents that are diverse, connected, interdependent and adaptive are the foundation of a complex system.

To understand how a complex system operates, it is necessary to think about the strength of each of these four elements. Imagine each one has a dial that can be turned from settings of zero to ten. At a setting of one, the system is uninteresting. It may have the elements of complexity, but nothing much is going on. Diversity is low, connectedness and interdependence are weak and there is almost no learning or adaptation taking place. At a setting of ten, the system is chaotic. Agents receive too much information from too many sources and are stymied in their decision making by conflicting and overwhelming signals.

Where complexity is most intriguing is in what Scott Page of the University of Michigan calls the "interesting in-between." This means the dials are set somewhere between three and seven, with each dial different from the others. This allows a good flow of information, interaction and learning among diverse agents, but not so much that the system becomes chaotic. This is the heart of complexity—a system that continuously produces surprising results without breaking down.

Two further characteristics of complex systems are of the utmost importance in our consideration of their application to currency markets and the dollar. These are emergent properties and phase transitions.

Saying a system has an emergent property is like saying the whole is more than the sum of its parts. Tasting a delicious, warm apple pie is more interesting than looking at the dough, sugar, apples and butter that went into it. When systems are highly complex, emergent properties are far more powerful and unexpected. Climate is one of the most complex systems ever studied. It is extremely difficult to model, and reliable weather forecasts can be made only about four days in advance. Hurricanes are emergent properties of climate. Their ingredients, such as low air pressure, warm water, convection and the like, are all easily observed, but the exact timing and location at which hurricanes will emerge is impossible to predict. We know them when we see them.

The best example of an emergent property is probably human consciousness. The human body is composed of oxygen, carbon and hydrogen, with traces of copper and zinc thrown in for good measure. If one were to combine these ingredients in a vat, stir carefully and even jolt the mixture with electricity, nothing would happen. The same ingredients combined through DNA coding, however, produces a human being. There's nothing in a carbon molecule that suggests thought and nothing in an oxygen molecule that suggests speech or writing. Yet the power of complexity produces exactly those capabilities using exactly those ingredients. Thought emerges from the human mind in the same complex, dynamic way that hurricanes emerge from the climate.

Phase transitions are a way to describe what happens when a complex system changes its state. When a volcano erupts, its state goes from dormant to active. When the stock market drops 20 percent in one day, its state goes from well behaved to disorderly. If the price of gold were to double in one week, the state of the dollar would go from stable to free fall. These are all examples of phase transitions in complex systems.

Not every complex system is poised for a phase transition—the system itself must be in a "critical state." This means that the agents in the system are assembled in such a way that the actions of one trigger the actions of another until the whole system changes radically. A good example of a phase transition in a critical state system is an avalanche. A normal snowfield on a flat surface is fairly stable, yet the same amount of snow on a steep incline may be in a critical state. New snow may fall for a while, but eventually one snowflake will disturb a few others. Those others will disturb more adjacent flakes until a small slide begins that takes more snow with it, getting larger along the way until the entire mountainside comes loose. One could blame the snowflake, but it is more correct to blame the unstable state of the mountainside of snow. The snowfield was in a critical state—it was likely to collapse sooner or later, and if one snowflake did not start the avalanche, the next one could have.

The same process occurs in a stock market crash. Buy and sell orders hit the market all the time just like snowflakes on the mountain. Sometimes the buyers and sellers are arranged in highly unstable ways so that one sell order triggers a few others, which are then reported by the exchange, triggering even more sell orders by nervous investors. Soon the cascade gets out of control, and more sell orders placed in advance and triggered by "stop-loss" rules are automatically executed. The process feeds on itself. Sometimes the process dies out; after all there are many small disturbances in the snow that do little harm. Sometimes the process grows exponentially until something outside the system intervenes. This intervention can take the form of trading halts, efforts by buying syndicates to reverse the flow or even closing the exchange. Once the cascade stops, the complex system can return to a stable, noncritical state—until the next time.

The recent multiple catastrophes near Sendai, Japan, perfectly illustrate how phase transitions occur in nature and society and how collapse can spread from one system to another when all are in the critical state. Tectonic plates, oceans, uranium and stock markets are all examples of separate complex systems. However, they can interact in a kind of metasystemic collapse. On March 11, 2011, shifting tectonic plates under the Pacific Ocean off the eastern coast of Japan caused an extremely violent 9.0 earthquake. The thrusting of the ocean floor then transferred energy from one system, the earth's crust, to another system, the ocean, causing a ten-meter-high tsunami. The tsunami smashed into several nuclear reactors, again transferring energy and causing another catastrophe, this time a partial meltdown in uranium and plutonium fuel rods used in the reactors. Finally, the fear induced by the meltdown in the reactors contributed to a meltdown in the Tokyo stock market, which crashed over 20 percent in two days. The earthquake and tsunami were natural systems. The reactor was a hybrid of natural uranium and man-made design, while the stock exchange is totally man-made. Yet they all operated under the same critical state dynamics embedded in complex systems.

Importantly, phase transitions can produce catastrophic effects from small causes—a single snowflake can cause a village to be destroyed by an avalanche. This is one secret behind so-called black swans. Nassim Nicholas Taleb popularized the term "black swan" in his book of the same name. In that book, Taleb rightly demolished the normal distribution—the bell curve—as a way of understanding risk. The problem is that he demolished one paradigm but did not produce another to replace it. Taleb expressed some disdain for mathematical modeling in general, preferring to take on the mantle of a philosopher. He dubbed all improbably catastrophic events "black swans," as if to say, "Stuff happens," and he left it at that. The term is widely used by analysts and policy makers who understand the "Stuff happens" part but don't understand the critical state dynamics and complexity behind it. Yet it is possible to do better than throw up one's hands.

A forest fire caused by lightning is a highly instructive example. Whether the fire destroys a single tree or a million acres, it is caused by *a single bolt of lightning*. Simple intuition might hold that large bolts cause large fires and small bolts cause small fires, but that is not true. The same bolt of lightning can cause no fire or a catastrophic fire *depending on the critical state*. This is one reason why black swans take us by surprise. They are called extreme events, but it would be more accurate to call them extreme results from everyday events. Extreme results will happen with some frequency; it is the everyday events that trigger them that we don't see coming precisely because they are so mundane. Studying the system shows us how the everyday event morphs into the black swan. As in the case of the avalanche, what really matters is not the snowflake but the snow.

Two more concepts are needed to round out our understanding of complexity theory. The first involves the frequency of extreme events relative to mild events in a complex system, referred to as a degree distribution. The second is the concept of scale.

The bell-curve degree distribution used in financial economics says that mild events happen all the time and highly extreme events practically never. Yet the bell curve is only one kind of degree distribution; there are many others. The degree distribution that describes many events in complex systems is called a power law. A curve that corresponds to a power law is shown below as Figure 2.

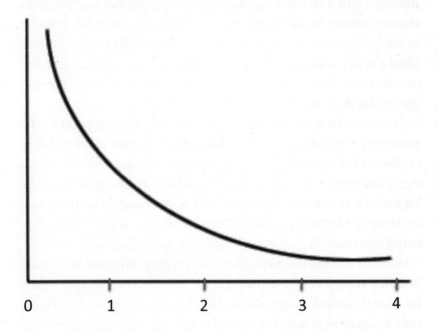

0   1   2   3   4

FIGURE 2: A curve illustrating a power-law degree distribution

In this degree distribution, the frequency of events appears on the vertical axis and the severity of events appears on the horizontal axis. As in a bell curve, extreme events occur less frequently than mild events. This is why the curve slopes downward (less frequent events) as it moves off to the right (more extreme events). However, there are some crucial differences between the power law and the bell curve. For one thing, the bell curve (see Figure 1) is "fatter" in the region close to the vertical axis. This means that mild events happen more frequently in bell curve distributions and less frequently in power law distributions. Crucially, this power law curve never comes as close to the horizontal axis as the bell curve. The "tail" of the curve continues for a long distance to the right and remains separated from the horizontal axis. This is the famous "fat tail," which in contrast with the tail on the bell curve does not appear to touch the horizontal axis. This means that *extreme events happen more frequently* in power law distributions.

Television and blogs are filled with discussions of fat tails, although the usage often seems more like cliché than technical understanding. What is even less understood is the role of scale. The curve shown above in Figure 2 ends at some point for convenience. Yet in theory it could continue forever to the right without hitting the horizontal axis. This continuation would take the extent of possible catastrophes into unimaginable realms, like a 10.0 earthquake, something never recorded.

Is there a limit to the length of the tail? Yes, at some point the fat tail drops vertically to the horizontal axis. This truncation marks the limit of the system. The size of the greatest catastrophe in a system is limited by the scale of the system itself. An example would be an active volcano on a remote island. The volcano and the island make up a complex dynamic system in a critical state. Eruptions may take place over centuries, doing various degrees of damage. Finally the volcano completely explodes and the island sinks, leaving nothing behind. The event would be extreme, but limited by the scale of the system—one island. *The catastrophe cannot be bigger than the system in which it occurs.*

That's the good news. The bad news is that man-made systems

increase in scale all the time. Power grids get larger and more connected, road systems are expanded, the Internet adds nodes and switches. The worse news is that the relationship between catastrophic risk and scale is exponential. This means that if the size of a system is doubled, the risk does not merely double—it increases by a factor of ten. If the system size is doubled again, risk increases by a factor of a hundred. Double it again and risk increases by a factor of a thousand, and so forth.

Financial markets are complex systems nonpareil. Millions of traders, investors and speculators are the autonomous agents. These agents are diverse in their resources, preferences and risk appetites. They are bulls and bears, longs and shorts. Some will risk billions of dollars, others only a few hundred. These agents are densely connected. They trade and invest within networks of exchanges, brokers, automated execution systems and information flows.

Interdependence is also characteristic of markets. When the subprime mortgage crisis struck in early August 2007, stocks in Tokyo fell sharply. Some Japanese analysts were initially baffled about why a U.S. mortgage crisis should impact Japanese stocks. The reason was that Japanese stocks were liquid and could be sold to raise cash for margin calls on the U.S. mortgage positions. This kind of financial contagion is interdependence with a vengeance.

Finally, traders and investors are nothing if not adaptive. They observe trading flows and group reactions; learn on a continuous basis through information services, television, market prices, chat rooms, social media and face-to-face; and respond accordingly.

Capital and currency markets exhibit other indicia of complex systems. Emergent properties are seen in the recurring price patterns that technicians are so fond of. The peaks and valleys, "double tops," "head and shoulders" and other technical chart patterns are examples of emergence from the complexity of the overall system. Phase transitions—rapid extreme changes—are present in the form of market bubbles and crashes.

Much of the work on capital markets as complex systems is still theoretical. However, there is strong empirical evidence, first reported by Benoît Mandelbrot, that the magnitude and frequency of certain market prices plot out as a power-law degree distribution. Mandelbrot showed that a time series chart of these price moves exhibited what he called a "fractal dimension." A fractal dimension is a dimension greater than one and less than two, expressed as a fraction such as 1½; the word "fractal" is just short for "fractional." A line has one dimension (length) and a square has two dimensions (length and width). A fractal dimension of 1½ is something in between.

A familiar example is the ubiquitous stock market chart of the kind shown in daily papers and financial websites. The chart itself consists of more than a single line (it has hundreds of small lines) but is less than an entire square (there is lots of unfilled space away from the lines). So it has a fractal dimension between one and two. The irregular pattern of ups and downs is an emergent property and a sharp crash is a phase transition.

A similar fractal pattern appears whether the chart is magnified to cover hours, days, months or years, and similar results come from looking at other charts in currency, bond and derivatives markets. Such charts show price movements, and therefore risk, distributed according to a power law and chart patterns with a fractal dimension significantly greater than 1.0. These features are at odds with a normal distribution of risk and are consistent with the power-law degree distribution of events in complex systems. While more work needs to be done in this area, so far the case for understanding capital markets as complex systems with power-law degree distributions is compelling.

This brings the analysis back to the question of scale. What is the scale of currency and capital markets, and how does it affect risk? If catastrophic collapses are an exponential function of scale, then every increase in scale causes a much greater increase in risk. Capital markets continually increase in scale, which is why the black swans keep coming in greater numbers and intensity.

Thinking about scale in capital markets today is like trying to measure the size of a field before the invention of the foot, the yard or the meter. There is no commonly agreed scaling metric for computing market risk using complexity and critical state dynamics.

This lack is not unprecedented. Earthquakes have been known throughout history, yet the Richter scale used to measure the intensity and frequency of earthquakes was invented only in 1935. Earthquakes are phase transitions in complex tectonic plate systems, and their frequency and intensity measured by the Richter scale also correspond to a power law. The similarity of stock market charts to seismographic readings (seen in Figure 3 below) is not coincidental.

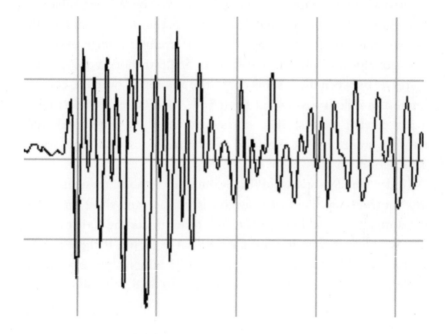

FIGURE 3: A sample seismograph reading

It will take some time for empirical work to catch up to theoretical work in this field. However, Nobel Prizes in economics likely await those who discover the best scaling metrics and accurately compute the slope of the power curve. But there is no need to wait for that work before drawing sound conclusions from the theory. Putting buildings on a known fault line was a bad idea even before the Richter scale was invented. Ignoring complexity and power laws in capital markets is a bad idea today even in the absence of empirical perfection. The edifice of capitalism may collapse in the meantime.

Even now one can make valuable inferences about the statistical properties of risk in capital and currency markets. There is no question that the scale of these markets, however best measured, has increased dramatically in the past ten years. A series of exchange mergers have created global megaexchanges. Deregulation has allowed commercial banks and investment banks to combine activities. Off–balance sheet activities and separate conduit vehicles have created a second shadow banking system as large as the visible system. Between June 2000 and June 2007, just prior to the start of the market collapse, the amount of over-the-counter foreign exchange derivatives went from $15.7 trillion to $57.6 trillion, a 367 percent increase. Between those same dates, the amount of over-the-counter interest rate derivatives went from $64.7 trillion to $381.4 trillion, a 589 percent increase. The amount of over-the-counter equity derivatives went from $1.9 trillion to $9.5 trillion in that same seven-year period, an increase of 503 percent.

Under Wall Street's usual risk evaluation methods, these increases are not troubling. Because they consist of long and short positions, the amounts are netted against each other under the VaR method. For Wall Street, risk is always in the net position. If there is a $1 billion long position in a security and a $1 billion short position in a highly similar security, methods such as VaR will *subtract* the short from the long and conclude the risk is quite low, sometimes close to zero.

Under complexity analysis, the view is completely different. In complex systems analysis, shorts are not subtracted from longs— they are *added* together. Every dollar of notional value represents some linkage between agents in the system. Every dollar of notional value creates some interdependence. If a counterparty fails, what started out as a net position for a particular bank instantaneously becomes a gross position, because the "hedge" has disappeared. Fundamentally, the risk is in the gross position, not the net. When gross positions increase by 500 percent, the theoretical risk increases by 5,000 percent or more because of the exponential relationship between scale and catastrophic event size.

This is why the financial system crashed so spectacularly in 2008.

Subprime mortgages were like the snowflakes that start an avalanche. Actual subprime mortgage losses are still less than $300 billion, a small amount compared to the total losses in the panic. However, when the avalanche began, everything else was swept up in it and the entire banking system was put at risk. When derivatives and other instruments are included, total losses reached over $6 trillion, an order of magnitude greater than actual losses on real mortgages. Failure to consider critical state dynamics and scaling metrics explains why regulators "did not see it coming" and why bankers were constantly "surprised" at the magnitude of the problem. Regulators and bankers were using the wrong tools and the wrong metrics. Unfortunately, they still are.

When a natural system reaches the point of criticality and collapses through a phase transition, it goes through a simplification process that results in greatly reduced systemic scale, which also reduces the risk of another megaevent. This is not true in all manmade complex systems. Government intervention in the form of bailouts and money printing can temporarily arrest the cascade of failures. Yet it cannot make the risk go away. The risk is latent in the system, waiting for the next destabilizing event.

One solution to the problem of risk that comes from allowing a system to grow to a megascale is to make the system smaller, which is called descaling. This is why a mountain ski patrol throws dynamite on unstable slopes before skiing starts for the day. It is reducing avalanche danger by descaling, or simplifying, the snow mass. In global finance today, the opposite is happening. The financial ski patrol of central bankers is shoveling more snow onto the mountain. The financial system is now larger and more concentrated than immediately prior to the beginning of the market collapse in 2007.

In addition to global financial descaling, another solution to complexity risk is to maintain the system size but make it more robust by not letting any one component grow too large. The equivalent in banking would be to have more banks, but smaller ones with the same total system assets. It was not that many years ago that the current JPMorgan Chase existed as four separate banks: J. P. Morgan, Chase Manhattan, Manufacturers Hanover and Chemical. A breakup today would make the financial system more robust. Instead U.S. banks are bigger and their derivatives books are larger today than in 2008. This makes a new collapse, larger than the one in 2008, not just a possibility but a certainty. Next time, however, it really will be different. Based on theoretical scaling metrics, the next collapse will not be stopped by governments, because it will be larger than governments. The five-meter seawall will face the ten-meter tsunami and the wall will fall.

▪ Complexity, Energy and Money

Using behavioral and complexity theory tools in tandem provides great insight into how the currency wars will evolve if money printing and debt expansion are not arrested soon. The course of the currency war will consist of a series of victories for the dollar followed by a decisive dollar defeat. The victories, at least as the Fed defines them, will arise as monetary ease creates inflation that forces other countries to revalue their currencies. The result will be a greatly depreciated dollar—exactly what the Fed wants. The dollar's defeat will occur through a global political consensus to replace the dollar as the reserve currency and a private consensus to abandon it altogether.

When the dollar collapse comes, it will happen two ways—gradually and then suddenly. That formula, famously used by Hemingway to describe how one goes bankrupt, is an apt description of critical state dynamics in complex systems. The gradual part is a snowflake disturbing a small patch of snow, while the sudden part is the avalanche. The snowflake is random yet the avalanche is inevitable. Both ideas are easy to grasp. What is difficult to grasp is the critical state of the system in which the random event occurs.

In the case of currency wars, the system is the international monetary system based principally on the dollar. Every other market—stocks, bonds and derivatives—is based on this system because it provides the dollar values of the assets themselves. So when the dollar finally collapses, all financial activity will collapse with it.

Faith in the dollar among foreign investors may remain strong as long as U.S. citizens themselves maintain that faith. However, a loss of confidence in the dollar among U.S. citizens spells a loss of confidence globally. A simple model will illustrate how a small loss of faith in the dollar, for any reason, can lead to a complete collapse in confidence.

Start with the population of the United States as the system. For convenience, the population is set at 311,001,000 people, very close to the actual value. The population is divided based on individual critical thresholds, called a T value in this model. The critical threshold T of an individual in the system represents the number of other people who must lose confidence in the dollar before that individual also losses confidence. The value T is a measure of whether individuals react at the first potential sign of change or wait until a process is far advanced before responding. It is an individual tipping point; however, different actors will have different tipping points. It is like asking how many people must run from a crowded theater before the next person decides to run. Some people will run out at the first sign of trouble. Others will sit nervously but not move until most of the audience has already begun to run. Someone else will be the last one out of the theater. There can be as many critical thresholds as there are actors in the system.

The T values are grouped into five broad bands to show the potential influence of one group on the other. In the first case, shown in Table 1 below, the bands are divided from the lowest critical thresholds to the highest as follows:

Table 1: HYPOTHETICAL CRITICAL THRESHOLDS (T)
FOR DOLLAR REPUDIATION IN U.S. POPULATION

For the first 1,000 people	T = 500
For the next 1 million people	T = 10,000
For the next 10 million people	T = 100,000
For the next 100 million people	T = 10,000,000
For the next 200 million people	T = 50,000,000

The test case begins by asking what would happen if one hundred people suddenly repudiated the dollar. Repudiation means an individual rejects the dollar's traditional functions as a medium of exchange, store of value and reliable way to set prices and perform other counting functions. These one hundred people would not willingly hold dollars and would consistently convert any dollars they obtained into hard assets such as precious metals, land, buildings and art. They would not rely on their ability to reconvert these hard assets into dollars in the future and would look only to the intrinsic value of the assets. They would avoid paper assets denominated in dollars, such as stocks, bonds and bank accounts.

The result in this test case of repudiation by a hundred people is that nothing would happen. This is because the lowest critical threshold shared by any group of individuals in the system is represented by T = 500. This means that it takes repudiation by five hundred people or more to cause this first group to also repudiate the dollar. Since only one hundred people have repudiated the dollar in our hypothetical case, the critical threshold of T = 500 for the most sensitive group has not been reached and the group as a whole is unaffected by the behavior of the one hundred. Since all of the remaining T values are higher than T = 500, the behavior of those groups is also unaffected. None of the critical thresholds has been triggered. This is an example of a random event dying out in the system. Something happened initially, yet nothing else happened as a result. If the largest group that would initially repudiate the dollar is fixed at one hundred, this system is said to be subcritical, meaning it is not vulnerable to a chain reaction of dollar repudiation.

Consider a second hypothetical case, shown in Table 2 below. The groupings of individuals by size of group are identical to Table 1. This system of critical thresholds is identical to the system in Table 1 with *two small differences*. The critical threshold for the first group has been changed from T = 500 people to T = 100 people. The critical threshold for the second group has been changed from T = 10,000 people to T = 1,000 people, while all the other values of T for the remaining three groups are unchanged. Put differently, we have changed the preferences of 0.3 percent of the population and left the preferences of 99.7 percent of the population unchanged. Here is the new table of thresholds with the two small changes shown in bold:

Table 2: HYPOTHETICAL CRITICAL THRESHOLDS (T) FOR DOLLAR REPUDIATION IN U.S. POPULATION	
For the first 1,000 people	T = **100**
For the next 1 million people	T = **1,000**
For the next 10 million people	T = 100,000
For the next 100 million people	T = 10,000,000
For the next 200 million people	T = 50,000,000

Now what happens when the same one hundred citizens repudiate the dollar as in the first case? In this second case, one hundred rejections will trigger the critical threshold for one thousand people who now also reject the dollar. Metaphorically, more people are running from the movie theater. This new rejection by a thousand people now triggers the critical threshold for the next one million people, and they too repudiate the dollar. Now that one million have repudiated the dollar, the next threshold of one hundred thousand is easily surpassed, and an additional ten million people repudiate the dollar. At this point, the collapse is unstoppable. With ten million people repudiating the dollar, another one hundred million join in, and soon thereafter the remaining two hundred million repudiate at once—the rejection of the dollar by the entire U.S. population is complete. The dollar has collapsed both internally and internationally as a monetary unit. This second system is said to be supercritical, and has collapsed catastrophically.

A number of important caveats apply. These thresholds are hypothetical; the actual values of T are unknown and possibly unknowable. The T values were broken into five bands for convenience. In the real world, there would be millions of separate critical thresholds, so the reality is immensely more complex than shown here. The process of collapse might not be immediate from threshold to threshold but might play out over time as information spreads slowly and reaction times vary.

None of these caveats, however, detracts from the main point, which is that *minutely small changes in initial conditions can lead to catastrophically different results.* In the first case there was no reaction to the initial repudiation by a hundred people, while in the second example the entire system collapsed. Yet the catalyst was the same, as were the preferences of 99.7 percent of the people. Small changes in the preferences of just 0.3 percent of the population were enough to change the outcome from nonevent to complete collapse. The system went from subcritical to supercritical based on almost zero systemic change.

This is a sobering thought for central bankers and proponents of deficits. Policy makers often work from models that assume policies can continue in a steplike manner without unpredictable nonlinear breakdowns. Money printing and inflation are considered to be the answer to the lack of aggregate demand. Deficits are considered to be an acceptable policy tool to increase aggregate demand by stimulus spending in the public sector. Printing money and deficit spending continue from year to year as if the system is always subcritical and more of the same will have no extreme impact. The model shows this is not necessarily true. A phase transition from stability to collapse can begin in imperceptible ways based on tiny changes in individual preferences impossible to detect in real time. These weaknesses are not discovered until the system actually collapses. But then it is too late.

With this example of how complex systems operate and how vulnerable the dollar may be to a loss of confidence, we can now look to the front lines of the currency war to see how these theoretical constructs might manifest in the real world.

The history of Currency Wars I and II shows that currency wars are last-ditch responses to much larger macroeconomic problems. Over the past one hundred years, those problems have involved excessive and unpayable debts. Today, for the third time in a century, the debt overhang is choking growth and inciting currency war, and the problem is global. Europe's sovereign borrowers and banks are in worse shape than those in America. Housing booms in Ireland, Spain and elsewhere were as reckless as the boom in the United States. Even China, which has enjoyed relatively strong growth and large trade surpluses in recent years, has an overleveraged shadow banking system run by provincial authorities, a massively expanding money supply and a housing bubble that could burst at any moment.

The post-2010 world may be different in many ways from the 1920s and the 1970s, but the massive overhang of unpayable, unsustainable debt is producing the same dynamic of deleveraging and deflation by the private sector offset by efforts at inflation and devaluation by governments. The fact that these policies of inflation and devaluation have led to economic debacles in the past does not stop them from being tried again.

What are the prospects for avoiding these adverse outcomes? How might the global debt overhang be reduced in a way that could encourage growth? Some analysts posit that the political struggle on government spending is just posturing and that once matters become urgent and key elections are over sober minds will sit down and do the right thing. Others rely on highly debatable projections of growth, interest rates, unemployment and other key factors to put deficits on a glide path to sustainability. There is good reason to view these forecasts with doubt, even pessimism. The reason has to do with the dynamics of society itself. Just as currency wars and capital markets are examples of complex systems, so those systems form part of larger complex systems with which they interact. The structure and dynamics of these larger systems are the same—except the scale is greater and the potential for collapse greater still.

Complexity theorists Eric J. Chaisson and Joseph A. Tainter supply the tools required to understand why spending discipline will likely fail and why currency wars and a dollar collapse may follow. Chaisson, an astrophysicist, is a leading theorist of complexity in evolution. Tainter, an anthropologist, is also a leading theorist of complexity as it relates to the collapse of civilization. Their theories, taken together and applied to capital markets as affected by contemporary politics, should give us pause.

Chaisson considers all complex systems from the cosmic to the subatomic and zeroes in on life generally and humans in particular as being among the most complex systems ever discovered. In his book *Cosmic Evolution,* he considers the energy requirements associated with increasing complexity and, in particular, the "energy density" of a system, which relates energy, time, complexity and scale.

Chaisson posits that the universe is best understood as the constant flow of energy between radiation and matter. The flow dynamics create more energy than is needed in the conversion, providing "free energy" needed to support complexity. Chaisson's contribution was to define complexity empirically as a ratio of free energy flow to density in a system. Stated simply, the more complex a system is, the more energy it needs to maintain its size and space. Chaisson's theories are well supported, starting with the original laws of thermodynamics through more recent sophisticated local observations of increasing order and complexity in the universe.

It is well understood that the sun uses far more energy than a human brain. Yet the sun is vastly more massive than a brain. When these differences in mass are taken into account, it turns out that the brain uses 75,000 times as much energy as the sun, measured in Chaisson's standard units. Chaisson has also identified one entity vastly more complex than the human brain: society itself in its civilized form. This is not surprising; after all, a society of brainy individuals should produce something more complex than the individuals themselves. This is wholly consistent with complexity theory, civilization being just an emergent property of individual agents with the whole greater than the sum of its parts. Chaisson's key finding is that civilization, adjusted for density, uses 250,000 times the energy used by the sun and one million times the energy used by the Milky Way.

To see the implications of this for macroeconomics and capital markets, begin with the understanding that money is stored energy. The classic definition of money includes the expression "store of value," but exactly what value is being stored? Typically value is the output of labor and capital, both of which are energy intensive. In the simplest case, a baker makes a loaf of bread using ingredients, equipment and her own labor, all of which use energy or are the product of other forms of energy. When the baker sells the loaf for money, the money represents the stored energy that went into making the bread. This energy can be unlocked when the baker purchases some goods or services, such as house painting, by paying the painter. The energy in the money is now released in the form of the time, effort, equipment and materials of the painter. Money works exactly like a battery. A battery takes a charge of energy, stores it for a period of time and rereleases the energy when needed. Money stores energy in the same way.

This translation of energy into money is needed to apply Chaisson's work to the actual operation of markets and society. Chaisson deals at the highest macro level by estimating the total mass, density and energy flow of human society. At the level of individual economic interactions within society, it is necessary to have a unit to measure Chaisson's free energy flows. Money is the most convenient and quantifiable unit for this purpose.

The anthropologist Joseph A. Tainter picks up this thread by proposing a related yet subtler input-output flow analysis that also utilizes complexity theory. An understanding of Tainter's theory is also facilitated by the use of the money-as-energy model.

Tainter's specialty is the collapse of civilizations. That's been a favorite theme of historians and students since Herodotus documented the rise and fall of ancient Persia in the fifth century BC. In his most ambitious work, *The Collapse of Complex Societies,* Tainter analyzes the collapse of twenty-seven separate civilizations over a 4,500-year period, from the little-known Kachin civilization of highland Burma to the widely known cases of the Roman Empire and ancient Egypt. He considers an enormous range of possible factors explaining collapse, including resource depletion, natural disaster, invasions, economic distress, social dysfunction, religion and bureaucratic incompetence. His work is a tour de force of the history, supposed causes and processes of civilizational collapse.

Tainter stakes out some of the same ground as Chaisson and complexity theorists in general by demonstrating that civilizations are complex systems. He demonstrates that as the complexity of society increases, the inputs needed to maintain society increase exponentially—exactly what Chaisson would later quantify with regard to complexity in general. By inputs, Tainter refers not specifically to units of energy the way Chaisson does, but to a variety of potentially stored energy values, including labor, irrigation, crops and commodities, all of which can be converted into money and frequently are for transactional purposes. Tainter, however, takes the analysis a step further and shows that not only do inputs increase exponentially with the scale of civilization, but the outputs of civilizations and governments *decline* per unit of input when measured in terms of public goods and services provided.

Here is a phenomenon familiar to every first-semester microeconomics student—the law of diminishing returns. In effect, society asks its members to pay progressively *more* in taxes and they get progressively *less* in government services. The phenomenon of marginal returns produces an arc that rises nicely at first, then flattens out, and then declines. In this thesis, the familiar arc of marginal returns mirrors the arc of the rise, decline and fall of civilizations.

Tainter's main point is that the relationship between people and their society in terms of benefits and burdens changes materially over time. Debates about whether government is "good" or "bad" or whether taxes are "high" or "low" are best resolved first by situating society on the return curve. In the beginning of a civilization, returns to investment in complexity, usually in the form of government, are typically extremely high. A relatively small investment of time and effort in an irrigation project can yield huge returns in terms of food output per farmer. Short periods of military service shared across the entire population can yield huge gains in peace and security. A relatively lean bureaucracy to organize irrigation, defense and other efforts of this type can be highly efficient as opposed to ad hoc supervision.

At the beginning of civilization, the research budget for the invention of fire was zero, while the benefits of fire were incalculable. Compare this to the development costs of the next generation of Boeing aircraft relative to the small improvements in air travel. This dynamic has enormous implications for the presumed benefits of increases in government spending beyond some low base.

Over time and with increasing complexity, returns on investment in society begin to level off and turn negative. Once the easy irrigation projects are completed, society begins progressively larger projects covering longer conduits with progressively smaller amounts of water produced. Bureaucracies that started out as efficient organizers turn into inefficient obstacles to improvement more concerned with their own perpetuation than with service to society. Elites who manage the institutions of society slowly become more concerned with their own share of a shrinking pie than with the welfare of society as a whole. The elite echelons of society go from leading to leeching. Elites behave like parasites on the host body of society and engage in what economists call "rent seeking," or the accumulation of wealth through nonproductive means—postmodern finance being one example.

By 2011, evidence had accumulated to show that the United States was well down the return curve to the point where greater exertions by more people produced less for society while elites captured most of the growth in income and profits. Twenty-five hedge fund managers were reported to have made over $22 billion for themselves in 2010 while forty-four million Americans were on food stamps. CEO pay increased 27 percent in 2010 versus 2009 while over twenty million Americans either were unemployed or had dropped out of the labor force but wanted a job. Of Americans with jobs, more worked for the government than in construction, farming, fishing, forestry, manufacturing, mining and utilities combined.

One of the best measures of the rent seeking relationship between elites and citizens in a stagnant economy is the Gini coefficient, a measure of income inequality; a higher coefficient means greater income inequality. In 2006, shortly before the recent recession began, the coefficient for the United States reached an all-time high of 47, which contrasts sharply with the all-time low of 38.6, recorded in 1968 after two decades of stable gold-backed money. The Gini coefficient trended lower in 2007 but was near the all-time high again by 2009 and trending higher. The Gini coefficient for the

United States is now approaching that of Mexico, which is a classic oligarchic society characterized by gross income inequality and concentration of wealth in elite hands.

Another measure of elite rent seeking is the ratio of amounts earned by the top 20 percent of Americans compared to amounts earned by those living below the poverty line. This ratio went from a low of 7.7 to 1 in 1968 to a high of 14.5 to 1 in 2010. These trends in both the Gini coefficient and the wealth-to-poverty income ratio in the United States are consistent with Tainter's findings on civilizations nearing collapse. When society offers its masses negative returns on inputs, those masses opt out of society, which is ultimately destabilizing for masses and elites.

In this theory of diminishing returns, Tainter finds the explanatory variable for civilizational collapse. More traditional historians have pointed to factors such as earthquakes, droughts or barbarian invasions, but Tainter shows that civilizations that were finally brought down by barbarians had repelled barbarians many times before and civilizations that were destroyed by earthquakes had rebuilt from earthquakes many times before. What matters in the end is not the invasion or the earthquake, but the *response*. Societies that are not overtaxed or overburdened can respond vigorously to a crisis and rebuild after disaster, while those that are overtaxed and overburdened may simply give up. When the barbarians finally overran the Roman Empire, they did not encounter resistance from the farmers; instead they were met with open arms. The farmers had suffered for centuries from Roman policies of debased currency and heavy taxation with little in return, so to their minds the barbarians could not possibly be worse than Rome. In fact, because the barbarians were operating at a considerably less complex level than the Roman Empire, they were able to offer farmers basic protections at a very low cost.

Tainter makes one additional point that is particularly relevant to twenty-first-century society. There is a difference between civilizational collapse and the collapse of individual societies or nations within a civilization. When Rome fell, it was a civilizational collapse because there was no independent society to take its place. Conversely, European civilization did not collapse again after the sixth-century AD, because for every state that collapsed there was another state ready to fill the void. The decline of Spain or Venice was met by the rise of England or the Netherlands. From the perspective of complexity theory, today's highly integrated, networked and globalized world more closely resembles the codependent states of the Roman Empire than the autonomous states of medieval and modern Europe. In Tainter's view, "Collapse, if and when it comes again, will this time be global. No longer can any individual nation collapse. World civilization will disintegrate as a whole."

In sum, Chaisson shows how highly complex systems such as civilizations require exponentially greater energy inputs to grow, while Tainter shows how those civilizations come to produce negative outputs in exchange for the inputs and eventually collapse. Money serves as an input-output measure applicable to a Chaisson model because it is a form of stored energy. Capital and currency markets are powerful complex systems nested within the larger Tainter model of civilization. As society becomes more complex, it requires exponentially greater amounts of money for support. At some point productivity and taxation can no longer sustain society, and elites attempt to cheat the input process with credit, leverage, debasement and other forms of pseudomoney that facilitate rent seeking over production. These methods work for a brief period before the illusion of debt-fueled pseudogrowth is overtaken by the reality of lost wealth amid growing income inequality.

At that point society has three choices: simplification, conquest or collapse. Simplification is a voluntary effort to descale society and return the input-output ratio to a more sustainable and productive level. An example of contemporary systemic simplification would be to devolve political power and economic resources from Washington, D.C., to the fifty states under a reinvigorated federal system. Conquest is the effort to take resources from neighbors by force in order to provide new inputs. Currency wars are just an attempt at conquest without violence. Collapse is a sudden, involuntary and chaotic form of simplification.

Is Washington the New Rome? Have Washington and other sovereigns gone so far down the road of higher taxes, more regulation, more bureaucracy and self-interested behavior that social inputs produce negative returns? Are certain business, financial and institutional elites so linked to government that they are aligned in the receipt of outsized tribute for negative social utility? Are so-called markets now so distorted by manipulation, intervention and bailouts that they no longer offer reliable price signals for the allocation of resources? Are the parties most responsible for distorting the price signals also those receiving the misallocated resources? When the barbarians arrive next time, in whatever form, what is the payoff for resistance by average citizens compared to allowing the collapse to proceed and letting the elites fend for themselves?

History and complexity theory suggest that these questions are not ideological. Instead they are analytic questions whose relevance is borne out by the experience of scores of civilizations over five millennia and the study of ten billion years of increasing complexity in nature. Science and history have provided a complete framework using energy, money and complexity to understand the risks of a dollar collapse in the midst of a currency war.

What is most important is that the systems of immediate concern—currencies, capital markets and derivatives—are social inventions and therefore can be changed by society. The worst-case dynamics are daunting, but they are not inevitable. It is not too late to step back from the brink of collapse and restore some margin of safety in the global dollar-based monetary system. Unfortunately, the deck is stacked against commonsense solutions by the elites who control the system and feed at the trough of complexity. Diminishing marginal returns are bad for society, but they feel great for those on the receiving end of the inputs—at least until the inputs run dry. Today, the financial resources being extracted from society and directed toward elites take the form of taxes, bailout costs, mortgage frauds, usurious consumer rates and fees, deceptive derivatives and bonuses. As citizens are crushed under the weight of this rent extraction, collapse grows more likely. Finance must be returned to its proper role as the facilitator of commerce rather than a grotesque end in itself. Complexity theory points the way to safety through simplified and smaller-sized institutions. Incredibly, Treasury Secretary Geithner and the White House are actively facilitating a larger-scale and more concentrated banking industry, including a protoglobal central bank housed at the IMF. Any success in this endeavor will simply hasten the dollar's dénouement.

CHAPTER 11

Endgame—Paper, Gold or Chaos?

> "I just want to make it clear to everybody that our policy has been and will always be . . . that a strong dollar is in our interest as a country, and we will never embrace a strategy of trying to weaken our currency to gain economic advantage at the expense of our trading partners."
>
> **U.S. Treasury Secretary Timothy F. Geithner, April 26, 2011**

> "No, they cannot touch me for coining, I am the king himself."
>
> **William Shakespeare, *King Lear***

Few economists or policy makers at the IMF or global central banks would subscribe to the complexity-based, money-as-energy model outlined in the previous chapter. Although the physics and behavioral science are well founded, mainstream economists do not greet interdisciplinary approaches warmly. Central bankers do not have a sudden dollar collapse in their models. Yet mainstream economists and central bankers alike are well aware of dollar weakness and the risks to international monetary stability from the new currency wars. Taking a range of views from the conventional to the cutting-edge, we can foresee four outcomes in prospect for the dollar—call them The Four Horsemen of the Dollar Apocalypse. In order of disruptive potential from smallest to greatest, they are: multiple reserve currencies, special drawing rights, gold and chaos.

■ Multiple Reserve Currencies

A country's reserves are something like an individual's savings account. An individual can have current income from a job and have various forms of debt, yet still maintain some savings for future use or a rainy day. These savings can be invested in stocks and commodities or just left in the bank. A country has the same choices with its reserves. It can use a sovereign wealth fund to invest in stocks or other asset classes, or it can keep a portion in liquid instruments or gold. The liquid instruments can involve bonds denominated in a number of different currencies, each called a reserve currency, because countries use them to invest and diversify their reserves.

Since Bretton Woods in 1944, the dollar has been by far the leading reserve currency; however, it has never been the sole reserve currency. The IMF maintains a global database showing the composition of official reserves, including U.S. dollars, euros, pounds sterling, yen and Swiss francs. Recent data show the U.S. dollar comprising just over 61 percent of identified reserves, while the next largest component, the euro, weighs in at just over 26 percent. The IMF reports a slow but steady decline for the dollar over the last ten years; in 2000 the dollar comprised 71 percent of total identified reserves. This decline in reserve status has been orderly, not precipitous, and is consistent with the expansion of trade between Europe and Asia and within Asia itself.

The continuation of the trend toward a diminished role for the dollar in international trade and the reserve balances begs the question of what happens when the dollar is no longer dominant but is just another reserve currency among several others? What is the tipping point for dollar dominance? Is it 49 percent of total reserves, or is it when the dollar is equivalent to the next largest currency, probably the euro?

Barry Eichengreen is the preeminent scholar on this topic and a leading proponent of the view that a world of multiple reserve currencies awaits. In a series of academic papers and more recent popular books and articles, Eichengreen and his collaborators have shown that the dollar's role as the leading reserve currency did not arise suddenly in 1944 as the result of Bretton Woods, but was actually achieved as early as the mid-1920s. He has also shown that the role of leading reserve currency shifted between the dollar and pounds sterling, with sterling losing the lead in the 1920s but regaining it after FDR's dollar devaluation in 1933. More broadly, the evidence suggests that a world of multiple reserve currencies is not only feasible but has occurred already, during the course of Currency War I.

This research has led Eichengreen to the plausible and fairly benign conclusion that a world of multiple reserve currencies, with no single dominant currency, may once again be in prospect, this time with the dollar and euro sharing the spotlight instead of the dollar and sterling. This view also opens the door to further changes over time, with the Chinese yuan eventually joining the dollar and euro in a coleading role.

What is missing in Eichengreen's optimistic interpretation is the role of a systemic anchor, such as the dollar or gold. As the dollar and sterling were trading places in the 1920s and 1930s, there was never a time when at least one was not anchored to gold. In effect, the dollar and sterling were substitutable because of their simultaneous equivalence to gold. Devaluations did occur, but after each devaluation the anchor was reset. After Bretton Woods, the anchor consisted of the dollar *and* gold, and since 1971 the anchor has consisted of the dollar as the leading reserve currency. Yet in the postwar world there has always been a reference point. Never before have multiple paper reserve currencies been used with no single anchor. Consequently, the world Eichengreen envisions is a world of reserve currencies adrift. Instead of a single central bank like the Fed abusing its privileges, it will be open season with several central banks invited to do the same at once. In that scenario, there would be no safe harbor reserve currency and markets would be more volatile and unstable.

One disturbing variation on Eichengreen's optimistic vision consists of regional currency blocs, with local dominance by the dollar, euro and yuan, and possibly the ruble in Russia's area of influence in Eastern Europe and Central Asia. Such blocs can arise spontaneously according to well-known models of self-organization in complex systems. Regional currency blocs could quickly devolve into regional trading blocs with diminished world trade, undoubtedly the opposite of what the advocates of multiple reserve currencies such as Eichengreen envision.

Eichengreen expects what he calls healthy competition among multiple reserve currencies. He discounts models of unhealthy competition and dysfunction—what economists call a "race to the bottom," which can arise when leading central banks lock in regional dominance through network effects and simultaneously abuse their reserve status by money printing. The best advice for advocates of the multiple reserve currency model is "Be careful what you wish for." This is an untested and untried model, absent gold or some single currency anchor. The missing-anchor problem may be one reason why the dollar continues to dominate despite its difficulties.

■ Special Drawing Rights

Perhaps no feature of the international monetary system is more shrouded in mystery and confusion for the nonexpert than the special drawing right, or SDR. This should not be the case, because the SDR is a straightforward device. The SDR is world money, controlled by the IMF, backed by nothing and printed at will. Once the IMF issues an SDR, it sits comfortably in the reserve accounts of the recipient like any other reserve currency. In international finance, the SDR captures the mood of the 1985 Dire Straits hit "Money for Nothing."

Experts object to the use of the word "money" in describing special drawing rights. After all, individual citizens can't obtain them, and if you walk into a liquor store and try paying for a few bottles of wine with SDRs, you will not get very far. However, SDRs do satisfy the traditional definition of money in many respects. SDRs are a *store of value* because nations maintain part of their reserves in SDR-denominated assets. They are a *medium of exchange* because nations that run trade deficits or surpluses can settle their local currency trade balances with other nations in SDR-denominated instruments. Finally, SDRs are a *unit of account* because the IMF keeps its books and records, its assets and liabilities in SDR units. What *is* different about SDRs is that citizens and corporations in private transactions cannot yet use them. But plans are already afoot inside the IMF to create just such a private market.

Another objection to treating SDRs as money is based on the fact that SDRs are defined as a basket of other currencies, such as dollars and euros. Analysts with this view say that SDRs have no value or purpose independent of the currencies in the basket and so they are not a separate form of money. This is incorrect for two reasons. The first reason is that the amount of issuance of SDRs is not limited by any amount of underlying currencies in the basket. Those underlying currencies are used to calculate value but not to limit quantity—SDRs can be issued in potentially unlimited amounts. This gives SDRs a quantity, or "float," which is not anchored to the currencies in the basket. The second reason is that the basket can be changed. In fact, the IMF has plans now under way to change the basket so as to reduce the role of the U.S. dollar and increase the role of the Chinese yuan. These two elements—unlimited new issuance and a changing basket—give the SDR a role as money in international finance independent of the underlying basket of currencies at any point in time.

The IMF created the SDR in 1969 at a time of international monetary distress. Recurrent exchange rate crises, rampant inflation and dollar devaluation were putting pressure on global liquidity and the reserve positions of many IMF members. Several SDR issues were distributed between 1969 and 1981; however, the amounts were relatively small, equivalent to about $33.8 billion at April 2011 exchange rates. After that, no SDRs were issued for the next twenty-eight years. Interestingly, the original SDR from 1969 was valued using a weight of gold. The gold SDR was abandoned in 1973 and replaced with the paper SDR currency basket still in use today.

In 2009 the world again faced an extreme liquidity shortage from losses incurred in the Panic of 2008 and the subsequent deleveraging of balance sheets of financial institutions and consumers. The world needed money fast, and the leaders of the international monetary system went to the 1970s playbook to find some. This time the effort was directed not by the IMF itself but by the G20 using the IMF as a tool of global monetary policy. The amounts were huge, equivalent to $289 billion at the April 2011 exchange rate. This global emergency money printing went almost unnoticed by a financial press that was preoccupied with the collapse of stock markets and home prices at the time. Yet it was the beginning of a new concerted effort by the G20 and the IMF to promote the use of SDRs as the global reserve currency alternative to the dollar.

Dollars, euros and yuan would not disappear under this new SDR global currency regime; rather they would still be of use in purely domestic transactions. Americans would still buy milk or gasoline using dollars, the same way Syrians could do the same locally using their Syrian pounds. However, on globally important transactions such as trade invoicing, international loan syndicates, bank bailouts and balance of payments settlements, the SDR would be the new world money and the dollar would be a subordinate part, subject to periodic devaluation and diminution in the basket according to the dictates of the G20.

In addition to the direct printing of SDRs, the IMF has more than doubled its SDR borrowing capacity from a precrisis level of about $250 billion (equivalent) to a new level of $580 billion as of March 2011. These expanded borrowings are accomplished by loans from IMF members to the IMF, which issues SDR notes in exchange. The borrowings were designed to give the IMF capacity to lend to members in distress. Now the IMF is positioned to perform the two key functions of a true central bank—money creation and lender of last resort—using the SDR as its form of money under the direction of the G20 as its de facto board of governors. The vision of the creators of the SDR in 1969 is now coming to fruition on a much grander scale. The day of the global central bank has well and truly arrived.

Even with these expanded issuance and borrowing facilities, the SDR is still far from being able to replace the dollar as the dominant international reserve currency. In order for the SDR to succeed as a reserve currency, SDR holders will require a large liquid pool of investible assets of various maturities that holders can invest their reserve balances in to achieve a return and preserve value. This requires an SDR bond market with public and private instruments and a network of primary dealers and derivatives to provide liquidity and leverage. Such markets can emerge piecemeal over long periods of time; however, the G20 and IMF do not have the luxury of time, because other liquidity sources are drying up. By 2011 the Fed was facing the limits of its ability to provide global liquidity singlehanded. The Chinese yuan was not yet ready to assume a reserve currency role. The euro had problems of its own, stemming from the sovereign debt crisis of its peripheral members. The IMF needed to fast-track the emergence of the SDR. Some kind of road map was required. On January 7, 2011, the IMF provided the map.

In a paper entitled "Enhancing International Monetary Stability—a Role for the SDR?," the IMF presented a blueprint for the creation of a liquid SDR bond market, the antecedent to replacing the dollar as the global reserve currency with SDRs. The IMF's paper identifies both potential issuers of SDR bonds, including the World Bank and regional development banks, and potential buyers, including sovereign wealth funds and global corporations. The study contains recommended maturity structures and pricing mechanisms, as well as detailed diagrams for the clearance, settlement and financing of such bonds. Suggestions are made to change the SDR basket over time so as to enhance the weight of the Chinese yuan and to diminish the weight of the dollar.

The IMF study is optimistic about the speed and stealth with which this could be accomplished. "Experience . . . suggests the process may be relatively fast and need not involve significant public support," it states. And the IMF took no pains to disguise its intentions, explaining, "These securities could constitute an embryo of global currency." The paper also lays out a schedule for SDR money printing, suggesting that $200 billion per year of new SDR issuance would get the global currency off to a good start.

Private organizations and scholars have also contributed to this debate. One group of multinational economists and central bankers, guided by Nobelist Joseph Stiglitz, has suggested that SDRs could be issued to IMF member countries and then deposited back with the IMF to fund its lending programs. This would accelerate the IMF's ascension to the role of global central bank even more quickly than the IMF itself has proposed. Adding the role of depository to the already implemented roles of currency issuer and lender of last resort would make the IMF a global central bank in all but name. The rise of a global central bank and a world currency would leave the U.S. dollar and the Federal Reserve in a subordinate position by default.

Here in all its technical IMF-speak glory is the global power elite's answer to the currency wars and the potential collapse of the dollar. Triffin's dilemma would be solved once and for all, because no longer would a single country bear the burden of providing global liquidity. Now money could be printed globally, unconstrained by the balance of trade of the leading reserve currency issuer.

Best of all, from the IMF's perspective, there would be no democratic oversight or accountability on its money printing operations. While the IMF was drawing up its plans for a global SDR currency, it also proposed more than doubling the IMF voting rights of Communist China at the expense of democratic members such as France, the United Kingdom and the Netherlands, among others. Interestingly, these new voting arrangements made the top twenty members of the IMF more closely resemble the list of the twenty nations in the G20. The two groups of twenty are not quite identical but they are converging quickly.

The IMF is explicit in its antidemocratic leanings, what it calls "political considerations." The SDR blueprint calls for the appointment of "an advisory board of eminent experts" to provide direction on the amount of money printing in the new SDR system. Perhaps these "eminent experts" would be selected from among the same economists and central bankers who led the international monetary system to the brink of destruction in 2008. In any case, they would be selected without the public hearings and press scrutiny that come in democratic societies and would be able to operate in secret once appointed.

John Maynard Keynes famously remarked, "There is no subtler, surer means of overturning the existing basis of society than to debauch the currency. The process engages all the hidden forces of economic law on the side of destruction, and does it in a manner which not one man in a million is able to diagnose." If not one man in a million understands debasement, perhaps not one in ten million understands the inner workings of the IMF. It remains to be seen whether we can gain a fuller understanding of those inner workings before the IMF implements its plan to displace the dollar with SDRs.

In the end, the IMF's plan for the SDR as announced in its blueprint document is an expedient, not a solution. It confronts the imminent sequential failure of fiat money regimes by creating a new fiat money. It papers over the problems of paper currencies with a new kind of paper.

However, the plan has two potentially fatal flaws that may stand in its way. The first is timing—could the IMF's new SDR solution be implemented before the next financial crisis? Creation of a new currency as envisioned by the IMF would take at least five years, perhaps longer. With growing budget deficits in the United States, an unresolved sovereign debt crisis in Europe and asset bubbles in China, the world may not make it to a widely available SDR without a collapse of the monetary system first.

The second flaw in the IMF's plan involves the role of the United States. The United States has enough voting power in the IMF to stop the SDR plan in its tracks. The expansion of SDR printing and borrowing since 2009 has been accomplished with U.S. agreement, in keeping with the Obama administration's preference for multilateral rather than unilateral solutions to global issues. A new U.S. administration in 2012 might take a different view, and there is room for the IMF's dollar replacement strategy to emerge as a 2012 campaign issue. But for now, the SDR is alive and well and a strong entrant in the global currency sweepstakes.

■ Return to the Gold Standard

Gold generates more impassioned advocacy, both for and against, than any other subject in international finance. Opponents of a gold standard are quick to pull out the old Keynes quote that gold is a "barbarous relic." Legendary investor Warren Buffett points out that all the gold in the world put in one place would just be a large block of shiny metal with no yield nor income-producing potential. Establishment figure Robert Zoellick caused elite fainting spells in November 2010 by merely mentioning the world "gold" in a speech, although he stopped far short of calling for a gold standard. Among elites in general, advocacy for gold is considered a trait of the dim, the slow-witted, those who do not appreciate the benefits of a "flexible" and "expanding" modern money supply.

Gold advocates are no less rigid in their view of modern central bankers as sorcerers who produce money from thin air in order to dilute the hard-earned savings of the working class. It is difficult to think of another financial issue on which there is less common ground between the opposing sides.

Unfortunately, the entrenched positions, pro and con, stand in the way of new thinking about how gold might work in a twenty-first-century monetary system. There is an unwillingness, rooted in ideology, to explore ways to reconcile the demonstrated stability of gold with the necessity for some degrees of freedom in the management of the money supply to respond to crises and correct mistakes. A reconciliation is overdue.

Gold is not a commodity. Gold is not an investment. Gold is money par excellence. It is truly scarce—all the gold ever produced in history would fit in a cube of twenty meters (about sixty feet) on each side, approximately the size of a small suburban office building. The supply of gold from new mining expands at a fairly slow and predictable pace—about 1.5 percent per year. This is far too slow to permit much inflation; in fact, a mild persistent deflation would be the most likely outcome under a gold standard. Gold has a high density; a considerable amount of weight is compressed into a small space relative to other metals that could be used as a monetary base. Gold is also of uniform grade, an element with fixed properties, atomic number 79 in the periodic table. Commodities such as oil or wheat that might be used to support a money supply come in many different grades, making their use far more complicated. Gold does not rust or tarnish and is practically impossible to destroy, except with special acids or explosives. It is malleable and therefore easily shaped into coins and bars. Finally, it has a longer track record as money—over five thousand years—than any rival, which shows its utility to many civilizations and cultures in varied circumstances.

Given these properties of scarcity, durability, uniformity and the rest, the case for gold as money seems strong. Yet modern central bankers and economists do not take gold seriously as a form of money. The reasons go back to CWI and CWII, to the causes of the Great Depression and the crack-up of Bretton Woods. A leading scholar of the Great Depression, Ben Bernanke, now the chairman of the Federal Reserve, is one of the most powerful intellectual opponents of gold as a monetary standard. His arguments need to be considered by advocates for gold, and ultimately refuted, if the debate is to move forward.

Bernanke's work on gold and the Great Depression draws in the first instance on a large body of work by Peter Temin, one of the leading scholars of the Great Depression, Barry Eichengreen and others that showed the linkages between the operation of the gold exchange standard from 1924 to 1936 and the world economy as a whole. Bernanke summarizes this work as follows:

> Countries that left gold were able to reflate their money supplies and price levels, and did so after some delay; countries remaining on gold were forced into further deflation. To an overwhelming degree, the evidence shows that countries that left the gold standard recovered from the Depression more quickly than countries that remained on gold. Indeed, no country exhibited significant economic recovery while remaining on the gold standard.

Empirical evidence bears out Bernanke's conclusions, but that evidence is just illustrative of the beggar-thy-neighbor dynamic at the heart of all currency wars. It is no different than saying if one country invades and loots another, it will be richer and the victim poorer—something that is also true. The question is whether it is a desirable economic model.

If France had gone off the gold standard in 1931 at the same time as England, the English advantage relative to France would have been negated. In fact, France waited until 1936 to devalue, allowing England to steal growth from France in the meantime. There is nothing remarkable about that result—in fact, it should be expected.

Today, under Bernanke's guidance, the United States is trying to do what England did in 1931—devalue. Bernanke has succeeded in devaluing the dollar on an absolute basis, as evidenced by the multiyear rise in the price of gold. Yet his effort to devalue the dollar on a relative basis against other currencies has been more protracted. The dollar fluctuates against other currencies but has not devalued significantly and consistently against all of them. What is happening instead is that all the major currencies are devaluing against gold at once. The result is global commodity inflation, so that beggar-thy-neighbor has been replaced with beggar-the-world.

In support of his thesis that gold is in part to blame for the severity and protracted nature of the Great Depression, Bernanke developed a useful six-factor model showing the relationships among a country's monetary base created by the central bank, the larger money supply created by the banking system, gold reserves broken down by quantity and price, and foreign exchange reserves.

Bernanke's model works like an upside-down pyramid, with some gold and foreign exchange on the bottom, money created by the Fed on top of the gold, and even more money created by banks on top of that. The trick is to have enough gold so the upside-down pyramid does not topple over. Until 1968, U.S. law required a minimum amount of gold at the bottom of the pyramid. At the time of the Great Depression the value of gold at a fixed price had to be at least 40 percent of the amount of Fed money. However, *there was no maximum*. This meant that the Fed money supply could contract *even if the gold supply was increasing.* This happened when bankers were reducing their leverage.

Bernanke observes:

> The money supplies of gold-standard countries—far from equaling the value of monetary gold, as might be suggested by a naive view of the gold standard—were often large multiples of the value of gold reserves. Total stocks of monetary gold continued to grow through the 1930s; hence, the observed sharp declines in . . . money supplies must be attributed entirely to contractions in the average money-gold ratio.

Bernanke gives two reasons for these contractions in money supply even in the presence of ample gold. The first reason involves policy choices of central bankers and the second involves the preferences of depositors and private bankers in response to banking panics. Based on these choices, Bernanke concludes that under the gold exchange standard there exist two money supply equilibria. One equilibrium exists where confidence is high and the leverage ratios are expanded. The other exists where confidence is low and the leverage ratios contract. Where a lack of confidence causes a contraction in money through deleveraging, that process can depress confidence, leading to a further contraction of bank balance sheets and declines in spending and investment. Bernanke concludes, "In its vulnerability to self-confirming expectations, the gold standard appears to have borne a strong analogy to a . . . banking system in the absence of deposit insurance." Here was Merton's self-fulfilling prophecy again.

For Bernanke, Eichengreen, Krugman and a generation of scholars who came into their own since the 1980s, this was the smoking gun. Gold was at the base of the money supply; therefore gold was the limiting factor on the expansion of money at a time when more money was needed. Here was analytic and historic evidence, backed up by Eichengreen's empirical evidence and Bernanke's model, that gold was a significant contributing factor to the Great Depression. In their minds, the evidence showed that gold had helped to cause the Great Depression and those who abandoned gold first recovered first. Gold has been discredited as a monetary instrument ever since. Case closed.

Despite the near unanimity on this point, the academic case against gold has one enormous flaw. The argument against gold has nothing to do with gold per se; it has to do with policy. One can see this by accepting Bernanke's model and then considering alternative scenarios in the context of the Great Depression.

For example, Bernanke points to the ratio of base money to total reserves of gold and foreign exchange, sometimes called the coverage ratio. As gold flowed into the United States during the early 1930s, the Federal Reserve could have allowed the base money supply to expand by up to 2.5 times the value of the gold. The Fed failed to do so and actually reduced money supply, in part to neutralize the expansionary impact of the gold inflows. So this was a policy *choice* by the Fed. Reducing money supply below what could otherwise be achieved can happen with or without gold and is a policy choice independent of the gold supply. It is historically and analytically false to blame gold for this money supply contraction.

Bernanke points to the banking panics of the early 1930s and the preference of banks and depositors to reduce the ratio of the broad money supply to the monetary base. In turn, bankers expressed a preference for gold over foreign exchange in the composition of their reserves. Both observations are historically correct but have no necessary relationship to gold. The reduction in the ratio of broad money supply to narrow money supply need not involve gold at all and can happen at any time—it has in fact been happening in the aftermath of the Panic of 2008. The substitution of gold for foreign exchange by central banks involves gold but represents yet another policy choice by the central banks. Those banks could just as easily have expressed the opposite preference and actually increased reserves.

In addition to this refutation of Bernanke's particular historical analysis, there are a number of actions central bankers could have taken in the 1930s to alleviate the tight money situation unconstrained by gold. The Fed could have purchased foreign exchange with newly printed dollars, an operation comparable to modern central bank currency swap lines, thereby expanding both U.S. and foreign reserve positions that could have supported even more money creation. SDRs were created in the 1960s to solve exactly this problem of inadequate reserves encountered in the 1930s. Were a 1930s-style global liquidity crisis to arise again, SDRs could be issued to provide the foreign exchange base from which money creation and trade finance could flow—exactly as they were in 2009. This would be done to head off a global contraction in world trade and a global depression. Again, this kind of money creation can take place without reference to gold at all. Any failure to do so is not a failure of gold; it is a failure of policy.

Central bankers in the 1930s, especially the Fed and the Banque de France, failed to expand the money supply as much as possible even under the gold exchange standard. This was one of the primary causes of the Great Depression; however, the limiting factor was not gold but rather the lack of foresight and imagination on the part of central banks.

One suspects that Bernanke's real objection to gold today is not that it was an actual constraint on increasing the money supply in the 1930s but that it *could become so at some point today.* There was a failure to use all of the money creation capacity that bankers had in the Great Depression, yet that capacity was never unlimited. Bernanke may want to preserve the ability of central bankers to create potentially unlimited amounts of money, which does require the abandonment of gold. Since 2009, Bernanke and the Fed have been able to test their policy of unlimited money creation in real-world conditions.

Blaming the Great Depression on gold is like blaming a bank robbery on the teller. The teller may have been present when the robbery took place, *but she did not commit the crime.* In the case of the Great Depression, the crime of tight money was not committed by gold but by the central bankers who engaged in a long series of avoidable policy blunders. In international finance, gold is not a policy; it is an instrument. Laying the tragedy of the Great Depression at the feet of the gold standard has been highly convenient for central bankers who seek unlimited money printing capacity. Central bankers, not gold, were responsible for the Great Depression and economists who continue to blame gold are merely looking for an excuse to justify fiat money without bounds.

If gold is rehabilitated from the false accusation of having caused the Great Depression, can it play a constructive role today? What would a gold standard for the twenty-first century look like?

Some of the most vociferous advocates for a gold standard on the ubiquitous blogs and chat rooms are unable to explain exactly what they mean by it. The general sense that money should be linked to something tangible and that central banks should not be able to create money without limit is clear. Turning that sentiment into a concrete monetary system that can deal with the periodic challenges of panic and depression is far more difficult.

The simplest kind of gold standard—call it the *pure* gold standard—is one in which the dollar is defined as a specific quantity of gold and the agency that issues dollars has enough gold to redeem the dollars outstanding on a one-for-one basis at the specified price. In this type of system, a paper dollar is really a warehouse receipt for a quantity of gold kept in trust for the holder of the dollar and redeemable at will. Under this pure gold standard, it is impossible to expand the money supply without expanding the gold supply through new mining output or other purchases. This system would inject a mild deflationary bias into the economy since global gold supply increases about 1.5 percent per year whereas the real economy seems capable of consistent 3.5 percent growth under ideal conditions. All things equal, prices would have to fall about 2 percent per year to equilibrate 3.5 percent real growth with a 1.5 percent increase in the money supply, and this deflation might discourage borrowing at the margin. The pure gold standard would allow for the creation of credit and debt through the exchange of money for notes, but it would not allow for the creation of money beyond the amount of gold on deposit. Such debt instruments might function in the economy as money substitutes or near-money, but they would not be money in the narrow sense.

All other forms of gold standard involve some form of leverage off the existing gold stock, and this can take two forms. The first involves the issuance of money in excess of the stock of gold. The second involves the use of gold substitutes, such as foreign exchange or SDRs, in the gold pool on which the money is based. These two forms of leverage can be used separately or in tandem. This type of gold standard—call it a *flexible* gold standard—requires consideration of a number of design questions. What is the minimum percentage of the money supply that must be in gold? Is 20 percent comfortable? Is 40 percent needed to instill confidence? Historically the Federal Reserve maintained about a 40 percent partial gold reserve against the base money supply. In early April 2011 that ratio was still about 17.5 percent. Although the United States had long since gone off a formal gold standard, a kind of shadow gold standard remained in the ratio of gold to base money, even in the early twenty-first century.

Other issues include the definition of money for purposes of calculating the money-gold ratio. There are different definitions of "money" in the banking system depending on the availability and liquidity of the instruments being counted. So-called base money, or M0, consists of notes and coins in circulation plus the reserves that banks have on deposit at the Fed. A broader definition of money is M1, which includes checking accounts and traveler's checks, but does not count bank reserves. The Fed also calculates M2, which is the same as M1 except that savings accounts and some time deposits are also included. Similar definitions are used by foreign central banks. In April 2011, U.S. M1 was about $1.9 trillion and M2 was about $8.9 trillion. Because M2 is so much larger than M1, the selection of a particular definition of "money" will have a large impact on the implied price of gold when calculating the ratio of gold to money.

Similar issues arise when deciding how much gold should be counted in the calculation. Should only official gold be counted for this purpose, or should gold held by private citizens be included? Should the calculation be done solely with reference to the United States, or should some effort be made to institute this standard using gold held by all major economies?

Some consideration must be given to the legal mechanism by

which a new gold standard would be enforced. A legal statute might be sufficient, but statutes can be changed. A U.S. constitutional amendment might be preferable, since that is more difficult to change and could therefore inspire the most confidence.

What should the dollar price of gold be under this new standard? Choosing the wrong price was the single biggest flaw in the gold exchange standard of the 1920s. The price level of $20.67 per ounce of gold used in 1925 was highly deflationary because it failed to take into account the massive money printing that had occurred in Europe during World War I. A price of perhaps $50 per ounce or even higher in 1925 might have been mildly inflationary and might have helped to avoid some of the worst effects of the Great Depression.

Taking the above factors into account produces some startling results. Without suggesting that there is any particular "right" level, the following implied gold prices result when using the factors indicated:

FLEXIBLE GOLD STANDARD FACTORS (As of April 2011)	IMPLIED PRICE OF GOLD
U.S. M1 money supply with 40% gold backing	$2,590 per ounce
U.S. M0 money supply with 40% gold backing	$3,337 per ounce
U.S. M1 money supply with 100% gold backing	$6,475 per ounce
U.S., China, ECB M1 money supply with 40% gold backing	$6,993 per ounce
U.S. M0 money supply with 100% gold backing	$8,342 per ounce
U.S. M2 money supply with 40% gold backing	$12,347 per ounce
U.S., China, ECB M2 money supply with 100% gold backing	$44,552 per ounce

In order to impose discipline on whatever regime was chosen, a free market in gold could be allowed to exist side by side with the official price. The central bank could then be required to conduct open market operations to maintain the market price at or near the official price.

Assume that the coverage ratio chosen is the one used in the United States in the 1930s, when the Fed was required to hold gold reserves equal to 40 percent of the base money supply. Using April 2011 data, that standard would cause the price of gold to be set at $3,337 per ounce. The Fed could establish a narrow band around that price of, say, 2.5 percent up or down. This means that if the market price fell 2.5 percent, to $3,254 per ounce, the Fed would be required to enter the market and buy gold until the price stabilized closer to $3,337 per ounce. Conversely, if the price rose 2.5 percent, to $3,420 per ounce, the Fed would have to enter the market as a seller until the price reverted to the $3,337 per ounce level. The Fed could maintain its freedom to adjust the money supply or to raise and lower interest rates as it saw fit, provided the coverage ratio was maintained and the free market price of gold remained stable at or near the official price.

The final issue to be considered is the degree of flexibility that should be permitted to central bankers to deviate from strict coverage ratios in cases of economic emergency. There are times, albeit rare, when a true liquidity crisis or deflationary spiral emerges and rapid money creation in excess of the money-gold coverage ratio might be desirable. This exceptional capacity would directly address the issue pertaining to gold claimed by Bernanke in his studies of monetary policy in the Great Depression. This is an extremely difficult political issue because it boils down to a question of trust between central banks and the citizens they ostensibly serve. The history of central banking in general has been one of broken promises when it comes to the convertibility of money into gold, while the history of central banking in the United States in particular has been one of promoting banking interests at the expense of the general interest. Given this history and the adversarial relationship between central banks and citizens, how can the requisite trust be engendered?

Two of the essential elements to creating confidence in a new gold-backed system have already been mentioned: a strong legal regime and mandatory open-market operations to stabilize prices. With those pillars in place, we can consider the circumstances under which the Fed could be allowed to create paper money and exceed the coverage ratio ceiling.

One approach would be to let the Fed exceed the ceiling on its own initiative with a public announcement. Presumably the Fed would do so only in extreme circumstances, such as a deflationary contraction of the kind England experienced in the 1920s. In these circumstances, the open market operations would constitute a kind of democratic referendum on the Fed's decision. If the market concurred with the Fed's judgment on deflation, then there should be no run on gold—in fact, the Fed might have to be a buyer of gold to maintain the price. Conversely, if the market questioned the Fed's judgment, then a rush to redeem paper for gold might result, which would be a powerful signal to the Fed that it needed to return to the original money-gold ratio. Based on what behavioral economists and sociologists have observed about the "wisdom of crowds" as reflected in market prices, this would seem to be a more reliable guide than relying on the narrow judgment of a few lawyers and economists gathered in the Fed's high-ceilinged boardroom.

A variation of this approach would be to allow the Fed to exceed the gold coverage ratio ceiling upon the announcement of a bona fide financial emergency by a joint declaration from the president of the United States and the speaker of the House. This would preclude the Fed from engaging in unilateral bailouts and monetary experiments and would subject it to democratic oversight if it needed to expand the money supply in case of true emergencies. This procedure would amount to a "double dose" of democracy, since elected officials would declare the original emergency and market participants would vote with their wallets to ratify the Fed's judgment by their decision to buy gold or not.

The implications of a new gold standard for the international monetary system would need to be addressed as well. The history of CWI and CWII is that international gold standards survive only until one member of the system suffers enough economic distress, usually because of excessive debt, that it decides to seek unilateral advantage against its trading partners by breaking with gold and devaluing its currency. One solution to this pattern of unilateral breakouts would be to create a gold-backed global currency of the kind suggested by Keynes at Bretton Woods. Perhaps the name Keynes suggested, the bancor, could be revived. Bancors would not be inflatable fiat money like today's SDRs but true money backed by gold. The bancor could be designated as the sole currency eligible to be used for international trade and the settlement of balance of payments. Domestic currencies would be pegged to the bancor, used for internal transactions and could be devalued against the bancor only with the consent of the IMF. This would make unilateral or disorderly devaluation, and therefore currency wars, impossible.

The issues involved in reestablishing a gold standard with enough flexibility to accommodate modern central banking practices deserve intensive study rather than disparagement. A technical institute created by the U.S. White House and Congress, or perhaps the G20, could be staffed with experts and tasked with developing a workable gold standard for implementation over a five-year horizon. This institute would address exactly the questions posed above with special attention paid to the appropriate price peg in order to avoid the mistakes of the 1920s.

Based on U.S. money supply and the size of the U.S. gold hoard, and using the 40 percent coverage ratio criteria, the price of gold would come out to approximately $3,500 per ounce. Given the loss of confidence by citizens in central banks and the continual experience of debasement by those banks, however, it seems likely that a broader money supply definition and higher coverage ratio might be required to secure confidence in a new gold standard. Conducting this exercise on a global basis would require even higher prices, because major economies such as China possess paper money supplies much larger than the United States and far less gold. The matter deserves extensive research, yet based on an expected need to restore confidence on a global basis, an approximate price of $7,500 per ounce would seem likely. To some observers, this may appear to be a huge change in the value of the dollar; however, the change has already occurred in substance. It simply has not been recognized by markets, central banks or economists.

The mere announcement of such an effort might have an immediate beneficial and stabilizing impact on the global economy, because markets would begin to price in future stability much as markets priced in European currency convergence years before the euro was launched. Once the appropriate price level was determined, it could be announced in advance and open market operations could commence immediately to stabilize currencies at the new gold equivalent. Finally, the currencies themselves could become pegged to gold, or a new global currency backed by gold could be launched with other currencies pegged to it. At that point the world's energies and creativity could be redirected from exploitation through fiat money manipulation toward technology, productivity improvements and other innovations. Global growth would be fueled by the creation of real rather than paper wealth.

■ Chaos

Perhaps the most likely outcome of the currency wars and the debasement of the dollar is a chaotic, catastrophic collapse of investor confidence resulting in emergency measures by governments to maintain some semblance of a functioning system of money, trade and investment. This would not be anyone's intention or plan; rather it would simply happen like an avalanche brought about by the layering of one last financial snowflake on an unstable mountainside of debt.

The instability of the financial system in recent years has been dialed up through the greatly increased diversity and interconnectedness of market participants. Embedded risk has been exponentially increased through the vastly expanded scale of notional derivatives contracts and leverage in the too-big-to-fail banks. The exact array of critical thresholds of all market participants is unknowable, but the overall system is certainly closer to criticality than ever before for reasons already discussed in detail. All that is required to initiate a collapse is a suitable catalyst relative to the lowest critical thresholds. This does not have to be a momentous event. Recall that both small and large fires are caused by the same-sized bolt of lightning, and what makes for conflagrations is not the lightning but the state of the world.

The catalyst might be noteworthy in its own right, yet the link between catalyst and collapse may not immediately be apparent. Following is one scenario for the catenation of collapse.

The triggering event happens at the start of the trading day in Europe. A Spanish government bond auction fails unexpectedly and Spain is briefly unable to roll over some maturing debt despite promises from the European Central Bank and China to support the Spanish bond market. A rescue package is quickly assembled by France and Germany, but the blow to confidence is severe. On the same day an obscure but systemically important French primary bond dealer files for bankruptcy. Normally trouble in Europe is good for the dollar, but now both the dollar and the euro come under siege. The double-barreled bad news from Spain and France is enough to cause a few Dutch pension fund dollar stalwarts to change their minds in favor of gold. Although not usually active in the to-and-fro of dollar trading, the Dutch push the dollar "sell" button and some snowflakes start to slide. In Geneva, another dollar-critical threshold is crossed at a hedge fund, and that fund pushes the "sell" button too. Now the slide is noticeable; now the avalanche has begun.

The dollar quickly moves outside its previous trading range and begins to hit new lows relative to the leading indices. Traders with preassigned stop-loss limits are forced to sell as those limits are hit, and this stop-loss trading just adds to the general momentum forcing the dollar down. As losses accumulate, hedge funds caught on the wrong side of the market begin to sell U.S. stocks to raise cash to cover margin calls. Gold, silver, platinum and oil all begin to surge upward. Brazilian, Australian and Chinese stocks start to look like safe havens.

As bank and hedge fund traders perceive that a generalized dollar collapse has begun, another thought occurs to them. If an underlying security is priced in dollars and the dollar is collapsing, then *the value of that security is collapsing too.* At this point, stress in the foreign exchange markets immediately transfers to the dollar-based stock, bond and derivatives markets in the same way that an earthquake morphs into a tsunami. The process is no longer rational, no longer considered. There is no more time. Shouts of "Sell everything!" are heard across trading floors. Markets in the dollar and dollar-based securities collapse indiscriminately while markets in commodities and non-U.S. stocks begin to spike. Dumping of dollar-denominated bonds is causing interest rates to surge as well. This has all happened before high noon in London.

New York traders, bankers and regulators are disturbed in their sleep by frantic calls from European colleagues and counterparts. They all awake to the same sea of red and rush to get to work. The usually sleepy 6:00 a.m. suburban commuter train is standing room only; the normal "no cell phone" etiquette is abandoned. The train looks like a trading floor on wheels, which it now is. By the time the bankers arrive in midtown Manhattan and Wall Street, the dollar index has dropped 20 percent and stock futures are down 1,000 points. Gold is up $200 per ounce as investors scramble to a safe haven to preserve wealth. The contrarians and bottom-feeders are nowhere in sight; they refuse to jump in front of a runaway train. Some securities have stopped trading because there are no bids at any price. The dollar panic is now in full swing.

Certain markets, notably stock exchanges, have automatic time-outs when losses exceed a certain amount. Other markets, such as futures exchanges, give officials extraordinary powers to deal with disorderly declines, including margin increases or position limits. These rules do not automatically apply in currencies or physical gold. In order to stop a panic, central banks and governments must intervene directly to fight back the waves of private selling. In the panic situation just described, massive coordinated buying of dollars and U.S. government bonds by central banks is the first line of defense.

The Fed, the ECB and the Bank of Japan quickly organize a conference call for 10:00 a.m. New York time to discuss coordinated buying of the U.S. dollar and U.S. Treasury debt. Before the call, the central bankers consult with their finance ministries and the U.S. Treasury to get the needed approvals and parameters. The official buying campaign begins at 2:00 p.m. New York time, at which point the Fed floods the major bank trading desks with "buy" orders on the dollar and U.S. Treasuries and "sell" orders on euros, yen, sterling, Canadian dollars and Swiss francs. Before the buying begins, Fed officials leak a story to their favorite reporters that the central banks will do "whatever it takes" to support the dollar and the Fed source specifically uses the phrase "no limits" in describing the central banks' buying power. The leaks soon hit the newswires and are seen on every trading floor around the world.

Historically, private market players begin to back off when governments intervene against them. Private investors have fewer resources than governments and are informed by the timeless admonition "Don't fight the Fed." At this point in most panics, traders are happy to close out their winning positions, take profits and go home. The central banks can then mop up the mess at taxpayer expense while traders live to fight another day. The panic soon runs its course.

This time, however, it's different. Bond buying by the Fed is seen as adding fuel to the fire because the Fed prints money when it buys bonds—exactly what the market was troubled by in the first place. Moreover, the Fed has printed so much money and bought so many bonds before the panic that, for the first time, the market questions the Fed's staying power. For once, the selling power of the panic outweighs the buying power of the Fed. Sellers don't fear the Fed and they "hit the bid," leaving the Fed holding a larger and larger bag of bonds. The sellers immediately dump their dollar proceeds from the bond sales and buy Canadian, Australian, Swiss and Korean currencies in addition to Asian stocks. The dollar collapse continues and U.S. interest rates spike higher. By the end of day one, the Fed is no longer spraying water on the fire—it is spraying gasoline.

Day two begins in Asia and there is no relief in sight. Even stock markets in the countries with supposedly stronger currencies, such as Australia and China, start to crash, because investors need to sell winning positions to make up for losses, and because other investors have now lost confidence in all stocks, bonds and government debt. The scramble for gold, silver, oil and farmland becomes a buying panic to match the selling panic on the side of paper assets. The price of gold has now doubled overnight. One by one officials close the Asian and European stock exchanges to give markets a chance to cool down and to give investors time to reconsider valuations. But the effect is the opposite of the one intended. Investors conclude that exchanges may never reopen and that their stock holdings have effectively been converted into illiquid private equity. Certain banks close their doors and some large hedge funds suspend redemptions. Many accounts cannot meet margin calls and are closed out by their brokers, but this merely shifts the bad assets to the brokers' accounts and some now face their own insolvencies. As the panic courses through Europe for the second day, all eyes slowly turn to the White House. A dollar collapse is tantamount to a loss of faith in the United States itself. The Fed and the Treasury have been overwhelmed and now only the president of the United States can restore confidence.

Military jargon is peppered with expressions like "nuclear option" and "doomsday machine" and other similar expressions used both literally and figuratively. In international finance, the president has a little-known nuclear option of immense power. This option is called the International Emergency Economic Powers Act of 1977, known as IEEPA, passed during the Carter administration as an updated version of the 1917 Trading with the Enemy Act. President Franklin Roosevelt had used the Trading with the Enemy Act to close banks and confiscate gold in 1933. Now a new president, faced with a crisis of comparable magnitude, would use the new version of that statute to take equally extreme measures.

The use of IEEPA is subject to two preconditions. There must be a threat to the national security or the economy of the United States, and the threat must originate from abroad. There is some after-the-fact notification to Congress, but in general the president possesses near dictatorial powers to respond to a national emergency. The circumstances now unfolding meet the conditions of IEEPA. The president meets with his economic and national security advisers and speechwriters to prepare the most dramatic economic address since the Nixon Shock of 1971. At 6:00 p.m. New York time on day two of the global dollar panic, the president gives a live address to an anxious world audience and issues an executive order consisting of the following actions, all effective immediately:

- The president will appoint a bipartisan commission consisting of seasoned veterans of capital markets and "eminent economists" to study the panic and make suitable recommendations for reform within thirty days.
- All private and foreign-owned gold held in custody at the Federal Reserve Bank of New York or depositories such as the HSBC and Scotiabank vaults in New York will be converted to the ownership of the U.S. Treasury and transferred to the U.S. gold depository at West Point. Former owners will receive suitable compensation, to be determined at a later time.
- All transfers of foreign holdings of U.S. Treasury obligations held in electronic book entry form in the system maintained by the Federal Reserve will be suspended immediately. Holders will receive interest and principal as agreed but no sales or transfers will be allowed.
- All financial institutions will record U.S. Treasury obligations on their books at par value and such securities will be held to maturity.
- Financial institutions and the Federal Reserve will coordinate efforts to purchase all new issuance of U.S. Treasury obligations in order to continue the smooth financing of U.S. deficits and the refinancing or redemption of any outstanding obligations.
- Stock exchanges will close immediately and remain closed until further notice.
- All exports of gold from the United States are prohibited.

This interim plan would stop the immediate crash in the Treasury bond market by freezing most holders in place and mandating future purchases by the banks. It would not offer a permanent solution and would at most buy a few weeks' time within which to develop more lasting solutions.

At this point policy makers would recognize that the paper dollar as currently understood had outlived its usefulness. Its claim to be a store of value had collapsed due to a total lack of trust and confidence, and as a result its other functions as a medium of exchange and unit of account have evaporated. A new currency is now required. More of the same would be unacceptable; therefore, the new currency would certainly have to be gold backed.

Now the hidden strength of the U.S. financial position would be revealed. By confiscating foreign official and most private gold on U.S. soil, the Treasury would now possess over seventeen thousand tons of gold, equal to 57 percent of all official gold reserves in the world. This would put the United States in about the same relative position it held in 1945 just after Bretton Woods, when it controlled 63 percent of all official gold. Such a hoard would enable the United States to do what it did at Bretton Woods—dictate the shape of the new global financial system.

The United States could declare the issuance of a "New United States Dollar" equal to ten old dollars. The new dollar would be convertible into gold at the price of one thousand new dollars per ounce—equal to $10,000 per ounce under the old dollar system. This would represent an 85 percent devaluation of the dollar when measured against the market price of gold in April 2011, and would be slightly greater than the 70 percent devaluation against gold engineered by FDR in 1933, but not a different order of magnitude. It would be far less than the 95 percent dollar devaluation measured in gold that occurred under Nixon, Ford and Carter from 1971 to 1980.

Because of its gold backing, the New United States Dollar would be the only desirable currency in the world—the ultimate victor in the currency wars. The Fed would be ordered to conduct open market operations to maintain the new price of gold as described under the flexible gold exchange standard above. A windfall profits tax of 90 percent would be imposed on all private gains from the upward revaluation of gold. The United States would then pledge generous concessionary loans and grants to Europe and China to provide liquidity to facilitate world trade, much as it had done under the Marshall Plan. Gradually, those parties whose gold had been confiscated, mostly European countries, would be allowed to buy back their gold at the new, higher price. There is little doubt that they would choose to store it in Europe in the future.

Confidence would slowly be restored, markets would reopen, new prices for goods and services would be discovered and life would continue with a New King Dollar at the center of the financial universe.

Or not. This scenario of chaos followed swiftly by the ascent of a new gold-backed dollar emerging phoenixlike from the ashes is only one possibility. Other possible scenarios would include an unstoppable financial collapse followed by the widespread breakdown of civil order and eventually a collapse of the physical infrastructure. These scenarios are familiar from popular films and novels, like Cormac McCarthy's *The Road*. The stories typically involve a post-apocalyptic survival tale in the wake of devastation caused by shooting wars, natural disasters or alien invaders. In principle, the destruction of wealth, savings, trust and confidence in the aftermath of a currency war and dollar collapse might be no less catastrophic than a hostile alien invasion. A person's net worth would consist of those things she can carry on her back.

Another possible response to a dollar collapse would be government intervention of a type that is far more extreme and coercive than the executive action permitted by IEEPA and described above. Such coercion would more likely occur in Asia or Russia and may involve wholesale nationalization of capital stock and intellectual property, closed borders and redirection of productive capacity to domestic needs rather than export. The world would retreat into a set of semiautarkic zones and world trade would collapse. The result would be the opposite of globalization. It would be the Beijing Consensus without the free riding—there would be no one left to ride.

Conclusion

The path of the dollar is unsustainable and therefore the dollar will not be sustained. In time, the dollar will join a crowd of multiple reserve currencies, be subordinated to SDRs, be rejuvenated by gold or descend into chaos with both redemptive and terminal possibilities. Of these four outcomes, the use of multiple reserve currencies seems least likely because it solves none of the problems of debt and deficits, but merely moves the problem around from country to country in a continuation of the classic currency war. The SDR solution is being promoted by some global elites in the G20 finance ministries and IMF executive suites, yet to the extent that it simply replaces national paper currencies with a global paper currency, it risks its own rejection and instability in time. A studied, expertly implemented return to the gold standard offers the best chance of stability but commands so little academic respect as to be a nonstarter in current debates. This leaves chaos as a strong possibility. Within chaos, however, there is a second chance to go for gold, albeit in a sudden, unstudied way. Finally, there is just chaos, followed by something worse.

The collapse of the dollar might be a particularly trying catastrophe of its own or occur as part of an even larger collapse of civilization. It might merely mark a turning away from the excesses of paper money or be a milepost on the way to a maelstrom. None of this is inevitable, yet all of it is possible.

It is not too late to step back from the brink of catastrophic collapse. Complexity starts out as a friend and ends up the enemy. Once complexity and large scale are seen to be the danger, the solution is a mixture of descaling, compartmentalization and simplification. This is why a ship whose hold is broken up by bulkheads is less likely to sink than a vessel with a single large hold. This is why forest rangers break up large tracts of timber with barren firebreaks. Every carpenter works by the phrase "The right tool for the right job." Economists should be no less diligent than carpenters in selecting the right tools.

As applied to capital and currency markets, the correct approach is to break up big banks and limit their activities to deposit taking, consumer and commercial loans, trade finance, payments, letters of credit and a few other useful services. Proprietary trading, underwriting and dealing should be banned from banking and confined to brokers and hedge funds. The idea that large banks are needed to do large deals is nonsense. Syndicates were invented for exactly this purpose and are excellent at spreading risk.

Derivatives should be banned except for standardized exchange-traded futures with daily margin and well-capitalized clearinghouses. Derivatives do not spread risk; they multiply it and concentrate it in a few too-big-to-fail hands. Derivatives do not serve customers; they serve banks and dealers through high fees and poorly understood terms. The models used to manage derivatives risk do not work and never will work because of the focus on net risk rather than gross risk.

A flexible gold standard should be adopted to reduce uncertainty about inflation, interest rates and exchange rates. Once businesses and investors have greater certainty and price stability, they can then take greater risk on new investments. There is enough uncertainty in entrepreneurship without adding inflation, deflation, interest rates and exchange rates to the list of barriers standing in the way of innovation. The U.S. economy as guided by the Fed has seen continual asset bubbles, crashes, panics, booms and busts in the forty years since the United States left gold. It is time to diminish the role of finance and empower the role of commerce. Gold produces the greatest price stability in prices and asset values and therefore provides the best visibility for investors.

The Taylor rule, named for its proponent economist, John B. Taylor, should guide monetary policy. The rule utilizes positive feedback loops by including actual inflation in its equation while offering simplicity and transparency. It is not perfect, but, to paraphrase Winston Churchill, it is better than all the others. The combination of the Taylor rule and a flexible gold standard should make central banking a boring occupation, which is exactly the point. The more drama that can be removed from central banking, the more certainty that will be provided to entrepreneurs, who are the real source of jobs and wealth creation.

Other suggestions to reverse the impact of complexity include elimination of the corporate income tax, simplification of the personal income tax and reductions in government spending. Opposition to ever larger government is not ideological; it is merely prudent. When the risk of collapse is in the scale itself, the first-order benefits of government programs are dominated by the invisible second-order costs. Smaller is safer.

What the recommendations above have in common is that they all shrink or simplify the financial system or, in the case of gold, build bulkheads against collapse. Critics will say that many of these proposals are backward looking to a time of less government and less complexity in banking, fiscal policy and monetary policy. They will be right and that is exactly the point. When you have moved to the negative marginal-return section of the complexity input-output curve, going backward is a good thing to do because society will be more productive and more robust to catastrophe.

If remedial policies are not adopted and events do spiral out of control, the Pentagon will inevitably be called upon to restore order in ways that the Treasury and Fed cannot. The threats envisioned in the Pentagon's 2009 financial war game are becoming more real by the day. Secretary of Defense Robert Gates, upon being briefed on the financial war game, said it was "an eye-opening experience" that "reflected some shortcomings in the ability and willingness of different parts of the government to share information." Gates did not mention the U.S. Treasury by name; however, my experience is that the Treasury and the Fed need to work more closely with the national security community to help the country prepare for what may lie ahead.

As I noted at the outset, a book on currency wars is inevitably a book about the dollar and its fate. The dollar, for all its faults and weaknesses, is the pivot of the entire global system of currencies, stocks, bonds, derivatives and investments of all kinds. While all currencies by definition represent some store of value, the dollar is different. It is a store of economic value in a nation whose moral values are historically exceptional and therefore a light to the world. The debasement of the dollar cannot proceed without the debasement of those values and that exceptionalism. This book has tried to offer fair warning of the dangers ahead and be a compass to help steer away.

Social and financial collapses have happened many times but are easily ignored or forgotten. Yet history does not forget, nor do complex systems refrain from doing what they are wont to do. Complex systems begin on a benign organizing principle and end by absorbing all available energy while destroying the system itself. Capital and currency markets are complex systems and will collapse in the end unless they are broken up, contained, compartmentalized and descaled. Currency wars are ultimately about the dollar, yet the dollar today is just a jumped-up version of a former self due to derivatives, leverage, printing and the derogation of gold. It is not past time to save it. Still, the time grows short.

ACKNOWLEDGMENTS

My sincere gratitude to those who helped me with this book begins with thanks to Melissa Flashman, my literary agent, who was instrumental in moving *Currency Wars* from concept to project to reality. Her support never wavered and that was a comfort through long months of research and writing.

I owe thanks and gratitude to Adrian Zackheim at Penguin/Portfolio for green-lighting this book and taking a chance on a first-time author. We both had the sense in 2010 that the currency wars had far to run. Unfortunately for the world economy, we were right. My editor, Courtney Young, editorial assistant Eric Meyers and the rest of the team at Penguin contributed expertly to the making of the book. Enormous thanks are owed to my copy editor, Nicholas LoVecchio, whose meticulous scrutiny added to the consistency and flow of the finished work. Thank you all for your skill and patience.

I am enormously grateful to my partners at Omnis in McLean, Virginia, for allowing me to bring Wall Street to the world of national security. Randy Tauss, Chris Ray, Joe Pesce and Charlie Duelfer are all American heroes of the quiet, unsung type. It is a privilege to work with them. Our prayers are with our late partner, Zack Warfield.

I thank my associates inside the national security community, who cannot be mentioned by name. You know who you are. America may not know your names, but she is lucky to have you in her service.

Thank you to the leaders at the Applied Physics Laboratory who allowed me to think outside the box while sitting inside the gates. Duncan Brown, Ted Smyth, Ron Luman and Peggy Harlow never rest in their threat assessments and forward-leaning thinking about how to counter those threats. They were kind to include me in their efforts.

I owe an enormous debt incurred over many years to my legal mentors Tom Puccio, Phil Harris, Mel Immergut, Mary Whalen and Ivan Schlager. Even lawyers need lawyers and they are the best.

Thank you to my economics mentors, John Makin, Greg "the Hawk" Hawkins, David Mullins, Jr., Myron Scholes and Bob Barbera. Given my heterodox theoretic approach to their field, I thank them for listening and sharing their thoughts and views.

Thanks also to my market mentors, Ted Knetzger, Bill Rainer, John Meriwether, Jim McEntee, Gordon Eberts, Chris Whalen, Peter Moran and Dave "Davos" Nolan. Davos and I shorted Fannie Mae stock at $45 per share in 2005 and lost money when it went to $65. Today it trades for 39 cents. Timing is everything.

With Washington, D.C., now the financial as well as political center of the universe, a book like this could not have been written without the support and encouragement of, and many sets of intellectual ping-pong with, those who are closest to the power. Thank you to Taylor Griffin, Rob Saliterman, Blain Rethmeier, Tony Fratto, Tim Burger, Teddy Downey, Mike Allen, Jon Ward, Juan Zarate and Eamon Javers for guiding me through the thickets of the New Rome.

When a military perspective was needed, one could do no better than turn to Brigadier General Joe Shaefer and Rear Admiral Steve Baker. Thank you both. When I met General Shaefer, he was the only active-duty general with an SEC license to trade securities options. Priceless. Thanks also to Greg Burgess of the Office of the Secretary of Defense for his vision and persistence in sponsoring the financial war game that makes up the first part of this book. I am indebted to Greg for inviting me to play and including me on the China team. Maybe we can play the game again when China has more gold.

The War Games chapters of this book would not exist without the efforts of the "Wall Street Irregulars" I recruited to join me on the global financial chessboard set up by the Pentagon. Thank you Steve Halliwell and Bill O'Donnell for your friendship, your willingness to participate and for allowing me to tell your stories. We'll meet again at Ten Twenty Post, where the war game really began.

Thank you to Lori Ann LaRocco of CNBC, Amanda Lang of CBC and Eric King of King World News for inviting me on your air to discuss the economic analysis that makes up so much of this book. There is nothing like live TV with smart anchors to force you to hone your thinking.

Thanks to the folks who took time to read various sections of the manuscript at different stages of completion and offered a thoughtful mix of questions, critiques and encouragement. They read not as economists but as concerned citizens with mortgages, children, bills to pay and a desire to make sense of a financial world turned upside down. Their comments made this a better book. Thank you, Joan, Glen and Diane.

There is simply no way to live with your spouse and write a book without the spouse becoming a huge part of the writing. You discuss it, debate it, argue about it, live it and breathe it. Thank you, Ann, for a thousand little things and the one big thing of helping me to be a better writer. All my love.

Jon Faust of the Johns Hopkins Center for Financial Economics and Sebastian Mallaby of the Council on Foreign Relations were both generous with their time in reading the manuscript and offering expert comments. Of course, the views expressed in this book are mine and not necessarily theirs. Thank you both.

This time I really did save the best for last. Enormous thanks and highest professional respect are owed to Will Rickards, pride of the University of Colorado and Taft School, for serving as my research assistant and editorial assistant. Any clarity and coherence in this book emerged under his watchful and demanding eye. Any errors that remain are mine alone.

NOTES

Chapter 1

3 *"The current international currency system is the . . ."* "Q&A with Hu Jintao," *Wall Street Journal*, January 18, 2011, http://online.wsj.com/article/ SB10001424052748703551604576085514147521334.html.

3 *The Applied Physics Laboratory, located on four hundred acres . . .* Information on the history and activities of the Applied Physics Laboratory is from the center's website, www.jhuapl.edu.

4 *It was for this purpose, the conduct of a war game sponsored by the Pentagon . . .* Details about the financial war game sponsored by the Office of the Secretary of Defense and hosted by the Warfare Analysis Laboratory of the Applied Physics Laboratory are from the author's recollection and contemporaneous notes and from voluminous materials provided by the Applied Physics Laboratory, including agendas, seating charts, invitational e-mails and game materials: "Economic and Finance Game Player Book," "Economic & Finance Game Mechanics," "Economic & Finance Game Overview," "Administrative Instructions—Global Economic Seminar 7–8 October 2008," "Administrative Instructions—Global Economic & Finance Game Design Planning Seminar 18–19 November 2008," "Economic and Financial Game Baseline Scenario—March 17, 2009," "Global Economic Impacts on the DoD Final Report 31 March, 2010," and "Global Economic Study: Appendix D: Economic Game 17–18 March 2009."

Chapter 3

37 *"We're in the midst of an international . . ."* Jonathan Wheatly, "Brazil in 'Currency War' Alert," *Financial Times*, September 27, 2010.

37 *"I don't like the expression . . ."* Interview with Dominique Strauss-Kahn by *Stern* magazine, November 18, 2010, www.imf.org/external/np/ vc/2010/111810.htm.

44 *The classical gold standard was not devised at an international conference* . . . This extended discussion of the classical gold standard draws upon Giulio M. Gallarotti, *The Anatomy of an International Monetary Regime: The Classical Gold Standard, 1880–1914*, New York: Oxford University Press, 1995.

45 *"Among that group of nations that eventually gravitated to gold standards . . ."* Gallarotti, op. cit.

45 *This highly positive assessment by Gallarotti* . . . Michael David Bordo, "The Classical Gold Standard: Some Lessons for Today," Federal Reserve Bank of St. Louis, May 1981.

48 *This panic began amid a failed attempt by several New York banks* . . . This account of the Panic of 1907 draws upon Robert F. Bruner and Sean D. Carr, *The Panic of 1907: Lessons Learned from the Market's Perfect Storm*, Hoboken: Wiley, 2007.

50 *Now, literally in the rubble of the 1906 San Francisco earthquake* . . . This account of the creation of the Federal Reserve System draws upon Murray N. Rothbard, *The Case Against the Fed*, Auburn, Alabama: Ludwig von Mises Institute, 1994.

53 *However, a successful negotiation in Paris was by no means a foregone conclusion* . . . This account of the negotiations with respect to reparations at the end of World War I draws upon Margaret MacMillan, *Paris 1919: Six Months That Changed the World*, New York: Random House, 2001.

54 *The entire mechanism of credit and trade was frozen* . . . MacMillan, op. cit.

Chapter 4

58 *As inflation slowly began to take off in late 1921* . . . This account of the Weimar hyperinflation of 1921–1923 and its impact on the German people draws upon Adam Fergusson, *When Money Dies: The Nightmare of Deficit Spending, Devaluation, and Hyperinflation in Weimar Germany*, New York: Public Affairs, 2010.

61 *At exactly the same time the Weimar hyperinflation was spiraling out of control* . . . The accounts of the interwar beggar-thy-neighbor devaluations and international financial conferences intended to mitigate their effects draws upon Liaquat Ahamed, *Lords of Finance: The Bankers Who Broke the World*, New York: Penguin Press, 2009.

65 *Separately, the United States, after cutting interest rates in 1927* . . . For accounts of U.S. monetary policy in the years prior to the Great Depression and the conclusion that Federal Reserve monetary policy was unduly restrictive, see Milton Friedman and Anna Jacobson Schwartz, *A Monetary History of the United States, 1867–1960*, Princeton: Princeton University Press, 1963.

68 *However, Roosevelt would not be sworn in as president until March 1933* . . . For an account of the early years of the Franklin D. Roosevelt

administration and his actions with respect to the banking system and gold, see Allan H. Meltzer, *A History of the Federal Reserve, Volume 1: 1913–1951*, Chicago: University of Chicago Press, 2003.

71 *"I, Franklin D. Roosevelt . . . declare that . . ."* Executive Order 6102, April 5, 1933, www.presidency.ucsb.edu/ws/index.php?pid=14611&st=&st1=#axzz 1LXd02JEK.

Chapter 5

79 *Gross national product rose over 5 percent in the first year of the tax cuts . . .* All statistics for United States gross domestic product are from the United States Department of Commerce, Bureau of Economic Analysis, National Economic Accounts Data, www.bea.gov.

80 *Inflation, measured year over year, almost doubled from an acceptable 1.9 percent in 1965 . . .* All statistics for United States inflation (consumer price index) are from the United States Department of Labor, Bureau of Labor Statistics, http://data.bls.gov.

80 *The British balance of payments had been deteriorating since the early 1960s . . .* Richard Roberts, "Sterling and the End of Bretton Woods," XIV International Economic History Congress, University of Helsinki, Finland, 2006.

82 *He called for a return to the classical gold standard . . .* "Money: De Gaulle v. the Dollar," *Time*, February 12, 1965.

83 *revealed in a letter from Karl Blessing, president of the Deutsche Bundesbank . . .* Letter of Karl Blessing to William McChesney Martin, March 30, 1967, Lyndon Baines Johnson Library and Museum, Austin, Texas, www .lbjlibrary.org.

84 *On November 29, 1968, not long after the collapse of the London Gold Pool . . .* "The Monetary System: What's Wrong and What Might Be Done," *Time*, November 29, 1968.

86 *Nixon wrapped his actions in the American flag . . .* Richard M. Nixon, "Address to the Nation Outlining a New Economic Policy: 'The Challenge of Peace,'" August 15, 1971, www.presidency.ucsb.edu/ws/index. php?pid=3115#axzz1LXd02JEK.

Chapter 6

98 *"The purpose . . . is not to push the dollar down . . ."* Wall Street Journal, "Fed's Yellen Defends Bond-Purchase Plan," November 16, 2010, http://online. wsj.com/article/SB10001424052748703670004575617000774399856.html.

98 *"quantitative easing also works through exchange rates . . ."* Christina D. Romer, "The Debate That's Muting the Fed's Response," *New York Times*, February 26, 2011, www.nytimes.com/2011/02/27/business/27view.html.

101 *Today's currency war is marked by claims of Chinese undervaluation . . .* For a discussion on the history of exchange rate changes between the Chinese

yuan and the U.S. dollar, see Xiaohe Zhang, "The Economic Impact of the Chinese Yuan Revolution," paper prepared for the 18th Annual Conference of the Association for Chinese Economic Studies, Australia, July 13, 2006.

103 *The resulting decline* . . . Statistics on United States interest rates are from the Board of Governors of the Federal Reserve System, Statistics and Historic Data, www.federalreserve.gov/econresdata/releases/statisticsdata.htm.

104 *The speech, entitled "Deflation . . ."* "Deflation: Making Sure 'It' Doesn't Happen Here," remarks by Ben S. Bernanke, National Economists Club, November 21, 2002, www.federalreserve.gov/boarddocs/speeches/2002/20021121/default.htm.

104 *Bernanke spoke plainly about* . . . Bernanke, op. cit.

106 *In 2006, Senator Charles E. Schumer of New York called* . . . Press release from the office of United States Senator Charles E. Schumer, February 19, 2006, http://schumer.senate.gov/new_website/record.cfm?id=259425.

108 *In 1950, the United States had official gold reserves of over 20,000 metric tons* . . . All statistics on official gold holdings are from World Gold Council, Investment Statistics, Changes in World Official Gold Reserves, www.gold.org.

112 *A bipartisan group of U.S. senators* . . . "U.S. and China Agree to Negotiate Investment Treaty," Associated Press, June 19, 2008.

117 *By 2010, European sovereign finance was a gigantic complex web composed of cross-holdings of debt* . . . The discussion of European sovereign debt cross-holdings by banks is from "Europe's Web of Debt," *New York Times*, May 1, 2010, www.nytimes.com/interactive/2010/05/02/weekinreview/02marsh.html.

121 *As late as 1994, Brazil maintained a peg of its currency, the real, to the U.S. dollar* . . . The discussion of Brazilian currency crises and developments draws on Riordan Roett, *The New Brazil*, Washington, D.C.: Brookings Institute Press, 2010.

Chapter 7

127 *Author David Rothkopf brought this concept to light* . . . David Rothkopf, *Superclass: The Global Power Elite and the World They Are Making*, New York: Farrar, Straus and Giroux, 2008, 174–75.

127 *"We have a convening power here that is separate from the formal authority of our institution . . ."* Rothkopf, op. cit.

132 *The plan was contained in the official leaders' statement* . . . "Leaders' Statement: A Framework for Strong, Sustainable and Balanced Growth," G20 Pittsburgh Summit, September 24–25, 2009, www.cfr.org/world/g20-leaders-final-statement-pittsburgh-summit-framework-strong-sustainable-balanced-growth/p20299.

132 *"Our collective response to the crisis has . . ."* "Leaders' Statement," op. cit.

137 *"Policy makers in the emerging markets have a range of powerful . . ."* "Global Imbalances: Links to Economic and Financial Stability," speech by Chairman Ben S. Bernanke at the Banque de France Financial Stability Review Launch Event, Paris, France, February 18, 2011, www.federalreserve.gov/newsevents/speech/bernanke20110218a.htm.

139 *Instead of setting firm targets . . .* "Leaders' Declaration," G20 Seoul Summit, November 11–12, 2010, www.g20.utoronto.ca/2010/g20seoul.pdf.

Chapter 8

145 *"It is a doctrine of war not to assume the enemy will not come . . ."* Sun Tzu, *The Art of War*, Oxford: Oxford University Press, 1963.

146 *"U.S. officials and outside analysts said the Pentagon, the Treasury and U.S. intelligence agencies . . ."* Bill Gertz, "Financial Terrorism Suspected in 2008 Economic Crash," *Washington Times*, February 28, 2011, www.washingtontimes.com/news/2011/feb/28/financial-terrorism-suspected-in-08-economic-crash/print/.

149 *While these companies operated as private stock companies . . .* Material on mercantilism and the history of the East India Company and the Dutch East India Company draws from Stephen R. Brown, *Merchant Kings: When Companies Ruled the World, 1600–1900*, New York: St. Martin's, 2009.

160 *The clearest exposition of Chinese thinking on financial warfare . . .* Colonel Qiao Liang and Colonel Wang Xiangsui, *Unrestricted Warfare*, Panama City: Pan American Publishing, 2002.

163 *In a single transaction in 2009, SAFE transferred its entire position . . .* "China Admits to Building Up Stockpile of Gold," Reuters, April 24, 2009.

Chapter 9

171 *In the classic formulation of nineteenth-century economic writer Walter Bagehot . . .* All references to Bagehot's principles for central banking are from Walter Bagehot, *Lombard Street: A Description of the Money Market*, New York: Scribner, Armstrong, 1873.

174 *"We conclude this crisis was avoidable . . ."* The Financial Crisis Inquiry Report: Final Report of the National Commission on the Causes of the Financial and Economic Crisis in the United States, New York: Public Affairs, 2011, xvii.

175 *In 2009, Janet Yellen, then president of the Federal Reserve Bank of San Francisco . . .* "Fed Seeks Power to Issue Own Debt When Crisis Ebbs, Yellen Says," Bloomberg, March 26, 2009.

181 *Svensson's paper is the Rosetta stone of the currency wars . . .* Lars E. O. Svensson, "Escaping a Liquidity Trap and Deflation: The Foolproof Way and Others," Working Paper No. 10195, National Bureau of Economic Research, December 2003.

182 *"Even if the . . . interest rate is zero . . ."* Svensson, op. cit.

182 *"If the central bank could manipulate private-sector beliefs . . ."* Svensson, op. cit.

185 *In a famous study written just before the start of President Obama's administration . . .* Christina D. Romer and Jared Bernstein, "The Job Impact of the American Recovery and Reinvestment Plan," report prepared by the Council of Economic Advisers, January 9, 2009.

185 *One month after the Romer and Bernstein study . . .* John F. Cogan, Tobias Cwik, John B. Taylor and Volker Wieland, "New Keynesian Versus Old Keynesian Government Spending Multipliers," Working Paper No. 14782, National Bureau of Economic Research, February 2009, www.volkerwieland. com/docs/CCTW%20Mar%202.pdf

186 *Empirical support for Keynesian multipliers of less than one, in certain conditions, was reported in separate studies . . .* See Charles Freedman, Michael Kumhof, Douglas Laxton, Dirk Muir and Susanna Mursula, "Global Effects of Fiscal Stimulus during the Crisis," International Monetary Fund, February 25, 2010; Robert J. Barro and Charles J. Redlick, "Macroeconomic Effects from Government Purchases and Taxes," Working Paper No. 10-22, Mercatus Center, George Mason University, July 2010; and Michael Woodford, "Simple Analytics of the Government Expenditure Multiplier," paper presented at the meetings of the Allied Social Sciences Association, January 3, 2010.

187 *Christ was saying that the impact of Keynesian stimulus . . .* Carl F. Christ, "A Short-Run Aggregate-Demand Model of the Interdependence and Effects of Monetary and Fiscal Policies with Keynesian and Classical Interest Elasticities," *The American Economic Review* 57, no. 2, May 1967.

192 *The role of VaR in causing the Panic of 2008 is immense . . .* The House of Representatives held one hearing on this topic, at which sworn testimony was provided by *Black Swan* author Nassim Nicholas Taleb, bank analyst Christopher Whalen and myself, among others. This hearing was held by the Subcommittee on Investigations and Oversight of the Committee on Science, Space and Technology on September 10, 2009. The ostensible reason for using the Science Committee was that VaR is a quantitative and therefore scientific discipline; however, I was informed that this was actually done at the request of Financial Services Committee chairman Barney Frank in order to establish a record on VaR while avoiding the lobbyists who typically influence witness selection and questions in the Financial Services Committee. The consensus of the witnesses was that VaR is deeply flawed and contributed significantly to the financial crisis of 2007–2008. However, this hearing had little impact on the final form of the resulting Dodd-Frank legislation, as no limitations on the use of VaR were imposed. The record is available at http://gop.science.house.gov/Hearings/Detail.aspx?ID=166.

Chapter 10

197 *Robert K. Merton's most famous contribution . . .* Robert K. Merton, "The Self-Fulfilling Prophecy," *The Antioch Review* 8, no. 2 (Summer 1948): 193–210.

197 *A breakthrough in the impact of social psychology on economics* . . . This work on what became the foundation of behavioral economics is contained in two volumes: Daniel Kahneman and Amos Tversky, eds., *Choices, Values, and Frames*, Cambridge: Cambridge University Press, 2000; and Daniel Kahneman et al., eds., *Judgment under Uncertainty: Heuristics and Biases*, Cambridge: Cambridge University Press, 1982.

201 *If they are diverse they will respond differently to various inputs producing* . . . The extended analysis that follows, including elements of diversity, connectedness, interdependence and adaptability, draws on a series of lectures under the title "Understanding Complexity," delivered in 2009 by Professor Scott E. Page of the University of Michigan.

207 *However, there is strong empirical evidence, first reported by Benoît Mandelbrot* . . . This discussion of fractal dimensions in market prices draws on Benoît Mandelbrot and Richard L. Hudson, *The (Mis)Behavior of Markets: A Fractal View of Risk, Ruin, and Reward*, New York: Basic Books, 2004.

218 *Chaisson posits that the universe is best understood* . . . The discussion of Chaisson's theory of free energy rate densities is from Eric J. Chaisson, *Cosmic Evolution: The Rise of Complexity in Nature*, Cambridge: Harvard University Press, 2001. Chaisson's specific values for free energy rate densities are given as:

SOME ESTIMATED FREE ENERGY RATE DENSITIES		
Generic Structure	Approximate Age (10^9 y)	Average Φ_m (ERG S^{-1} G^{-1})
galaxies (Milky Way)	12	0.5
stars (Sun)	10	2
planets (Earth)	5	75
plants (biosphere)	3	900
animals (human body)	10^{-2}	20,000
brains (human cranium)	10^{-3}	150,000
society (modern culture)	0	500,000

219 *In his most ambitious work* . . . Joseph A. Tainter, *The Collapse of Complex Societies*, Cambridge: Cambridge University Press, 1988.

219 *Tainter stakes out some of the same ground as Chaisson* . . . Tainter, op. cit.

Chapter 11

227 *Barry Eichengreen is the preeminent scholar on this topic . . .* For Eichengreen's views on the prospects for multiple reserve currencies, see Barry Eichengreen, *Exorbitant Privilege: The Rise and Fall of the Dollar and the Future of the International Monetary System*, Oxford: Oxford University Press, 2011; and Barry Eichengreen, "The Dollar Dilemma: The World's Top Currency Faces Competition," *Foreign Affairs*, September/October 2009: 53–68.

236 *"Countries that left gold were able to reflate their money supplies . . ."* Ben Bernanke, "The Macroeconomics of the Great Depression: A Comparative Approach," *Journal of Money, Credit and Banking* 27 (1995): 1–28.

237 *In support of his thesis that gold is in part to blame . . .* Bernanke, op. cit. Bernanke's specific model states:

$$M1 = (M1/BASE) \times (BASE/RES) \times (RES/GOLD) \times PGOLD \times QGOLD$$

Where

M1 = M1 money supply (money and notes in circulation plus commercial bank deposits),

BASE = monetary base (money and notes in circulation plus reserves of commercial banks),

RES = international reserves of the central bank (foreign assets plus gold reserves), valued in domestic currency,

GOLD = gold reserves of the central bank, valued in domestic currency = PGOLD × QGOLD,

PGOLD = the official domestic currency price of gold, and

QGOLD = the physical quantity (for example, in metric tons) of gold reserves.

SELECTED SOURCES

ARTICLES

Ahamed, Liaquat. "Currency Wars, Then and Now: How Policymakers Can Avoid the Perils of the 1930s." *Foreign Affairs*, March/April 2011.

Bak, Per. "Catastrophes and Self-Organized Criticality." *Computers in Physics* 5 (1991): 430–33.

———. "The Devil's Staircase." *Physics Today* 39, no. 12 (1986): 38–45.

Barro, Robert J. "Are Government Bonds Net Wealth?" *Journal of Political Economy* 82 (1974): 1095–1117.

Barro, Robert J., and Charles J. Redlick. "Macroeconomic Effects from Government Purchases and Taxes." Working Paper No. 10–22, Mercatus Center, George Mason University, July 2010.

Bernanke, Ben. "Deflation: Making Sure 'It' Doesn't Happen Here." National Economists Club, November 21, 2002.

———. "Global Imbalances: Links to Economic and Financial Stability." Speech by Chairman Ben S. Bernanke at the Banque de France Financial Stability Review Launch Event, Paris, France, February 18, 2011.

———. "The Macroeconomics of the Great Depression: A Comparative Approach." *Journal of Money, Credit and Banking* 27, no. 1 (February 1995): 1–28.

Blanchard, Olivier, and Roberto Perotti. "An Empirical Characterization of the Dynamic Effects of Changes in Government Spending and Taxes on Output." *The Quarterly Journal of Economics* (2002): 1329–68.

Blessing, Karl. Letter of Karl Blessing to William McChesney Martin, March 30, 1967. Lyndon Baines Johnson Library and Museum, Austin, Texas.

Bordo, Michael David. "The Classical Gold Standard: Some Lessons for Today." Federal Reserve Bank of St. Louis, May 1981.

Buiter, Willem, et al. "Global Economics View: The Debt of Nations." Research report prepared for Citigroup Global Markets, January 7, 2011.

"Business: Nixon's Dollar and the Foreign Fallout." *Time*, September 6, 1971.

"China Admits to Building Up Stockpile of Gold." Reuters, April 24, 2009.

Christ, Carl F. "A Short-Run Aggregate-Demand Model of the Interdependence and Effects of Monetary and Fiscal Policies with Keynesian and Classical Interest Elasticities." *American Economic Review* 57, no. 2 (May 1967).

Cline, William R., and John Williamson. "Currency Wars?" Policy Brief, Peterson Institute for International Economics, November 2010.

Cogan, John F., and John B. Taylor. "The Obama Stimulus Impact? Zero." *Wall Street Journal*, December 9, 2010.

Cogan, John F., et al. "New Keynesian Versus Old Keynesian Government Spending Multipliers." Working Paper No. 14782, National Bureau of Economic Research, March 2009.

"Communiqué." Presented at Meeting of Finance Ministers and Central Bank Governors, Gyeongju, Republic of Korea, October 23, 2010.

Cutler, David M., James M. Poterba and Lawrence H. Summers. "What Moves Stock Prices?" Working Paper No. 2538, National Bureau of Economic Research, March 1988.

De Rugy, Veronique, and Garett Jones. "Mercatus on Policy: Will the Stimulus Bill Crowd Out Good Economics?" Working Paper No. 58, Mercatus Center, George Mason University, September 2009.

"The Economy: The Advantages of the Unthinkable." *Time*, December 27, 1971.

"The Economy: Changing the World's Money." *Time*, October 4, 1971.

"The Economy: The Forthcoming Devaluation of the Dollar." *Time*, December 13, 1971.

"The Economy: Money: A Move Toward Disarmament." *Time*, October 11, 1971.

"The Economy: Money: The Dangers of the U.S. Hard Line." *Time*, September 27, 1971.

"The Economy: The Quiet Triumph of Devaluation." *Time*, December 27, 1971.

Eichengreen, Barry. "The Dollar Dilemma: The World's Top Currency Faces Competition." *Foreign Affairs*, September/October 2009: 53–68.

Eichengreen, Barry, and Douglas A. Irwin. "The Slide to Protectionism in the Great Depression: Who Succumbed and Why?" Working Paper No. 15142, National Bureau of Economic Research, July 2009.

———. "Trade Blocs, Currency Blocs, and the Reorientation of World Trade in the 1930s." *Journal of International Economics* 38 (1995): 1–24.

Eichengreen, Barry, and Marc Flandreau. "The Rise and Fall of the Dollar, or When Did the Dollar Replace Sterling as the Leading Reserve Currency?" Paper No. 6869, Centre for Economic Policy Research, June 2008.

"Europe's Web of Debt." *New York Times*, May 1, 2010.

"Fed Seeks Power to Issue Own Debt When Crisis Ebbs, Yellen Says." Bloomberg, March 26, 2009.

"Fed's Yellen Defends Bond-Purchase Plan." *Wall Street Journal*, November 16, 2010.

Ferguson, Niall. "Complexity and Collapse: Empires on the Edge of Chaos." *Foreign Affairs*, March/April 2010.

Forbes, Kristin. "Why Do Foreigners Invest in the United States?" Report prepared for International Monetary Fund's Conference on International Macro-Finance, May 29, 2008.

Freedman, Charles, Michael Kumhof, Douglas Laxton, Dirk Muir and Susanna Mursula. "Global Effects of Fiscal Stimulus during the Crisis." International Monetary Fund, February 25, 2010.

"G-20 Mutual Assessment Process and the Role of the Fund." Prepared for International Monetary Fund, December 2, 2009.

Gertz, Bill. "Financial Terrorism Suspected in 2008 Economic Crash." *Washington Times*, February 28, 2011.

Gilson, Ronald J., and Curtis J. Milhaupt. "Sovereign Wealth Funds and Corporate Governance: A Minimalist Response to the New Mercantilism." Social Science Research Network, February 18, 2008, http://ssrn.com/abstract=1095023.

Hayek, Friedrich. "The Use of Knowledge in Society." *The American Economic Review* 35, no. 4 (September 1945): 519–30.

Hetzel, Robert L. "Monetary Policy in the 2008–2009 Recession." *Economic Quarterly* 95 (2009): 201–33.

"IMF to Begin On-Market Sales of Gold." Press Release No. 10/44, International Monetary Fund, February 17, 2010.

Kahneman, Daniel. "A Perspective on Judgment and Choice: Mapping Bounded Rationality." *American Psychologist* 58, no. 9 (2003): 698–99.

"Leaders' Declaration." G20 Seoul Summit, November 11–12, 2010.

"Leaders' Statement: A Framework for Strong, Sustainable and Balanced Growth." G20 Pittsburgh Summit, September 24–25, 2009.

Lyons, Gerald. "State Capitalism: The Rise of Sovereign Wealth Funds," in "Thought Leadership." London: Standard Chartered Bank, October 15, 2007.

Makin, John H. "Inflation Is Better Than Deflation." Prepared for the American Enterprise Institute for Public Policy Research, March 2009.

Merton, Robert K. "The Self-Fulfilling Prophecy." *The Antioch Review* 8, no. 2 (Summer 1948): 193–210.

"The Mild Repercussions of a Deft Devaluation." *Time*, August 22, 1969.

Milgram, S. "Behavioral Study of Obedience." *Journal of Abnormal Social Psychology* 67, no. 4 (October 1963): 371–78.

"The Monetary System: What's Wrong and What Might Be Done." *Time*, November 29, 1968.

"Money: Aquarius in the Foreign Exchanges." *Time*, October 10, 1969.

"Money: De Gaulle v. the Dollar." *Time*, February 12, 1965.

"More Credit with Fewer Crises: Responsibly Meeting the World's Growing Demand for Credit." A World Economic Forum Report in Collaboration with McKinsey & Company, January 2010.

"Nations Act to Put Brakes on Yen's Rise." *Wall Street Journal*, March 18, 2011.

Newman, Mark. "Power Laws, Pareto Distributions and Zipf's Law." *Contemporary Physics* 46 (September 2005): 323–51.

Nixon, Richard M. "Address to the Nation Outlining a New Economic Policy: 'The Challenge of Peace,'" August 15, 1971.

Pastore, S., L. Ponta and S. Cincotti. "Heterogeneous Information-Based Artificial Stock Market." *New Journal of Physics* 12 (2010).

Plosser, Charles I. "Exit: Shadow Open Market Committee." Speech Given in New York, March 25, 2011.

———. "The Scope and Responsibility of Monetary Policy." Report prepared for GIC 2011 Global Conference Series: Monetary Policy and Central Banking in the Post-Crisis Environment, January 17, 2011.

"Proposal for a General Allocation of SDRs." Report prepared for International Monetary Fund, June 9, 2009.

Rajan, Raghuram. "Currencies Aren't the Problem: Fix Domestic Policy, Not Exchange Rates." Foreign Affairs, March/April 2011.

Reinhart, Carmen M., and M. Belen Sbrancia. "The Liquidation of Government Debt." Working Paper 11–10, Paterson Institute for International Economics, April 2011.

Rickards, James G. "A New Risk Management Model for Wall Street." The RMA Journal: The Journal of Enterprise Risk Management, March 2009: 20–24.

Roberts, Richard. "Sterling and the End of Bretton Woods." University of Sussex, from "A Reassessment of Sterling, 1945–2005," XIV International Economic History Congress, University of Helsinki, Helsinki, Finland, August 2006, www.helsinki.fi/iehc2006/papers1/Roberts.pdf.

Romer, Christina D. "The Debate That's Muting the Fed's Response." New York Times, February 26, 2011.

Romer, Christina D., and Jared Bernstein. "The Job Impact of the American Recovery and Reinvestment Plan." Report prepared by the Council of Economic Advisers, January 9, 2009.

Scheinkman, José A., and Michael Woodford. "Self-Organized Criticality and Economic Fluctuations." The American Economic Review 84, no. 2 (May 1994): 417–21.

Sornette, Didier. "Critical Market Crashes." Physics Reports 378 (2003): 1–98.

———. "Dragon-Kings, Black Swans and the Prediction of Crises." International Journal of Terraspace Science and Engineering, December 2009.

Sornette, Didier, and Ryan Woodward. "Financial Bubbles, Real Estate Bubbles, Derivative Bubbles, and the Financial and Economic Crisis." Report prepared for Proceedings of Applications of Physics and Financial Analysis Conference Series, May 2, 2009.

Stiglitz, Joseph E. "A Modest Proposal for the G-20." Project Syndicate, April 1, 2011.

Subbotin, Alexander. "A Multi-Horizon Scale for Volatility." Working paper prepared for Centre d'Économie de la Sorbonne, March 3, 2008.

Svensson, Lars E. O. "Escaping a Liquidity Trap and Deflation: The Foolproof Way and Others." Working Paper No. 10195, National Bureau of Economic Research, December 2003.

———. "The Zero Bound in an Open Economy: A Foolproof Way of Escaping from a Liquidity Trap." Working Paper No. 7957, National Bureau of Economic Research, October 2000.

"Systematic Risk and the Redesign of Financial Regulation." A Global Financial Stability Report, prepared for the International Monetary Fund, April 2010.

Taylor, John B. "Discretion Versus Policy Rules in Practice." Carnegie-Rochester Conference Series on Public Policy (1993): 195–214.

———. "Evaluating the TARP." Written testimony for the Committee on Banking, Housing and Urban Affairs, United States Senate, March 17, 2011.

"U.S. and China Agree to Negotiate Investment Treaty." Associated Press, June 19, 2008.

Weitzman, Martin L. "On Modeling and Interpreting the Economics of Catastrophic Climate Change." *The Review of Economics and Statistics*, February 2009.

Woodford, Michael. "Convergence in Macroeconomics: Elements of the New Synthesis." Paper prepared for annual meeting of the American Economics Association, New Orleans, January 4, 2008.

———. "Simple Analytics of the Government Expenditure Multiplier." Paper presented at the Allied Social Sciences Association, Atlanta, Georgia, January 3–5, 2010.

Zhang, Xiaohe. "The Economic Impact of the Chinese Yuan Revolution." Paper prepared for the 18th Annual Conference of the Association for Chinese Economic Studies, Australia, July 13, 2006.

Yellen, Janet L. "Improving the International Monetary and Financial System." Remarks delivered at the Banque de France International Symposium in Paris, France, March 4, 2011.

BOOKS

Ahamed, Liaquat. *Lords of Finance: The Bankers Who Broke the World*. New York: Penguin Press, 2009.

Ariely, Dan. *Predictably Irrational: The Hidden Forces That Shape Our Decisions*. New York: HarperCollins, 2008.

Authers, John. *The Fearful Rise of Markets*. Upper Saddle River, NJ: Financial Times Press, 2010.

Bagehot, Walter. *Lombard Street: A Description of the Money Market*. New York: Scribner, Armstrong, 1873.

Bak, Per. *How Nature Works: The Science of Self-Organized Criticality*. New York: Copernicus, 1996.

Barabási, Albert-László. *Linked*. New York: Plume, 2003.

Beinhocker, Eric D. *Origin of Wealth: Evolution, Complexity, and the Radical Remaking of Economics*. Cambridge: Harvard University Press, 2007.

Bernanke, Ben S. *Essays on the Great Depression*. Princeton: Princeton University Press, 2000.

Bernstein, Peter L. *Against the Gods: The Remarkable Story of Risk*. New York: Wiley, 1996.

———. *Capital Ideas: The Improbable Origins of Modern Wall Street*. Hoboken: Wiley, 2005.

Bernstein, William J. *A Splendid Exchange: How Trade Shaped the World*. New York: Atlantic Monthly Press, 2008.

Bhagwati, Jagdish. *A Stream of Windows: Unsettling Reflections on Trade, Immigration, and Democracy*. Cambridge: MIT Press, 1998.

Bookstaber, Richard. *A Demon of Our Own Design: Markets, Hedge Funds, and the Perils of Financial Innovation.* Hoboken: Wiley, 2007.

Braudel, Fernand. *The Structures of Everyday Life: Civilization and Capitalism, 15th–18th Century, Volume 1.* New York: Harper and Row, 1979.

———. *The Wheels of Commerce: Civilization and Capitalism, 15th–18th Century, Volume 2.* New York: Harper and Row, 1979.

Brown, Cynthia Stokes. *Big History: From the Big Bang to the Present.* New York: New Press, 2007.

Brown, Stephen R. *Merchant Kings: When Companies Ruled the World, 1600–1900.* New York: St. Martin's, 2009.

Bruner, Robert F., and Sean D. Carr. *The Panic of 1907: Lessons Learned from the Market's Perfect Storm.* Hoboken: Wiley, 2007.

Buchanan, Mark. *Ubiquity: The Science of History, or Why the World Is Simpler Than We Think.* New York: Crown, 2001.

Capie, Forrest. *Depression and Protectionism: Britain Between the Wars.* London: Allen and Unwin, 1983.

Chaisson, Eric J. *Cosmic Evolution: The Rise of Complexity in Nature.* Cambridge: Harvard University Press, 2001.

Christian, David. *Maps of Time: An Introduction to Big History.* Berkeley: University of California Press, 2004.

Davies, G. *A History of Money: From Ancient Times to the Present Day.* Cardiff: University of Wales Press, 2002.

Dawson, Christopher. *Dynamics of World History.* Wilmington, DE: ISI Books, 2002.

Dunbar, Nicholas. *Inventing Money: The Story of Long-Term Capital Management and the Legends Behind It.* Chichester, UK: Wiley, 2000.

Eichengreen, Barry. *Exorbitant Privilege: The Rise and Fall of the Dollar and the Future of the International Monetary System.* Oxford: Oxford University Press, 2011.

———. *Global Imbalances and the Lessons of Bretton Woods.* Cambridge: MIT Press, 2007.

———. *Globalizing Capital: A History of the International Monetary System,* 2nd ed. Princeton: Princeton University Press, 2008.

———. *Golden Fetters: The Gold Standard and the Great Depression, 1919–1939.* New York: Oxford University Press, 1995.

Elliott, J. H. *Empires of the Atlantic World: Britain and Spain in America, 1492–1830.* New Haven: Yale University Press, 2006.

Ferguson, Niall. *The Ascent of Money: A Financial History of the World.* New York: Penguin, 2008.

Fergusson, Adam. *When Money Dies: The Nightmare of Deficit Spending, Devaluation, and Hyperinflation in Weimar Germany.* New York: Public Affairs, 2010.

The Financial Crisis Inquiry Report: Final Report of the National Commission on the Causes of the Financial and Economic Crisis in the United States. New York: Public Affairs, 2011.

Findlay, Ronald, and Kevin H. O'Rourke. *Power and Plenty: Trade, War, and the World Economy in the Second Millennium.* Princeton: Princeton University Press, 2007.

Fox, Justin. *The Myth of the Rational Market*. New York: HarperCollins, 2009.

Friedman, Milton, and Anna Jacobson Schwartz. *A Monetary History of the United States, 1867–1960*. Princeton: Princeton University Press, 1963.

Frydman, Roman, and Michael D. Goldberg. *Imperfect Knowledge Economics: Exchange Rates and Risks*. Princeton: Princeton University Press, 2007.

Gallarotti, Giulio M. *The Anatomy of an International Monetary Regime: The Classical Gold Standard, 1880–1914*. New York: Oxford University Press, 1995.

Gasparino, Charles. *The Sellout: How Three Decades of Wall Street Greed and Government Mismanagement Destroyed the Global Financial System*. New York: Harper Business, 2009.

Gleick, James. *Chaos: Making a New Science*. New York: Viking, 1987.

Hackett Fischer, David. *The Great Wave: Price Revolutions and the Rhythm of History*. Oxford: Oxford University Press, 1996.

Hahn, Robert W., and Paul C. Tetlock, eds. *Information Markets: A New Way of Making Decisions*. Washington, D.C.: AEI Press, 2006.

Hamilton, Alexander. *Writings*. New York: Literary Classics of the United States, 2001.

Hayek, F. A. *The Fortunes of Liberalism: Essays on Austrian Economics and the Ideal of Freedom*. Peter G. Klein, ed. Indianapolis: Liberty Fund, 1992.

———. *Good Money, Part I: The New World*. Stephen Kresge, ed. Indianapolis: Liberty Fund, 1999.

———. *Good Money, Part II: The Standard*. Stephen Kresge, ed. Indianapolis: Liberty Fund, 1999.

Homer, Sidney. *A History of Interest Rates*, 2nd ed. New Brunswick, NJ: Rutgers University Press, 1963.

Irwin, Douglas A. *Against the Tide: An Intellectual History of Free Trade*. Princeton: Princeton University Press, 1996.

Israel, Jonathan I. *The Dutch Republic: Its Rise, Greatness, and Fall, 1477–1806*. Oxford: Oxford University Press, 1995.

Janis, Irving L. *Groupthink: Psychological Studies of Policy Decisions and Fiascoes*. Boston: Houghton Mifflin, 1982.

Jensen, Henrik Jeldtoft. *Self-Organized Critically: Emergent Complex Behavior in Physical and Biological Systems*. New York: Cambridge University Press, 1998.

Johnson, Clark H. *Gold, France, and the Great Depression: 1919–1932*. New Haven: Yale University Press, 1997.

Johnson, Simon, and James Kwak. *13 Bankers: The Wall Street Takeover and the Next Financial Meltdown*. New York: Pantheon, 2010.

Kahneman, Daniel, and Amos Tversky, eds. *Choices, Values, and Frames*. Cambridge: Cambridge University Press, 2000.

Kahneman, Daniel, et al., eds. *Judgment under Uncertainty: Heuristics and Biases*. Cambridge: Cambridge University Press, 1982.

Kambhu, John, et al. *New Directions for Understanding Systematic Risk*. Washington, D.C.: National Academy Press, 2007.

Keynes, John Maynard. *The Economic Consequences of the Peace*. London: Macmillan, 1920.

———. *The General Theory of Employment, Interest, and Money.* San Diego: Harcourt, 1964.

———. *A Tract on Monetary Reform.* Amherst, NY: Prometheus Books, 1999.

———. *Treatise on Money, Volume I: The Pure Theory of Money.* London: Macmillan, 1950 [1930].

———. *Treatise on Money, Volume II: The Applied Theory of Money.* London: Macmillan, 1950 [1930].

Kindleberger, Charles P. *Manias, Panics, and Crashes: A History of Financial Crises,* rev. ed. New York: Basic Books, 1989.

———. *The World in Depression, 1929–1939.* Berkeley: University of California Press, 1986.

Knapp, Georg Friedrich. *The State Theory of Money.* San Diego: Simon Publications, 1924.

Kuhn, Thomas S. *The Structure of Scientific Revolutions.* Chicago: University of Chicago Press, 1996.

Liang, Qiao, and Wang Xiangsui. *Unrestricted Warfare.* Panama City: Pan American Publishing, 2002.

Lowenstein, Roger. *When Genius Failed: The Rise and Fall of Long-Term Capital Management.* New York: Random House, 2000.

Luman, Ronald R., ed. *Unrestricted Warfare Symposium,* three volumes. Laurel, MD: Johns Hopkins University Applied Physics Laboratory, 2007–2009.

MacMillan, Margaret. *Paris 1919: Six Months That Changed the World.* New York: Random House, 2001.

Makin, John H. *The Global Debt Crisis: America's Growing Involvement.* New York: Basic Books, 1984.

Mallaby, Sebastian. *More Money Than God.* New York: Penguin, 2010.

Mandelbrot, Benoît, and Richard L. Hudson. *The (Mis)Behavior of Markets: A Fractal View of Risk, Ruin, and Reward.* New York: Basic Books, 2004.

Mead, Walter Russell. *God and Gold: Britain, America, and the Making of the Modern World.* New York: Random House, 2007.

Meltzer, Allan H. *A History of the Federal Reserve, Volume 1: 1913–1951.* Chicago: University of Chicago Press, 2003.

Mihm, Stephen. *A Nation of Counterfeiters: Capitalism, Con Men, and the Making of the United States.* Cambridge: Harvard University Press, 2007.

Milgram, Stanley. *The Individual in a Social World: Essays and Experiments,* 2nd ed. New York: McGraw-Hill, 1992.

Mitchell, Melanie. *Complexity: A Guided Tour.* New York: Oxford University Press, 2009.

Newman, Mark, Albert-László Barabási and Duncan J. Watts. *The Structure and Dynamics of Networks.* Princeton: Princeton University Press, 2006.

Peters, Edgar E. *Chaos and Order in the Capital Markets: A New View of Cycles, Prices, and Market Volatility.* New York: Wiley, 1991.

———. *Fractal Market Analysis: Applying Chaos Theory to Investment and Economics.* New York: Wiley, 1994.

Rajan, Raghuram G. *Fault Lines: How Hidden Fractures Still Threaten the World Economy.* Princeton: Princeton University Press, 2010.

Ray, Christina. *Extreme Risk Management: Revolutionary Approaches to Evaluating and Measuring Risk.* New York: McGraw-Hill, 2010.

Reinhart, Carmen M., and Kenneth S. Rogoff. *This Time Is Different: Eight Centuries of Financial Folly.* Princeton: Princeton University Press, 2009.

Roett, Riordan. *The New Brazil.* Washington, D.C.: Brookings Institute Press, 2010.

Rothbard, Murray N. *The Case Against the Fed.* Auburn, AL: Ludwig von Mises Institute, 1994.

———. *A History of Money and Banking in the United States: The Colonial Era to World War II.* Auburn, AL: Ludwig von Mises Institute, 2005.

———. *What Has Government Done to Our Money?* Auburn, AL: Ludwig von Mises Institute, 2005.

Rothkopf, David. *Superclass: The Global Power Elite and the World They Are Making.* New York: Farrar, Straus and Giroux, 2008.

Samuelson, Paul A., and William D. Nordhaus. *Economics,* 19th ed. New York: McGraw-Hill, 2010.

Sanger, David. *The Inheritance: The World Obama Confronts and the Challenges to American Power.* New York: Harmony Books, 2009.

Schelling, Thomas C. *Micromotives and Macrobehavior.* New York: Norton, 1978.

———. *The Strategy of Conflict.* Cambridge: Harvard University Press, 1980.

Schumpeter, Joseph A. *Capitalism, Socialism and Democracy.* London: Allen and Unwin, 1976.

Shlaes, Amity. *The Forgotten Man: A New History of the Great Depression.* New York: HarperCollins, 2007.

Shleifer, Andrei. *Inefficient Markets: An Introduction to Behavioral Finance.* Oxford: Oxford University Press, 2000.

Sowell, Thomas. *Applied Economics: Thinking Beyond Stage One.* New York: Basic Books, 2004.

———. *Basic Economics: A Common Sense Guide to the Economy.* New York: Basic Books, 2011.

Steil, Benn, and Manuel Hinds. *Money, Markets and Sovereignty.* New Haven: Yale University Press, 2009.

Steil, Benn, and Robert E. Litan. *Financial Statecraft: The Role of Financial Markets in American Policy.* New Haven: Yale University Press, 2006.

Stewart, Bruce H., and J. M. Thompson. *Nonlinear Dynamics and Chaos,* 2nd ed. Chichester, UK: Wiley, 2002.

Surowiecki, James. *The Wisdom of Crowds.* New York: Doubleday, 2004.

Tainter, Joseph A. *The Collapse of Complex Societies.* Cambridge: Cambridge University Press, 1988.

Taleb, Nassim Nicholas. *The Black Swan: The Impact of the Highly Improbable.* New York: Random House, 2007.

Tarnoff, Ben. *Moneymakers: The Wicked Lives and Surprising Adventures of Three Notorious Counterfeiters.* New York: Penguin Press, 2011.

Taylor, John B. *Getting Off Track: How Government Actions and Interventions Caused, Prolonged, and Worsened the Financial Crisis.* Stanford: Hoover Institution Press, 2009.

————. *Global Financial Warriors: The Untold Story of International Finance in the Post-9/11 World*. New York: Norton, 2007.

Temin, Peter. *Lessons from the Great Depression*. Cambridge: MIT Press, 1989.

Thaler, Richard H., and Cass R. Sunstein. *Nudge: Improving Decisions about Health, Wealth, and Happiness*. New York: Penguin, 2009.

Thompson, J.M.T., and H. B. Stewart. *Nonlinear Dynamics and Chaos*, 2nd ed. New York: Wiley, 2002.

Tilden, Freeman. *A World in Debt*. Toronto: Friedberg Commodity Management, 1983.

Von Mises, Ludwig. *The Theory of Money and Credit*. Indianapolis: Liberty Fund, 1980.

Von Mises, Ludwig, et al. *The Austrian Theory of the Trade Cycle and Other Essays*. Richard M. Ebeling, ed. Auburn, AL: Ludwig von Mises Institute, 1996.

Von Neumann, John, and Oskar Morgenstern. *The Theory of Games and Economic Behavior*. Princeton: Princeton University Press, 1944.

Waldrop, Mitchell. *Complexity: The Emerging Science at the Edge of Order and Chaos*. New York: Simon and Schuster, 1992.

Watts, Duncan J. *Six Degrees: The Science of a Connected Age*. New York: Norton, 2003.

Whalen, Christopher R. *Inflated: How Money and Debt Built the American Dream*. Hoboken: Wiley, 2011.

Woodward, Bob. *Maestro: Greenspan's Fed and the American Boom*. New York: Simon and Schuster, 2000.

Wriston, Walter B. *The Twilight of Sovereignty: How the Information Revolution Is Transforming Our World*. New York: Charles Scribner's Sons, 1992.

Yergen, Daniel, and Joseph Stanislaw. *The Commanding Heights: The Battle between Government and the Marketplace That Is Remaking the Modern World*. New York: Simon and Schuster, 1998.

INDEX